ENVISIONING
AFRICAN
INTERSEX

ENVISIONING
AFRICAN
INTERSEX

Challenging Colonial

and Racist Legacies in

South African Medicine

AMANDA LOCK SWARR

DUKE UNIVERSITY PRESS
Durham and London   2023

All rights reserved. Designed by Courtney Leigh Richardson and typeset in Avenir and Minion Pro by Westchester Publishing Services

Library of Congress Cataloging-in-Publication Data
Names: Swarr, Amanda Lock, author.
Title: Envisioning African intersex : challenging colonial and racist legacies in South African medicine / Amanda Lock Swarr. Description: Durham : Duke University Press, 2023. | Includes biblio-graphical references and index.
Identifiers: LCCN 2022039542 (print)
LCCN 2022039543 (ebook)
ISBN 9781478019619 (paperback)
ISBN 9781478016977 (hardcover)
ISBN 9781478024248 (ebook)
Subjects: LCSH: Gross, Sally, 1953–2014. | Semenya, Caster, 1991– | Intersex people—Medical care—South Africa. | Intersex people—Political activity—South Africa. | Discrimination against intersex people—South Africa. | Racism in medicine—South Africa. | Scientific racism—South Africa.
Classification: LCC HQ78.2.S6 S94 2023 (print) | LCC HQ78.2.S6 (ebook) | DDC 306.76/850968—dc23/eng/20221107
LC record available at https://lccn.loc.gov/2022039542
LC ebook record available at https://lccn.loc.gov/2022039543

Author's royalties from *Envisioning African Intersex* will be donated to Intersex South Africa.

For Sally

CONTENTS

Introduction. Pathologizing Gender Binaries:
Intersex Images and Citational Chains • 1

PART I. UNCOVERING: COLONIAL AND APARTHEID LEGACIES

1   Colonial Observations and Fallacies: "Hermaphroditism"
in Histories of South Africa • 23

2   "Intersex in Four South African Racial Groups in Durban":
Visualizing Scientific Racism and Gendered Medicine • 49

PART II. RECOVERING: DECOLONIAL INTERSEX INTERVENTIONS

3   Defying Medical Violence and Social Death: Sally Gross
and the Inception of South African Intersex Activism • 73

4   #HandsOffCaster: Caster Semenya's Refusals
and the Decolonization of Gender Testing • 102

5   Toward an "African Intersex Reference of Intelligence":
Directions in Intersex Organizing • 132

Epilogue. Reframing Visions of South African Intersex • 156

Acknowledgments • 161

Appendix 1: Compilation of Works by
and Featuring Sally Gross • 165

Appendix 2: Cited Twitter Posts Referencing
Caster Semenya • 167

Appendix 3: African Intersex Movement
Priorities (2017, 2019, 2020) • 169

Notes • 171

References • 207

Index • 231

Introduction. Pathologizing Gender Binaries
Intersex Images and Citational Chains

In 2009, South African Caster Semenya won the 800-meter event at the World Championships in Athletics in track and field. But instead of celebrating her victory, Semenya faced accusations that her body was "too masculine" for her to compete in women's sport. Sporting authorities, doctors, and the media claimed that Semenya was intersex. Over the following decade, she was subjected to international scrutiny: her body was photographed, she endured explorations of her reproductive organs, and her chromosomes and hormones were evaluated to determine her eligibility to compete in women's sport. Decisions about the "truth" of her gender changed again and again over the following decade, as supposed experts fought over the parameters of womanhood and the course of her life.

Now with two Olympic gold medals to her name, Semenya continues to contest regulations that currently bar her from her sport. The latest decisions of the International Olympic Organizing Committee prohibit Semenya from competing in the 800-meter event unless she undertakes surgery or pharmaceutically alters her natural testosterone levels (an intervention that previously made her physically ill). Recent headlines indicate the global importance of these conversations, declaring "Caster Semenya Case among 'Most Pivotal' Ever Heard" and "A Sports Arbitration Court Must Determine the Definition of a Woman," and Semenya was named one of *Time* magazine's 100 most influential people.

But while Semenya's treatment is significant, and continuing international debates over her body are hailed as deciding who counts as a woman or a man, it is far from isolated. This book exposes how scientists and doctors have scrutinized innumerable South Africans' bodies over the past four centuries to try to prove that intersex is more common among black people than among white people. Countless studies in medical journals and books, film and television representations, and media discussions repeat the same claim. I debunk this erroneous claim and replace it with a new assertion. In *Envisioning African Intersex*, I argue that colonial histories and scientific racism—a contrived comparison of bodies to justify white supremacy—form the basis for all intersex medicine. I foreground the work of African intersex activists who expose the material effects of such medicine and challenge their own pathologization.

Writing this book has taken me more than twenty years. In 1997, while researching trans and intersex medical literature as a graduate student, I came across several articles that all made the same unbelievable claim about the frequency of black intersex in South Africa. Well aware of racist histories of science and medicine, I began tracing the origins and repetitions of this assertion, growing a bibliography of publications focused on race and "intersex." I never had the chance to explore this claim fully in my previous work, but I continued to query the wide acceptance of this problematic assertion, turning it over in my head and in conversations with activists and scholars. As the years went by, the implications of associating intersex with blackness across the Global South have made a deeper exploration of these histories urgent. This book thus explores why physicians and scientists continue to assert disproportionate black intersex frequency and the repercussions of the uncritical acceptance of this assertion.

Scientific definitions of intersex are pathologizing and taxonomic, encompassing up to sixty diagnoses affecting genitals, reproductive organs, chromosomes, hormones, and more. The term *intersex* has its etymological roots in the early 1800s and was widely taken up by medical professionals in the 1950s.[1] Since the 1990s, intersex has also been reclaimed as a term of self-identification, a reclamation that I will explore. Most contemporary discussions about intersex begin with questions about its frequency. As Iain Morland points out, both scholarly and popular considerations of intersex start with citations of statistics about the prevalence of intersex conditions. This gives false impressions that the "truth" of bodies can be separated from discourse and that maleness and femaleness are actually unambiguous most of the time. Morland refuses to define intersex and rehearse figures because, as he puts it, "both are in dispute" (2011, 147). Instead, he suggests, "Let us suspend the assumption that we can know what intersex is, to explore how and why knowledge about intersex is produced" (147). Keguro Macharia mounts a related critique of research and statistics in queer African studies in which archival creation and the collection of data to gain NGO funding or state support have "tended to produce work where numbers matter more than names and lives. The African queer, the focus of so much attention, has disappeared into a mass of acronyms and percentages" (2015, 145). I follow Morland and Macharia's cautions about quantification and terminologies. Instead of providing numbers and definitions, this book sifts through these concepts and histories as inherently fraught.

Historians explain the longue durée of an idea as a shift that occurs imperceptibly over an extended period. This book demonstrates that the longue durée of racialized intersex takes place through efforts to create proof, especially visual proof, of gendered difference focused on bodies of people of color in the Global South. I argue that this slow imposition of ideas of raced gender "abnormality" as innate has materialized in two ways: through citational chains and objectifying scrutiny.

Assumptions of gender binarism enmeshed with race have become so commonplace that they function as quotidian, as invisible and part of the everyday. They seep into public consciousness through what I refer to as *citational chains*. Citational chains are references that build on each other to create truth claims despite fundamentally flawed foundations of the original works cited. These chains can include bibliographical citations of publications or citations of ideas that become repeated norms.[2] They create fictions that are repeated so often and circulated so widely that their origins are masked. Erroneous observations by colonial explorers and scientists' troubled claims about Africans' bodies are replicated in citational chains that span decades and centuries. Their scholarship positions "hermaphroditism" and intersex as always already connected to blackness, and it garners wide acceptance through insidious reach in academia, popular culture, journalism, and social media.[3]

Objectifying scrutiny, leering, and what it means to "see" are also integral to fusing race and intersex. Intersex medicine relies on doctors' and scientists' diagnoses with their eyes; they observe what they view as difference on the body, and then they test the body and invade it to try to see more.[4] They document what they want to see through medical photography to provide visual data and evidence to each other. They rely on medical imaging—a wide range of technologies such as X-rays that create visual representations of the body for analysis—to reveal internal structures of the body and justify medical treatment. Images are also manipulated to convince readers and viewers of raced gender binaries in texts and media, while fetishizing scrutiny ranges from colonial travel postcards to visual surveillance by the state.

Despite the deep roots of repeated and spectacularized depictions of intersex, these representations have always been challenged. In individual refusals that span centuries and collective actions that began in the 1990s, intersex South Africans have confronted medical violence, secrecy, and stigma by speaking openly. Reclaiming visual representations and creating their own media, those self-defined as intersex refuse exploitative imaging. African intersex activists share their theories and images through photography, film, and video, especially on social media, intervening in views of their lives not just for casual observers but for other intersex people in solidarity and mutual affirmation. The illusion that man/woman divides are unassailable and timeless requires constant surveillance, and because this illusion is always failing, institutionalized violence has enforced rigid gender binaries. But South African activists are creating new literal and figurative visions, refusing pathologizing histories, and decolonizing intersex.

Decolonial Visions of South African Intersex

African feminist scholars have pointed to the damage caused by the colonial imposition of gender dimorphism for many decades. Ifi Amadiume's *Male Daughters, Female Husbands: Gender and Sex in an African Society* (1987) contends that in precolonial times, the association of gendered roles with bodies was not present among the Igbo. Her analyses of a "flexible gender system" center local ideologies and disrupt universalizations about gender.[5] Oyèrónkẹ́ Oyěwùmí (1997) also famously argues that the category of "woman" did not predate colonialism in Yorùbáland; there were many ways to classify and interpret human bodies, and concepts of power were unconnected to genital anatomy. Oyěwùmí contends that colonial science and what she terms a "bio-logic" imposed dualistic gender as an unquestionable understanding of the social world. She thus asserts that the gendering and denigration of "women" (designated as "anafemales" in her ungendered assessment) were crucial to colonization.[6] Macharia discusses Oyěwùmí's insights, recognizing their archival limits but asking, "If we take African gendering practices as theoretically significant, what might become possible in thinking through African and Afro-diasporic queer and trans politics?" (2019, 26). I share these insights not to generalize over regions and times or to romanticize a precolonial past but to emphasize that African feminists have long unsettled the presumptions of the gendered body in ways that are often overlooked by those in the Global North.[7] These kinds of critiques—at the core of decolonial feminist approaches adopted by African feminists today—form the grounding for what I describe as intersex decoloniality.[8]

Intersex decoloniality is a way of articulating the inseparability of colonialism, race, and gender binarism. I conceptualize it in two parts: (1) an uncovering of colonial representations of hermaphroditism and intersex and their continued impact, and (2) a decolonial reconceptualization of gender centered in intersex self-determination and solidarity. African feminist decolonial approaches are integral to this thinking. In *Decolonization and Afro-Feminism*, Sylvia Tamale articulates that while Africa is burdened by deep and irreversible histories that pervade every aspect of life, decolonial feminist work undermines "the structural, institutional and psychological linkages that still link Africa to Western neocolonial interests and exploitation" (2020, 18).[9] Olajumoke Yacob-Haliso (2021) also describes the importance of dismantling colonial hierarchies and the white gaze. She asserts the need to recenter Africa as a way to rewrite problematic theories and histories.[10]

For Tamale, "The prefix 'de-' in the terms 'decolonization' and 'decoloniality' connotes an active action of undoing or reversal" (2020, 20). There are many approaches to this undoing among African feminists. Yvette Abrahams explains how decolonization takes place in everyday actions. She unlearns the effects of colonization by undoing them: "Centimetre by centimetre my body begins to feel decolonised, brain cell by brain cell I begin to appreciate how deeply I have been colonised" (2021, 277). The deeply personal work of African intersex activists discussed in this book likewise both revises colonial scripts and reverses the violence of gender enforcement that they have experienced. I center arguments about such undoing and redoing in this text, merging decolonial feminist with critical intersex approaches to challenge the coloniality and racist science of gender binaries.[11]

Envisioning African Intersex is conceptualized in two parts that reflect this decolonial framing. The first part of this book seeks to expose and rupture colonial legacies of gendered bodies. Racialized, capitalist, and gender oppression constitute what María Lugones calls the "coloniality of gender," and, as in Tamale's view, she suggests that decolonial feminism offers strategies for overcoming this oppression. Although much as been written on masculinity and femininity as produced by colonialism, widespread assumptions that material bodies (or "sex") are innately dualistic require deeper examination. Lugones's theorizations that colonialized people could not fit categories of man/woman by design inform a decolonial intersex critique. As she puts it, "Only the civilized are men or

women. Indigenous peoples of the Americas and enslaved Africans were classified as not human in species—as animals, uncontrollably sexual and wild"
(2010, 743). This animalization of those who were colonized and enslaved was
integrally connected to their representations as "hermaphroditic" or "without
gender" (Lugones 2007, 203). Lugones argues that colonizers imagined indigenous people of the Americas as "hermaphrodites or intersexed, with large
penises and breasts with flowing milk" (195).[12]

In different but related ways, the ascription of hermaphroditic bodies
can be found throughout African colonial and diasporic histories. Hortense
Spillers famously refers to US enslavement as producing "flesh ungendered," in
which Black bodies are "a territory of cultural and political maneuver, not at all
gender-related, gender-specific" (1987, 67).[13] Forcible ungendering, to draw on
Spillers's useful language, unsettles the innateness of gender binaries. The racist
and colonial imposition of gender binarism further relied on what Sylvia Wynter
describes as the long association of white people with "true" man/woman and
Others as "untrue" (quoted in Scott 2000, 174). These parameters of truth marked
African and African diasporic Others as "defective humans," stripped of personhood (Wynter 2000, 25). Taken together, thinkers including Lugones, Spillers,
and Wynter critically assess how certain people are construed outside binary gender and as primitive, defective, and animalistic. In the space of ungendering that
Envisioning African Intersex follows to the present, there is a condemnation of
those whose bodies are judged as ambiguous or hermaphroditic. I expose and
trace histories of these colonial associations, especially in southern Africa, in
chapters 1 and 2.

If objectifying colonial gazes see so-called hermaphrodites as "primitive"
and rigidly differentiated gendered bodies as "civilized," where does this leave
those who are diagnosed or who self-identify as intersex? C. Riley Snorton
usefully interprets how Spillers's conception of flesh ungendered manifests in
Black trans history. He writes that if, as Spillers explains, "the capacity for gender differentiation was lost in the outcome of the New World, ordered by the
violent theft of body and land, it would stand to reason that gender indefiniteness would become a critical modality of political and cultural maneuvering
within figurations of blackness" (2017, 56). *Envisioning African Intersex* thinks
Snorton's "gender indefiniteness" with intersex decoloniality to explore spaces
of political and cultural maneuvering and reconceptualizing.

Of course decoloniality must do more than remind us of the enduring legacies of colonialism (Rao 2020). The second part of this book thus consists
of decolonizing intersex interventions that seek to reconceptualize colonial
ideas of gender in three distinct chapters. Violence that targets intersex people

has always been met with resistance. Intersex activists have worked together against such violence across national borders since the 1990s, perhaps most strikingly in the African Intersex Movement (AIM) initiative formed by organizers from seven countries in 2017.[14] Solidarity in African decolonial activism is grounded in common values and "shared and endured legacies of enslavement, colonialism, racism and neoliberalism" (Tamale 2020, 11).[15] While Africa is a diverse continent, the violent mistreatment of those diagnosed as intersex has had striking commonalities that span geographical contexts. The three chapters in the second part of this book highlight different African activists' approaches to challenging the silence and lies of colonially based science and medicine.

In addition to engaging African decolonial feminisms, this book equally relies on the insights of critical intersex studies. To date, the field has had what philosopher Hil Malatino smartly describes as two emphases: documenting histories and reforming medicine. Early work in intersex studies had importantly practical intent. But new work like Malatino's eschews academic convention and construes "intersexuality as something other than the product of a positivist pathology whose roots must be discovered and clarified in order for treatment to be reconsidered and reformed" (2019, 3). Critical intersex studies rather follows intersex "to see where it goes, how it works, what arguments, assertions, and understandings of gender, sex, and sexuality it enables and disables" (3). In so doing, Malatino and other thinkers in the field create space to disrupt pathologization, looking at how gender is shaped by power and working toward a kind of undoing and reversal that dovetails with African feminist decoloniality. Morland follows a similar agenda in critical intersex studies, rejecting the fetishization that accounts of intersex often obligate. Morland refuses to spectacularize intersex in his work. He explains, "I will tell you about particular anatomies by telling you about the ethics and politics of medical and critical discourse, which is where anatomies are typically located anyway, together with the surgeries performed on them" (2011, 147).

Malatino and Morland's work converges with other important recent scholarship that analyzes, for instance, how colonial science racially and geographically coded difference in intersex bodies (Eckert 2017) and explores how this science is challenged by contemporary intersex activists working transnationally (Rubin 2017). Critical intersex studies has also been closely intertwined with trans studies, where overt discussions of decoloniality have proliferated for over a decade.[16] Trans and intersex decolonial analyses jointly call for interrogations of medical and administrative violence, appropriation, and homogenized understandings of gender and bodies.[17] Mauro Cabral's positionality as "an intersex and trans* guy from a Latin American country (Argentina)," trained as a historian and philosopher and working full-time directing an international trans* organization, informs his analyses. For Cabral, decolonizing means addressing complicated relationships to both colonial and gendered language; challenging "the production of trans* and intersex people as 'proper objects,' 'privileged examples,' and, in general, valuable goods in the theoretical primitive accumulation of flesh"; and analyzing scientific and medical classification through the logics of international capitalism (quoted in Boellstorff et al. 2014, 422–23). These thinkers and areas of inquiry deeply inform the framing of this book. *Envisioning African Intersex* refuses to objectify intersex subjects, instead turning the gaze on institutions and practitioners. This book theorizes the creation of gender binarisms through the critical interventions of intersex theorists and activists.

Intersex Imaginaries and Images in the Global South

Anthropology and biomedicine have jointly shaped conceptions of intersex, and one of the most prominent efforts to classify gender in transnational contexts occurred in historical research on those labeled as *third gender*. The concept of "third gender" has been used to describe gender expressions outside man/woman binaries across time and geography, often in the Global South. The use of the numeric word *third* throughout scholarship focused on intersex and trans people already reinscribes a dual gender system (plus one). Those identified as "third gender" are represented as foreign or primitive, their lives denigrated as evidence of Euro-American superiority or romanticized as transcending gender. Evan B. Towle and Lynn M. Morgan (2002, 484) were among the first authors to critique this idea: "The 'third gender' concept is by nature flawed because it subsumes all non-Western, nonbinary identities, practice, terminologies, and histories. Thus it becomes as junk drawer into which a great non-Western miscellany is carelessly dumped. Ethnographic examples can come from distinct societies located in Thailand, Polynesia, Melanesia, Native America, India, western Africa, and elsewhere and from any point in history, from ancient Greece to sixteenth-century Brazil to nineteenth-century England to contemporary North America." "Third gender" designations turn on the judgment of gender ambiguity as timeless—both primordial and predated—and are reductionist, as these global generalizations group varied cultures and expressions together under one category. This kind of cross-cultural appropriation marks such gender expressions as generic, representative of a paradox of both inferiority and an "idealized existence in a utopian time and place" (477) in both academic and activist accounts. Some contemporary discussions of intersex similarly generalize and romanticize those in the Global South as having escaped medical intervention and sometimes as linked to mythological historical and literary figures of hermaphroditism. Such efforts, while often well intentioned, are appropriative. As Towle and Morgan put it, "We do not believe that the goal of dismantling gender oppression and the binary gender system should seek legitimacy in narrow or sanctified appropriations of non-Western cultural histories or practices, although this method is used in anthropology and in the popular literature" (471). In short, "third gender" and other cross-cultural generalizations have promoted homogenization and appropriation at the expense of intersex people in the Global South.

Research intended to "discover" intersex communities and collect "evidence" demonstrates the disturbing reach of dominant imaginings embedded in ideas like "third gender." Three locations—in Africa (broadly construed), the Dominican Republic, and Papua New Guinea—have been referenced as exemplars of exoticism for the past fifty years. Building on colonial histories, academic studies that drew attention to these locales all originated in the 1970s. Since that time, these three sites have continued to govern scholarly and public imaginations. Research in South Africa, the Dominican Republic, and Papua New Guinea collectively illustrates concerns at the core of decolonial intersex analysis.

The first of these sites is the animating force behind this book. Researchers assert that black people in Africa are more likely to be intersex than people in the rest of the world. The colonial roots of this claim, addressed in chapter 1, focus on black people's bodies, and especially on their genitals, as not clearly male or female, and South Africa is the dominant location for this claim. The racist science and medicine of comparative anatomy has long been codified in scholarly literature across the African continent. Architects of colonialism and apartheid—a system of white supremacy manifested in policies of political, economic, and social separateness—violently controlled South Africans' relationships, movements, and access to services. Policing gender binaries was integral to this power and control. Further, from the 1970s onward, published medical studies reinforced ideas of disproportionate intersex in black bodies. Scientists' and doctors' arguments primarily rested on visual data, especially physical exams of bodies and medical photography, as contrived evidence of their claims. In the chapters to come, this imaging is contrasted with self-representations and efforts of activists such as Sally Gross—one of the first openly intersex activists in Africa, who initiated globally pioneering intersex legislation—and the growing chorus of intersex South African activists mobilizing social media and changing policy.[18]

The second site brought under scrutiny is the Dominican Republic, initiated by the work of epidemiologist Julianne Imperato-McGinley in the 1970s.

In the town of Salinas, children locally referred to as Guevedoces (interpreted to mean "penis at twelve") are raised as girls until puberty, when they develop anatomical traits often thought of as masculine. Imperato-McGinley's scholarship pathologizes them as having a genetic condition—5α-reductase deficiency—and residents of Salinas have come to be seen as representative of intersex physical difference. Beginning with her first publication in 1974, Imperato-McGinley's work evoked global fascination and objectification, continued through ongoing academic research, pharmaceutical investigations, TV/film explorations, and hundreds of international news reports. The bodies of those scrutinized are represented as rare and exotic, and their community is described with words such as "remote," "primitive," and "mysterious." Even pharmaceutical giant Merck has capitalized on this community, conducting research to develop what has become the best-selling drug finasteride (Propecia/Proscar), a drug that mimics 5α-reductase deficiency to block testosterone production and treat prostate issues and baldness.[19] Imperato-McGinley's scholarship and the varied scientific and popular accounts that have followed it reflect a fear of sudden intersex "afflictions," and these accounts compare 5α-reductase deficiency to a debilitating illness that can strike suddenly and unexpectedly. Academic and popular representations alike consistently express stunned disbelief at locals' reported acceptance of Guevedoces in contrast to their own biases.

While most analyses to date focus on dissecting the bodies of Dominicans as a source of scientific data, I reverse this gaze to examine those doing the scrutinizing. Why has this community remained a focus of fascination and become representative of the Global South for more than fifty years? One answer to this question rests on visual depictions of those in Salinas that begin with disturbing photographs in Imperato-McGinley's research (e.g., Peterson et al. 1977). In the tradition of intersex medical photography that I interrogate in chapter 2, the eyes of Dominicans are obscured with a white bar. But this bar does little to disguise the physical and emotional distress of those facing the camera's gaze.

In Imperato-McGinley's research, exploratory surgeries and photographic documentation are justified in the name of science but without benefit to community members who became unwitting patients. One image represents a crying eighteen-month-old baby reaching for someone just outside the photographic frame. Viewers see pain in the face of a twelve-year-old posed nude (except for socks) with large postsurgical bandages on their abdomen. Another photograph shows three relatives together against a Lamprey grid—a backdrop of measured squares invented in the late 1800s and popularized in anthropometric photography as a means to measure indigenous bodies and quantify their inferiority.[20] They are pictured shirtless, and captions compare their musculature and hair.

There is no discussion of individual patients pictured, most of whom are not seeking care for illness but who are experimented on for the sake of research itself. In numerous unsettling photos, children's genitals are portrayed with unidentified white fingers spreading labia for the camera. The captions of all these photographs boldly describe them as universally representative of disorder and aged development.

While these photographs from the 1970s were first published in medical journals, they have continued to be reprinted and to represent 5α-reductase deficiency and intersex in the Global South. The current website for the Urological Sciences Research Foundation (2022) includes black and white photographs from Imperato-McGinley's co-authored 1977 publication. Their framing invites voyeurism: the eyes of those pictured are covered with a white bar while viewers gaze at their nude bodies. The photos are positioned next to a map showing the location of the Dominican Republic and a short description of "The 'Guevedoces' of the Dominican Republic." Speaking for the Urological Sciences Research Foundation, the unnamed author explains 5α-reductase deficiency with bizarrely inaccurate and unscientific language: "These children appeared to be girls at birth, but at puberty these 'girls' sprout muscles, testes, and a penis" (Urological Sciences Research Foundation 2022). This representation positions those in Salinas as primitive and of the past, while also depicting photographs from fifty years ago as if they were in the present moment.

Innumerable film and television representations mirror this website's content, tone, and presentism. A Science Channel television program (*Through the Wormhole*) includes the black and white photos in a segment on embryonic gender development narrated by Morgan Freeman (Acutt 2016), and a documentary by the BBC as part of a program called *Countdown to Life* uses the images similarly (Austin and Johnson 2015). A tweet from the Science Channel advertising *Through the Wormhole* (September 13, 2016) consists of Imperato-McGinley's photograph of three shirtless people against a Lamprey grid with white bars over their eyes and the text "A person's apparent sex can change during puberty."[21] *The Third Sex* (Roberts 2004), a film aired on television in the United States and Europe and then distributed via video, goes as far as staging an enactment of actors exploring a set intended to look like a remote village. Film footage is altered to look like grainy black and white, accompanied by spooky music, while a narrator describes Imperato-McGinley's work at length for general viewers. The imagined creation of this scene is one of colonial anthropological discovery.[22]

These same images are reproduced in contexts that do not even feign scientific agendas. My Google image searches documented their repeated inclusion on pornographic websites. Journalists have also consistently used the images; old and new images together accompany dozens of headlines that exclaim, for example, "Inside the Baffling Caribbean Village where Little Girls Turn into Boys at the Age of 12 . . . and Even Suddenly Grow Penises" (Godden 2017), "The Mysterious Caribbean Village Where Young Girls Morph into Boys" (Petkar 2017), and "There's a Village in the Caribbean Where 'Girls' Grow Penises at Age 12" (*Pink News* 2017). The "mysterious" descriptions of the intrigue of residents who "transform," "morph" or "grow penises" follow familiar colonial tropes of exotic rarity. In these varied accounts, Dominicans are reified for gender pathologies based on contrived research conducted at the expense of people in Salinas.

Attention to the third site in the Global South was incited by the influential research of anthropologist Gilbert Herdt on "hermaphrodites" among the pseudonymic Sambia in Papua New Guinea.[23] Herdt's research began, like Imperato-McGinley's, in 1974.[24] This scholarship presents another unsettling representation that eschews ethics in problematic efforts to expose and discover unknown and titillating gendered secrets. Herdt engaged in decades of research on sexuality and gender in Papua New Guinea, including well-known studies of ritualized homosexuality and semen transfer among men (e.g., Herdt 1987). He collaborated at different times with psychiatrist Robert Stoller and later with endocrinologist Julian Davidson on what, of particular note here, Herdt labels "clinical ethnography" (1985, 115) in the region.

Herdt and Stoller focus their attention on a reportedly intersex shaman named Sakulambei, and their research exemplifies the inherent problems of research on intersex in the Global South. In a 1979 interview, Herdt and Stoller persuade the reluctant Sakulambei to discuss his body by convincing him of their interest in his shamanic activities and knowledge (Herdt and Stoller 1985). But their real goal, as they state in their writing, is to gain Sakulambei's trust to learn about his body. In a conversation between Herdt and Stoller that took place in front of Sakulambei but was not translated for him, they explain their decision to lie.[25]

HERDT: I'm going to do something that's not quite ethical, but I'm going to leave the language vague enough so that he may suspect that you are . . . you may have some hermaphroditic qualities . . . [pause].

STOLLER: Good. [I do, in the sense that I can work with hermaphroditic patients in such a way that a few thought I was a hermaphrodite. That is why I said "good" and felt that it was not unethical.]

FOOTNOTE 27, HERDT: I'd forgotten I'd done this until translating the tapes in 1981–1982. It amounts to a lie: I as much as said [Stoller] was a hermaphrodite. I don't think it was harmful; the circumstances of the interview were extraordinary. I never lie with informants, but fudged in this instance. I think it helped; but readers may disagree with this tack. [S: One should never, in doing research, lie in order to get information. Supervision corrects such mistakes.] (Herdt and Stoller 1985, 135, bracket insertions in original)

Admitted deceptions include falsely leading Sakulambei to believe that Stoller is intersex ("fudging"), which he admits he is not, and promising to keep secrets about Sakulambei's body that are later exposed as the subject of their multiple publications. They observe in this same publication that Sakulambei is "a good liar" (1985, 136) and does not trust them, but with good reason. It is Herdt and Stoller who continue to seek a "truth" of his body using dishonesty.[26]

As in South Africa and the Dominican Republic, Herdt's research on intersex in Papua New Guinea hinges on visual scrutiny as an indicator of truth and pathology. In Herdt and Stoller's discussions with Sakulambei, they learn of a German businessman named Gronemann who visited Papua New Guinea around 1960. Sakulambei explains to them that at ten years old, he was undressed and photographed by Gronemann, and he remained extremely upset that he was never paid for this privilege. Two years after this interview, Herdt also learned that Gronemann had had sex with the young Sakulambei before taking these photos, raising unanswered questions of sexual exploitation and pornography (Herdt and Stoller 1985, 142). Herdt and Stoller believe that the photo being taken at all is evidence that Sakulambei's body is visibly hermaphroditic. Lena Eckert's careful analysis of this situation suggests that the authors believe Gronemann's photography "testifies to the existence of something that needs to be displayed as exceptional" (2017, 147). Even though they do not reprint the businessman's photographs, they invoke their existence as proof of intersex, relying on the businessman's gaze as trustworthy and authentic. This use of images is what Eckert refers to as the myth of photographic truth and its invocation of realism.[27] In the exploitation of Sakulambei, as in other colonial travel and research, photography was considered positivist evidence and even more accurate than the eye (Pinney 2011).

Images have the power to create meaning, boundaries, and realities rather than just reflecting and observing them. Those deemed intersex in all three of these contexts are similarly subjected to documentation of their bodies. All photographs are stenciled off the real, like a footprint, rather than an unassailable representation of reality, and photographs of people deemed intersex are inherently interpretive, dwelling in the "usually shady commerce between art and truth" (Sontag 1977, 6). From the inception of the camera in 1839, the coupling of evidence and photography positioned some bodies as superior to others. Photography has been critical to state and scientific practices such as surveillance and record keeping of gendered and racialized differences.[28] Recorded images were crucial to burgeoning racial science, in Anne McClintock's words, as a source of "mechanical and therefore objectively sound 'factual' knowledge about racial 'types,' 'specimens,' and 'tribes'" (1995, 124) and to endorse eugenic control. As scientifically justified means to create illusions of some people as civilized and others as primitive, "photography became the servant of imperial progress" (125), and violence enacted with cameras captured moments that then transcended time.[29] With increasing reproduction and distribution, photographs widely established a fallacy of realism in the service of institutional power.

Taken together, representations of these locales in the Global South serve as critical contexts for "seeing" in the science of raced gender. There is no better tool than photographs to create a sense of truth and, as Sontag puts it, to "help people take possession of the space in which they are insecure" (1977, 9). Reproduced images of intersex and race are traced throughout this book. But rather than accepting the realities such images seek to create, *Envisioning African Intersex* turns the scrutinizing gaze back to the photographers, critiques the reach of their photos, and centers the perspectives of photographic subjects. Throughout these chapters, images are shown to be sites of violence in their creation and reproduction, codifying false realities of intersex in South Africa and the Global South more broadly. But these same images are reclaimed and reframed by activists seeking to create new decolonial realities.

Unsettling Approaches to Intersex

Envisioning African Intersex grew out of my relationship with South African intersex activist Sally Gross, which began in 2000, and it is grounded in my research and activism in South Africa over more than two decades. Queer African scholarship is integral to my methodology (my approach to this book) and my choices of methods (what I did to write it). Central to this work are critiques of who sets the parameters of knowledge and challenges to understandings of who counts as a theorist and what counts as theory. With these ideas in mind, this book not only unsettles claims of scientists and doctors but asks questions, including, What does it mean to position Gross, the activist who started the first intersex organization on the African continent, as a gender theorist? Can social media like Twitter be read as sites for Semenya's views on gender testing in sport? How do videos on YouTube articulate the visions of South African activists refusing and reframing intersex stigmatization? My effort to answer these questions is centered in insights from African scholars and activists, methodologically challenging generalizations about gender and sexuality based in the Global North that do not travel and translate well.

Much work in queer and transgender studies transnationally has been invested in the recuperative project of finding and creating archives and genealogies. But scholars including Zethu Matebeni (2014a, 2021), Keguro Macharia (2015), and Anjali Arondekar (2005) urge us to interrogate colonial archives of sexuality and gender as subjects of inquiry rather than as sources of them.[30] Extractive methodologies of "mining" archives for evidence of contemporary sexual and gender identifications recall South Africa's destructive past of unethical research as well as literal mining of the earth for diamonds and gold. I instead aim to trace alternate histories, refusing the discovery of intersex patients and the fetishization at the center of medico-science, reading South African histories to expose doctors' and scientists' racialized practices of gendering under colonialism and apartheid.

These methodologies compelled me to seek sources outside conventional archives and publications. This book thus draws on a complex of materials— colonial archival documents, a wide range of African scientific and medical literature spanning a century, popular publications on gender binaries in the Global South, films on intersex in various African contexts, personal materials and interviews from the GALA Queer Archive at the University of the Witwatersrand, life histories and interviews I conducted from 1997 to the present, participant observation in South African LGBTQI organizations, decades of media by and about African intersex people, and online sources, including websites of organizations, YouTube videos, and social media posts.[31] Recognizing the impossibility of a comprehensive genealogy necessitated embracing partiality and anecdotal accounts as an antidote to positivist analyses of intersex.

Many of my methodological decisions have been similarly driven by decisions about what not to do. I write extensively about and describe photographs, especially in medical contexts, but I do not feel comfortable reproducing photography that was so often taken under duress and with questionable consent. I have chosen not to seek out intersex folks in the public eye for interviews; instead, I represent their opinions through writings and online postings where they have chosen to express themselves. Cross-culturally, many scholars who have written about intersex have been secretive in conducting their research and exploitative in their decisions to reveal others' secrets. I have been privy to secrets and conducted interviews with those who have cautiously revealed themselves to be intersex since 1997, but I chose not to discuss these experiences rather than to betray trust or risk lives.

In researching medical and popular histories of intersex, many of my efforts to search for relevant materials evoked confused terminology of the past or yielded minimal results. Historically, the term *hermaphrodite* has been deployed in various ways and expressed in contexts ranging from Greek mythology to derogatory slurs. In this book, I leave the archaic descriptor *hermaphrodite* in the past, except when historically indicated or reclaimed by activists. As mentioned earlier, *intersex* can refer to a vast range of gendered bodily formations or be a term of self-identification, and its use varies widely over time and place.[32] While highly contested since its adoption in 2005, disorders of sex development (DSD) is another phrase used medically.[33] I rely on the more widely used term *intersex* in accordance with activists' conventions and concerns about DSD referring to some bodies as "disordered."[34] Gross put it this way: "I do not use the recent label 'DSD' because, as introduced, the first 'D' stands for 'disorders' and I deny that intersex is pathological or a disorder" (2013).

Direct recommendations, such as this one made by a collaboration of South African intersex activists, further guide my decisions about language; they state, "Use the term intersex. Stigmatising language leads to poor mental health, marginalisation, and exclusion from human rights and social institutions. The term intersex promotes equality and human rights for people born with atypical sex characteristics" (*National Dialogue* 2018, 30). I follow these activists' directives and their urgings to "uncomplicate" the term *intersex* as a means of increasing conversations that are "understandable across educational and classed backgrounds" (32). I also use the concept *intersex medicine* to signify a range of theories and protocols used to pathologize and treat people under this rubric. Rather than beginning this book with a description of medical conditions and their histories, I reserve these discussions for chapters where I trace said nuances and genealogies.

Some reading this book may wonder about my thinking behind use of the words *gender* and *race*. One of the earliest interventions of feminist studies was to distinguish between *sex* as the body—male/female—and *gender* as social roles and obligations—masculine/feminine. But following the work of feminist and queer theorists over the past thirty years, I instead refer to the entirety of the man/woman binary as *gender*. As this book discusses in many different ways, distinctions between male/female bodies (as sex) are neither natural nor consistent, and bodies are historically and geographically produced. Let me put it plainly: I think the distinction between sex and gender is artificial and replicates problematic scientific notions of the gendered body. For these reasons, I do not find the word *sex* very useful, and I choose not to use it in order to highlight the production of gender and its assumptions about the body.

Race also presents an ungrounded shifting invention that I engage and question throughout this book. Efforts to fabricate empirical evidence to justify colonial hierarchies created taxonomies and pathologies, including slippery "scientific" concepts such as tribe, nation, ethnicity, language, and population. In South Africa such concepts were intended to produce "racial purity" and to guide colonial and apartheid policies (Braun and Hammonds 2014). Analyzing the use of this overlapping and changing terminology points to its emptiness while recognizing the violent strength of its imposition. I also follow many South African scholars' preference not to capitalize racial terms, including *black*, following historical discussions about race and enforced capitalization under colonialism and apartheid.[35] Scholars such as Asanda Ngoasheng (2021) refuse capitalization as a reminder that race is socially constituted and to push back on lexicons imposed by the Global North.[36] In thinking about both gender and race, I find it more useful to analyze the concepts themselves and the questions they raise than to evaluate the skewed evidence they attempt to produce.

Tamale exhorts, "It is extremely important for Africa's decolonization/decolonial project that Europe's manipulation of history and the imperialist intellectual deceit is uncovered" (2020, 17). In the chapters to come, I work to uncover the historical deceit that imposed fallacies about raced and gendered bodies and that denigrated intersex people. The first two chapters of this book focus on colonization and apartheid in South Africa, exposing gendered deceptions perpetuated through citational chains and visual exploitation. Chapter 1 traces current ideas back to their historical roots to theorize colonial representations of "hermaphroditism" and four centuries of unsubstantiated claims. This chapter disproves three historical fictions of Africans' bodies as inferior and disproportionately hermaphroditic. First, I demonstrate that the racist fantasy of the "Hottentot apron" is meritless. Second, I parallel South African histories with the emergence of medical notions of "true hermaphroditism" in colonial Europe. I consider why and how this diagnosis eventually excluded Europeans and instead could only be "discovered" in the colonies, especially in Africa. Following this genealogy to the 1900s and then to the inception of apartheid in 1948, I explore how the problematic invention of Bantu Gynaecology—a field that claimed African women were physically different from and inferior to European women—and theories of race and gender plasticity popularized in the 1950s converge in the new field of intersex medicine in South Africa.

Chapter 2 investigates the claim popularized by H. J. Grace's influential 1970 master's thesis at the University of KwaZulu-Natal that "intersexuality on the whole is more common in the Bantu than in other races" (3–4). The intention of Grace's thesis was to prove an inordinate commonality of intersex among black South Africans, but he was unable to do so. Nevertheless, as this chapter explains, since that time, Grace's work has been cited by scientists worldwide as definitive proof of racialized claims about intersex. Through a close reading of this thesis and a review of related medical publications, I follow a citational chain of literature that continued to parrot its erroneous assertions over the following fifty years. This pathological creation of intersex difference relies on visual representations, especially on exploitative medical photography, to create a sense of truth. In this chapter, I establish how a set of interrelated strategies—definition, scrutiny, repetition, and justification—codified claims about disproportionate intersex and blackness with lasting transnational influence.

The second part of this book continues to dismantle colonial and apartheid gendered fallacies by centering South African activists' strategies. Chapters 3, 4, and 5 each foreground decolonizing intersex praxis, retaining a focus on South Africa while also including collaborations that span the continent. In chapter 3, I analyze the inception of intersex activism in Africa. In 1999, anti-apartheid activist Sally Gross established the first intersex organization on the African continent—Intersex South Africa—and she was the driving force behind a host of legal transformations with global significance until her untimely death in 2014. Chapter 3 explores Gross's interventions into issues as complex as the contentious implementation of discredited medical protocols in South Africa, class-based complications of whiteness and intersex in South Africa, and the intersection of intersex with environmental racism and DDT. Throughout her life, Gross mounted strong critiques of teratology, the colonial science of monstrosity, and of prominent scientists such as John Money to detail damage caused by theories and protocols imposed from the Global North. My conversations with Gross and her diverse writing and film work elucidate how she shifted public opinion about intersex science and its colonial roots.

Chapter 4 analyzes gender regulations and medically unnecessary procedures—including clitoridectomy and gonadectomy—forced on Caster Semenya and other athletes by sporting authorities with neocolonial agendas. These procedures rely on the same colonial citations and claims about disproportionate intersex frequency problematized in chapters 1 and 2. In this chapter, I challenge histories of race and geopolitics in gender testing and the racially biased agendas of the orchestrators of gendered policies. But this chapter also demonstrates that Semenya and other athletes refuse to acquiesce to the leaders of global sport, who reiterate colonial rhetoric and falsely claim disproportionate rates of intersex in the Global South. Social media campaigns #HandsOffCaster and #IAAFMustFall, as well as Semenya's declarations on platforms such as Instagram and Twitter, have created new dialogues that challenge colonial claims and redefine what it means to be a woman. Chapter 4 exposes racist sport science and foregrounds Semenya, her contemporaries, and her supporters' decolonizing interventions into the shifting parameters of gender.

How do contemporary intersex activists in Africa decolonize and retheorize gender through their self-representations? The fifth and final chapter of this book explores the priorities of activists, including those in the African Intersex Movement and the establishment of what they term an "African intersex reference of intelligence" (AIM 2017, 2020). Since 2017, activists from seven countries have worked together under the auspices of AIM to issue a set of unified demands, including ending nonconsensual surgeries and establishing new legal policies. In this chapter, the visual exploitations that began this book are rejected. Instead, contemporary activists interrogate medical protocols and navigate challenges of visibility through campaigns that use videos and photographs in new ways. Activists' self-representations on social media and film starkly contrast the anonymity and violence that characterize histories of intersex medicine. Their critiques of medical protocols and their policy demands expand understandings of gender, as they model new decolonial understandings and call for accountability and retribution.

Envisioning African Intersex demonstrates the impact of colonial ideologies that codified racialized gender distinctions and how their false claims became canonical. I show how images, film, and video enforce the dominant narrative of disproportionate African intersex, circulating far beyond medico-scientific contexts and beyond national borders. Activists who are disrupting these images and creating new representations provide important historical correctives with quotidian impact. Contemporary African intersex activists envision fresh understandings of gender, offering new, decolonial ways of seeing.

PART I

Uncovering

Colonial and Apartheid Legacies

1. Colonial Observations and Fallacies

"Hermaphroditism" in Histories of South Africa

The first time I cracked open a book called Bantu Gynaecology it fell to a picture of a "hermaphrodite." Were I to construct a fiction from that moment, it would say that I became aware that bantu-ness had something to do with sexual morphology, that there was something both dramatic about that morphology and that something traumatic happened to those who, like me, dared to look at it. . . . The [headless] picture made me uncomfortable, made me wonder if it told a truth about sex, a truth about me, about my own gender non-normativity. It made me wonder about the truth of bantu sex, a truth that was medically certified. —KEGURO MACHARIA, "On Caster Semenya"

* * *

Godfrey Phillips Charlewood's *Bantu Gynaecology* (1956) is a text built on hundreds of years of representations of Africans' bodies as innately "hermaphroditic."[1] The most obvious influences of works like Charlewood's were on scientists and doctors, but Macharia's experience encountering this book is perhaps even more notable, demonstrating the broad effects of its claims.

Theories and methods of categorizing and quantifying the body, such as measurements of skulls and blood, were used by scientists to assert that Africans were less evolved than and inferior to Europeans. But it is less well known that these taxonomies also portrayed Africans as outside male/female binaries and their genitals as inherently ambiguous. Bodies were gendered through scientific imaging and analyses of labial length, penis size, pelvis width, vaginal depth, testicular substance, and the composition of reproductive organs. These assessments relied on comparative anatomy, justifying violence by claiming that some bodies are inherently superior to others; and in gendered colonial taxonomies, hermaphroditism was spectacularized as primitive. This chapter traces centuries of representations and exploitation to theorize the role of gender dimorphism in colonial domination.

When I recently checked *Bantu Gynaecology* out of the library using interlibrary loan, the photograph of a person labeled as a "hermaphrodite" was missing; it had been ripped or cut out of the book (Charlewood 1956, 13–14).[2] This book contains dozens of photos, slides, and drawings of bodies illustrating disturbing moments of violent objectification. For example, the title page of the book is accompanied by a full-page photograph of an unnamed nude young person staring defiantly (or perhaps angrily?) into the camera, with the caption: "Congenital absence of one breast." So why were these two particular pages missing from the book? Had they been removed, perhaps, by a censoring librarian, a recalcitrant patient, or a fascinated voyeur? When, over the past sixty-five years, did this happen?

There are very few medically oriented books on African gendered pathologies, but I found that my interlibrary-loaned copy of Willem A. Van Niekerk's *True Hermaphroditism: Clinical, Morphologic and Cytogenetic Aspects*, also focused on South Africa, was similarly missing the pages with photographs of someone labeled as a "'true' hermaphrodite" (1974, 53–54).[3] I wondered how these removals and lacunae of medical photographs could be read. What had happened to these absent images initially posed under troubling circumstances in various periods? Perhaps this removal was an effort to possess the photograph, to tear it out so it could be consumed. *Envisioning African Intersex* explores how "true hermaphroditism"—the medical diagnosis personified in the missing photo—is enmeshed with scientific theories of race and objectifying consumptive gazes that persist to the present.

Since at least the 1600s, efforts to produce racial difference have focused on African people's genitalia as monstrous and abnormal, always already juxtaposed to white European bodies. Pumla Dineo Gqola identifies this "obsession with African genitalia" as a feature of colonialism and enslavement that continued into the apartheid era, traces of which can be seen now in what she refers to as "contemporary global racisms" (2015, 44). Colonialisms relied on genocide, territorialization, and economic domination, but they also fundamentally shaped and controlled how people think about and see themselves and the world. In South Africa, such colonialisms were not simply European impositions but multiplicitous colonialisms that included tangled and conflicting relations between colonizer and colonized and between fields and locations of science (Rassool and Hayes 2002; Rassool 2015). Colonial histories produced a range of violent efforts to locate difference in genitals that were grounded in what African historian Catherine Burns calls a "fascination with, and ultimately iconographic representation of African women's sexual organs" as exotic and sexualized (1995, 409). Travelers and naturalists' preoccupations with southern African women's genitals became an influential discourse of racialized gender binarism in the nineteenth century.

As in the exemplars from the Dominican Republic and Papua New Guinea discussed in the introduction, early representations of Africa aligned medico-scientific efforts to discover and racialize difference in genitals in ways now described as intersex. Many people have written about these colonial fixations with African genitals, and often these works include a brief mention of genitals as hermaphroditic. Although this use varied over time, Africans' genitals were almost always represented as anatomically abnormal or nonbinary and were constructed to support the superiority of the Global North. Hierarchical theories rested on clearly discernible differences between men's and women's bodies as visible markers of civilization and the reproductive dominance of the European (later white) race. Colonialists' fascination with body parts they represented as gendered created contrived notions of genitals that continue to be repeated in the present.

Colonial Scrutiny and the Fallacy of the "Hottentot Apron"

In southern Africa, anecdotal observations were critical to the development of science and put trust in explorers and their methods of recording what they purported to see. From the 1600s onward, a fixation with African men's genitalia centered on claims that they had one testicle and debates over whether their alleged monorchidism was innate, a traditional surgical practice to improve running speed, or a mythical claim to undermine men's virility (Gordon 1992). But while monorchidism and Africans' penises and breasts were of great interest to naturalists in this period, "nothing excited these men more than the elongation of the labia minora, or intervaginal lips, among the Hottentot" (Schiebinger 2013, 164). Dozens of publications centered on observations of the so-called Hottentot apron that began when Europeans colonized the Cape of Good Hope.[4]

Authors of accounts that spanned three hundred years regularly described African women's genitalia as elongated labia, as penile, and/or as hermaphroditic. Colonists defined inhabitants in southern Africa through their genitals. Indeed, the first scholarly interest in people indigenous to South Africa focused on the measurement of "Hottentot genitalia" (Gordon 1992, 186). Beginning with the earliest recorded narratives, the "Hottentot apron" was pronounced a "deformity" that departed from the European norm; explorers and naturalists declared the elongated labia they claimed to observe as a "vestige of Hottentots' animal origin" (Schiebinger 2013, 164).

Hermaphroditic genitals were strongly linked to primitiveness in colonial theories of the body. A few examples from southern Africa demonstrate the breadth of this assertion. Sir Thomas Herbert's *Some Yeares Travaile* (1634, 1638, 1665, 1677) "contained the usual enthralled description of female genitalia and 'semi-eunuchs'" (Gordon 1992, 190).[5] Explorer John Ovington (1697) wrote that assertions that people indigenous to the region were "Hermophradites" represented an accepted consensus. Captain Cook's famous scientific expedition of 1771 sought to determine the innateness of genital anatomy of those in the Cape of Good Hope; he writes, "We were very desirous to determine the great question among natural historians, whether the women of this country have or have not that fleshy flap or apron" (1797, 362). While the nuances and politics of European colonialism in the Cape were complex and varied over centuries, this focus persisted. These and scores of other early accounts were widely cited as justification for the violent oppression of colonialism and had vast subsequent influence on European scholars' hierarchical theories.[6] Carl Linnaeus was so enthralled by this supposed aspect of "Hottentot" anatomy that "he (quite mistakenly) made it a characteristic of the entire 'African' race" (Schiebinger 2013, 164). Similarly, in the eighteenth century, Voltaire (François-Marie Arouet) argued that African women's anatomy was so unusual that they likely belonged to a separate species of humans.

But despite centuries of innumerable claims of African hermaphroditism and genital difference, the validity of these observations has also been questioned since the 1600s. Some early naturalists found descriptions of elongated labia untrustworthy. Ovington was perhaps the first to suggest that this attribution was based on false supposition: "There is a vulgar Opinion which has formerly been receiv'd, that the Natives of this *Cape* were *Hermophradites*, which was founded only upon Conjecture; for two Gentlemen, who were resolv'd not to be liable to this Errour, assur'd me the Report was false, upon the Curiosity they had of knowing the Reason of it, which was becaufe the Female Parts were cut in the Fashion of small Teats hanging down" (1697, 497). Ovington suggested that misunderstandings—or perhaps local practices to intentionally elongate labia—had led to representations of a hermaphroditic "Hottentot apron" as congenital.

Ovington was in good company in the years to come. While European naturalists widely debated whether or not the "Hottentot apron" actually existed, in fact, "Few had actually seen African genitalia; much of the information filtering into European universities and academies was second- or third-hand—if not totally fabricated" (Schiebinger 2013, 165). In 1749, influential French naturalist Georges-Louise Leclerc, Comte de Buffon, described this *monstrueuse difformité* as a defining morphological feature of those he described as "Hottentots." Though he went on to deny existence of the "Hottentot apron" in 1766, his earlier views continued to be reprinted internationally, and "authors shamelessly poached his paragraphs on Hottentots in countless follow-up ethnographies" (Curran 2011, 110). These early inaccurate accounts became the first links in citational chains, repeated references to ideas and publications that built on each other over decades and centuries despite their problematic origins. The false claims about Africans' bodies derived a growing power from their repetition.

In Renaissance Europe, medical and biological theories of gender were composite, contradictory, and unstable (Huet 1993).[7] European and African women alike were feared for their reproductive capacity and considered threatening when they expressed independence or disdain for men. There was also an increasing tendency to absorb the "hermaphrodite" into the figure of the deviant woman in Europe (Jones and Stallybrass 1991, 90). With this context in mind, Gordon's speculation that explorers' depiction of the "Hottentot apron" may have been retaliatory merits close consideration. Women in the region were known for their autonomy from their husbands and for their disdain for Europeans; when met with exploitation, they responded by throwing stones and exposing themselves to insult explorers and force them to retreat.[8] He explains that this was intimidating and shocking to European travelers, musing, "Could it be that our intrepid explorers felt threatened by these autonomous females and thus tended not only to portray their menfolk as wimps, as semi-eunuchs, but also to exaggerate female genitalia?" (1992, 194).[9] Gordon's reflections fit among a range of critiques postulating that colonial explorers' biases explicitly influenced their genital representations.

Even among those who did believe in some observable genital difference, there were constant arguments about its cause. If the so-called Hottentot apron existed, some researchers questioned if "women created these flaps of skin by pulling, pinching, twisting, and wrapping normal labia around little sticks or twigs" (Schiebinger 2013, 165–66). Physician Matthew L. Hewat's *Bantu Folk Lore* (1905) claims that at puberty, Basuto women of southern Africa engaged in an unknown practice that elongated their labia (though "much difficulty is experienced in finding out what exactly takes place"), at which time, "the female thus converted into an animal of lust and desire" (1905, 107). Sander Gilman rejects this derogatory tone while similarly suggesting that such difference might simply be a result of "manipulation of the genitalia and considered beautiful by the Hottentots and Bushman as well as tribes in Basutoland and Dahomey" (1985, 85). But despite these substantive doubts, the unsubstantiated assertion of congenital difference among those indigenous to southern Africa prevailed. Outside these few exceptions, the vast majority of researchers increasingly described innate racialized difference as factual.[10]

Published drawings imparted further evidentiary weight to support the troubled claim of hermaphroditic genitals. For instance, in 1790, naturalist François Le Valliant describes pleading with a woman at the Cape of Good Hope to let him examine and draw her genitals. Le Valliant admitted that she very reluctantly succumbed to his request, but his resulting illustration was criticized by colonial geographer and travel writer John Barrow (1801) and by La Valliant's translator Elizabeth Helme (1790) as "more a product of his imagination than a true image of nature" (Schiebinger 2013, 168). It is not clear whether such images were intended to be deceptive. But even if observers were not willfully fraudulent, "In a very real sense they invented their own Hottentots before they saw them. . . . The first European writers had little precedent for describing what they observed, thus their descriptions are largely the manifestation of Europeans feelings about Africa. Most early writers were Renaissance 'meta-physicalists' who were largely stylists rather than seekers of facts. They were read for entertainment not documentation. Few of these intrepid writers spent more than a few days at the Cape. Instead they borrowed and plagiarised freely, which is why all these accounts are so tiringly similar" (Gordon 1992, 187–88). Furthermore, despite their inaccuracy, early drawings by explorers were cited as confirmation of inferiority. Functioning as visual evidence, they were presented to connote scientific certainty and pictorial confirmation of difference.

This depiction of African genitals as inherently or disproportionately hermaphroditic also became the basis for scientific and medical textbooks that preceded *Bantu Gynaecology*. J. J. Virey's (1819) dictionary of medical and scientific anatomical studies included drawings allegedly of "Hottentot" genitalia (Gilman 1985, 85). In Theodor Billroth's gynecology handbook, the so-called Hottentot apron is described as an error in the development of the female genitalia, an assertion that had become commonplace by 1877 (Gilman 1985, 89). *A Textbook of the Diseases of Women* by Henry Jacques Garrigues (1894) included similar descriptions and has now been in print for more than a century.[11] Garrigues's account includes drawings and descriptions of supposedly normative labia of unidentified women he contrasts to those in southern Africa, stating: "In all of the women of the Bushmen in South Africa and in some of the Hottentot women they hang halfway down to the knees, forming the so-called *Hottentot Apron*" (1854, 37). These pictorial representations are presented simply as facts. No consideration is given to the biases underpinning this fallacy and the deficiencies of sources in the ever-growing citational chain.

Perhaps even more influential was *Woman: An Historical, Gynaecological and Anthropological Compendium* (Ploss, Bartels, and Bartels [1885] 1935), three volumes referenced and reprinted across Britain, Continental Europe, and the United States for decades (Hodes 2017). The compendium includes a chapter titled "The Female Genitalia: Racial and Ethnographical Characteristics" that is more than one hundred pages long and purports to establish global racial hierarchies in women's bodies. Ten pages are dedicated to "The Hottentot Apron" (Ploss, Bartels, and Bartels [1885] 1935, 327–36), including exhaustive detail about colonial observers' unverified accounts and almost a dozen photographs of women's genitals.[12] Rebecca Hodes explains that many of these photographs of the "Hottentot vulva" were taken by German photographer Franz Seiner in 1910 while on a research trip and "were changed and manipulated both prior and subsequent to their publication in the *Ploss Compendium*" (2017, 124–25).[13] Ploss, Bartels, and Bartels also argue that the clitoris is "larger among tropical races" (especially "African races") than in cold climates, citing widespread representations in "native works of art" and including one drawing and photo of a figurine as proof of their contention ([1885] 1935, 336–39). Taken together, these assertions demonstrate reliance on images as evidentiary, manipulated to support erroneous colonial observations, and illustrate the power of racialized comparative anatomy to create notions of truth.

Africans in Exhibition: Scientific Racism and Genital Ambiguity

From the inception of colonialism in Africa, scientific racism and theories that preceded it have denigrated Africans as anatomically inferior to Europeans by falsely contending, for instance, that they had an additional layer of darker skin (Jean Riolan, 1618), blackish blue brains and other organs (Johann Friedrich Meckel, 1755), and pigmented blood, bile, and even sperm (Claude-Nicole

Le Cat, 1765). Fabricated claims about gendered body parts formed another means of creating the myth that there are only two kinds of "civilized" gendered bodies (male or female). These claims extended to exhibitions in Europe. Perhaps the most well-known African exploited and cited by scientists as demonstrating their theories was Sara Baartman.[14]

Baartman was abducted in South Africa and transported to Europe, where she was spectacularized in London and Paris from 1810 to 1815. As Zoë Wicomb puts it, "She encapsulates so much of the history of colonisation and exploitation in South Africa, also the extermination of the Khoe peoples, as well as the history of representation itself" (Wicomb 2021, 44). According to one newspaper account from 1810, Baartman was held in a cage "like a wild beast, and ordered to move backwards and forwards . . . more like a bear on a chain than a human being" (Lindfors 1983a, 9). Observers scrutinized and judged her body, and for an extra fee they could poke and prod her while she was on display. Europeans' primary interest was in her buttocks, deemed "steatopygic" and a common source of attention among comparative anatomists, and her genitals, which they deemed exemplary of the so-called Hottentot apron of early colonial lore.[15] Baartman resisted scientists' efforts to compel her to strip for examination of her genitals. Nevertheless, they still described in scientific and medical texts what they could not see, relying heavily on their imaginations. After her death, they cast her body in plaster and wax before dissecting, preserving, displaying, and storing her body parts, including her genitals, in the French Musée de l'Homme for decades.[16]

Baartman's body was an obsession of Georges Cuvier, an infamous scientist dedicated to comparative anatomy whose work codified the myth of African genital difference and inferiority. Cuvier hoped that his assessment of Baartman's dissected genitals would settle long-standing arguments; as he put it in his 1817 statement to the French Academy, "There is nothing more celebrated in natural history than the Hottentot apron, and at the same time there is nothing which has been the object of such great argumentation." Cuvier's intentions were twofold, "the likening of a female of the 'lowest' human species with the highest ape, the orangutan, and the description of the anomalies of the Hottentot's 'organ of generation'" (Gilman 1985, 85). Building on a citational chain of unsubstantiated information, Cuvier's descriptions relied on problematic travelers' accounts of African genitalia.[17] He compared colonial fears and fantasies of unknown and hidden geographies of Africa with Baartman's hidden genitals, both sites of violent discovery and conquest. The assessments of Cuvier and his colleague Henri de Blainville served as the basis for innumerable works to follow.[18] Gilman (1985, 88), for instance, cites many of the works extending this argument about the "Hottentot apron" in the subsequent decades, including Otto (1824), Müller (1834), Flower and Murie (1867), and Luschka, Koch, and Görtz (1869). All these scholars and countless others continued to argue that African genital inferiority justified colonial oppression.

How is the objectification and hypervisibility of Baartman, in colonial and contemporary accounts alike, linked to torn-out pages of books like *Bantu Gynaecology* and *True Hermaphroditism*? Images of Africans' exoticized genitals have long been visually violated and consumed. The violence Baartman faced included scrutiny of her living body, pictorial representations in scholarly and media accounts, and the dismemberment and display of her corpse. This manifold leering relied, in part, on genital fascination. The spectacularization of Baartman also follows centuries of attempts to render Africans' bodies abnormal and primitive gazingstocks. In fact, Baartman's own history is unique but sadly not exceptional; hundreds of Africans were transported to Europe by colonial observers and scientists for display as justification for colonial hierarchies.[19]

Throughout the nineteenth century, southern Africans were displayed as the antithesis of civilization and of normative European bodies, presented as the "missing link" between humans and animals. So-called Bushmen and Hottentots, in particular, were said to represent "the lowest exemplum of mankind on the great chain of being" (Gilman 1985, 83). Scientifically justified popular displays of people from Africa forced those enslaved to submit to examinations of their bodies and to perform European fantasies of their lives in tableaux.[20] Robert Knox, who studied under Cuvier in 1822, was known as a South African pioneer of physical anthropology and the first to lecture and publish on "South African Bushmen" (Knox 1850; Kirby 1940, 258). In 1847 he brought "a small party of Bushmen"—two men, two women, and a child born on the voyage—to Liverpool to lecture on their anatomies and to display them in public. Racial hierarchies and comparative anatomy were the basis for all of Knox's theories, and he recommended that dead "Bushmen" bodies be stuffed to preserve them, as he thought they would soon be extinct (Knox 1855).

Living exhibitions were tied to the development of museums as repositories that facilitated the spread of a science of gender and race. From 1877 onward, a cluster of museums developed throughout South Africa with chilling effect on the popular imagination. As Saul Dubow explains, "For a white public seeking to rationalise its social supremacy, it was not always necessary to have direct access to or understanding of the details of scientific debate; a broad awareness of the existence of a body of knowledge justifying racism was sufficient" (1995, 9).[21] The South African Museum was especially significant in this effort, as its curators took great scientific interest in documenting the bodies of indigenous "Bushmen"

(San) and "Hottentots" (Khoe), including a project that became the most influential rendering of Africans' bodies. "The Casting Project" (1907–1924) was this effort to plaster cast and photograph hundreds of "pure-bred" people of "nearly extinguished races" (Davison 1993, 168), which notably included a focus on supposed genital characteristics (Rassool 2015, 659).

Patricia Davison explains the particular intention of the project, premised on a notion of racial purity: to enshrine "women [who] would have steatopygia and elongated labia minora, and men would have semi-erect penises" (1993, 169).[22] Museum modeler James Drury was given explicit instructions for finding, posing, photographing, and casting people who would be the best "specimens." Genitals were considered to be "differentiating characteristics in taxonomic classification" (Davison 1993, 173).[23] Drury was directed to add genital molds to the representative statues he created; a "Memorandum about the Modelling" from 1908 directs: "Men are of course desirable; women still more so. You will be very careful to take all their peculiarities, including the 'apron.' A special moulding of the same to be added to the statue is very much wanted" (Louis Péringuey, quoted in Davison 1993, 172).

Drury's representation of the so-called Hottentot apron was extended in publications. While working for the museum, he copublished his own analysis in the *Medical Journal of South Africa*—"The Pudendal Parts of the South African Bush Race"—arguing that African women's genitals were "masculine" and alluding to them as hermaphroditic. Drury and his co-author, John Drennan, compared the bodies of those they cast to those of "ordinary" women, conceding that the supposedly innate difference was not readily visible: "On asking a woman of these tribes to remove their loin cloth or apron, one could not, at first sight, detect any difference between her and an ordinary woman, as far as the general configuration of the external genitals was concerned. On close observation, however, the vulva appeared to be situated more forward and higher up than in European women, whist the outer lips . . . were puffed up as if swollen" (Drury and Drennan 1926, 113). The authors go on to assert that they have proved and documented genital particularities, including regional differences on "two distinct types of the longinymph condition: the wattle type being characteristic of the Cape Bushwoman and the butterfly type of the Kalahari Bushwoman" (Drury and Drennan 1926, 117).[24] Fifteen long paragraphs describe in painstaking detail the genitals of those to whom they applied plaster casts—including measurements, shapes, and coloration—as well as the physical effects of the humiliating process of casting and the questioning that accompanied it.

The authors include four crude drawings to illustrate their theories. Drury and Drennan declare that the labia they observed are joined such that they could have been mistaken for a single organ and were "erectile" in various circumstances, pronouncing that the elongation of the labia of those in southern Africa is both "natural" and "infantile" (1926, 117). Nude photographs of the people subjected to this project and of the lifelike plaster casts of their genitals were published to support Drury's work and were reprinted in numerous publications over the following decade (e.g., A. M. Wilson 1911).

The effects of "The Casting Project" are immeasurable. For close to a century, countless museum visitors viewed exhibits created from this project. It was on display in various forms and constituted the South African Museum's biggest visitor attraction for decades, with the casts presented as timeless and likened to animal species (Davison 2018).[25] In an initiative intended to highlight the violence of these casts, artist Pippa Skotnes (1996, 2002) recounts her own observations of thousands of schoolchildren, teachers, tourists, and guides passing through the museum during weeks she spent in the exhibition in the 1990s. Guides began their discussions of "Bushmen" bodies with genitals presented as their most significant feature, an emphasis she traces back to colonial obsessions: "'The male penis,' bellowed one German guide speaking in English to his tourist group, 'is peculiar in that it stands erect at all times when at rest. The women's labia can hang to the knees'" (Skotnes 2002, 254–55). In these manifold ways, "The Casting Project" institutionalized race with supposed genital difference through popular depictions.[26]

Observation, representation, and display were at the heart of colonial scientific approaches (Rassool 2015, 658), with scrutiny and measurements functioning as a methodological center of violent regimes. South African historians Ciraj Rassool and Patricia Hayes analyze ocularization and the life of /Khanako, a ≠Khomani (N/u) and /?Auni speaker who lived in the southern Kalahari in the early twentieth century. /Khanako was a strong community leader, but a "feeding frenzy of the eye" rendered her representative of African indigeneity and inferiority (Rassool and Hayes 2002, 118). During her lifetime, /Khanako was reduced to a physical type, photographed, and recorded, and casts were made of her body, as well.[27] Rassool and Hayes trace how one photograph of her was dehistoricized and reproduced in books and museum exhibitions, even transformed into a postcard with a swastika imprinted on her buttocks (purportedly a commentary on German occupation of Namibia, circulating in the late 1930s).[28]

Europeans were widely exposed to travel literature and photographs of Africans from the 1700s onward, and postcards of /Khanako and many others played a particular role in their views of colonized people as temporally regressive. Postcards created an objectifying distance between those who acquired them and those considered inferior. A false sense of intimacy came from possessing these images, and Europeans often purported to "know" Africans quite well just from viewing photographs (Landau 2002). Postcards added an element of owner-ship to European armchair conquest, personalizing intimate interactions with individual portraits.[29] Such photos were also sexualized as part of what Anne McClintock (1995) calls the "porno-tropics," the colonial space of fantasy onto which Europe projected forbidden sexual desires and fears. Representations of African people as physically lascivious and hermaphroditic were common in European lore, and these representations were often eroticized. Just as the photographs in *Bantu Gynaecology* and *True Hermaphroditism* were torn out and likely taken into private possession, so too were postcards consumed and viewed as pornography.[30]

For prominent comparative anatomists such as Raymond Dart, South Africa itself was "a unique museum of human evolution" (Dubow 1996, 8). Dart's work was concerned with the supposed physical differences of Africans' genitals, ex-tending suppositions on the "Hottentot apron" as well as the penises he deemed innately "horizontal" (Dart 1937, 222–30). Scholars such as M. R. Drennan, a follower of Dart known to be even more contemptuous in his designation of Af-rican people as "anatomical curiosities or living fossils," continued this thinking into the twentieth century (Dubow 1995, 47). These scientists favored theories of evolutionary recapitulation, comparing adults of inferior groups (including "Bushmen") to children of superior groups and focusing on the former's sup-posed "childlike morphology and behaviour" (Dubow 1996, 30). Such ideologies were hugely influential. For instance, during a 1936 expedition, photographer James van Buskirk was "called upon to photograph the different varieties of fe-male labia identified by . . . physical examinations and according to criteria set out in an earlier [1926] study by Drury and Drennan" (Rassool and Hayes 2002, 136). The photographs resulting from this expedition were widely reproduced as yet another confirmation of racial difference and typologies.

Varied displays and images thus buttressed racialized gender binaries and European superiority in different ways, providing visual "proof" of supposed primitiveness. Catherine Burns describes the fascination with what she describes as "iconographic representation of African women's sexual organs (as exotic, highly sexualised and problematic sites of study)" as "an important theme of early travellers' accounts of African, and especially Khoisan women's sexual organs, which evolved in the nineteenth century into a highly developed discourse" (1995, 409). Taken together, these kinds of intimate representations were integral to hierarchies of civilization promoted by social Darwinists and eugenicists. In this era, scientists' visions and descriptions of Africans' genitals as abnormal or hermaphroditic compared them to earlier times and lower life forms. These iterations of African genital difference would continue to serve as a critical basis for emerging claims positioning South Africa as the site for some of the only "true hermaphrodites" in the world.

The Extinction of "True Hermaphroditism" in the Global North

The complicated fallacy of African genital ambiguity runs parallel to histories of "hermaphrodites" in Europe. As colonial explorers and naturalists imagined the "Hottentot apron," interpretations of bodies they deemed hermaphroditic reflected the contradictions of Renaissance gender theories. Biology and medicine did not exist in their present forms and had marginal influence in defining and producing gender in this era. European "hermaphrodites" and Africans alike were categorized as "monstrous," a category that encompassed a range of extraordinary bodies of sometimes valued and sometimes denigrated people. Ambroise Paré's widely circulated *Of Monsters and Prodigies* (1634) describes magical and medical monsters of all kinds as intertwined, representing so-called hermaphrodites as sensational yet natural in text and drawings. In some contexts, "hermaphrodites" had property rights and chose their own sexual identifications, while in others, they experienced violence and ostracism.

The word *hermaphrodite* described offspring of the Greek gods Hermes and Aphrodite reflected in two Greek origin myths.[31] The term and those designated as such has always been inconsistent, used to refer not only to the material body but to those who challenged expectations about gendered behaviors and relationships. But conceptions of "hermaphrodites" and others considered monsters who had been viewed as "prodigies, marvels, signs, and prophecies" were increasingly seen as scientific objects of investigation (Huet 1993, 36). The expansion of science and medicine represented a movement away from imagination and a panoply of ideas about how the world works to rationality, rules, and norms.

By the 1800s, European scientific and popular exhibitions spectacularized the bodies of European "hermaphrodites" alongside Baartman and other Africans and examined them with similarly invasive and violent curiosity. People whose bodies were seen to challenge gender binaries—from bearded women and unbearded men to those with visible genital anomalies—faced scientific and popular objectification, and so-called "hermaphrodites" were dismembered and animalized throughout the United States and Europe. In the nineteenth century, there was a strong trade among doctors and scientists who lent and sold each other wax casts, drawings, photographs, and preserved specimens taken from human "hermaphrodites" (Dreger 1998, 68). Scrutiny was the methodology that turned people into objects, available to the public and to scientists who used murderously obtained body parts "literally to place the world before their eyes without ever leaving their place of employ" (Fausto-Sterling 1995, 24). Public and museum displays engaged viewers' consumptive gazes to provide material for imagined abnormality, exoticism, and savagery. They presented normality and civilization as centered in Europe, regularizing the violence of colonialism, even as "hermaphrodites" and other so-called monsters existed in their midst.

European discourse about monstrosity and "hermaphrodites" provided the context for the classificatory science of teratology, founded by Étienne Geoffroy Saint-Hilaire and his son, Isidore Geoffroy Saint-Hilaire, in the 1830s. The younger Saint-Hilaire mentored Georges Cuvier, even collaborating to publish Cuvier's autopsy and analysis of Sara Baartman's body after her death. But he broke from Cuvier and many other scientists of the time to popularize teratology, coining the term derived from the Greek work *tera* for monster and focusing on bodies deemed congenitally abnormal. In prior centuries, thinking about monstrosity had been a diverse mix of fiction, legends, and facts that referred to the extraordinary. But with the codification of teratology, "hermaphrodites" and others considered monstrous were seen as predictable and bound by scientific rules and norms. As Marie-Hélène Huet points out, a science of teratology/ monsters would have been "inconceivable before the nineteenth century, if by 'science' we mean a discipline primarily concerned with finding and establishing laws" (1993, 109). Formalizing teratology shifted the focus of discourse about "hermaphrodites" from wonderings about conception and spiritual significance to a focus on their internal teleology. Within the science of teratology, "hermaphrodites" were no longer considered extraordinary but pathological. A teratological worldview redefined "hermaphroditism" as an unhealthy condition to be medically cured.

Saint-Hilaire's notions of cure rested on clear diagnoses of what he described as multiple hermaphroditisms. In his assessment, a combination of "male" and "female" characteristics within particular zones of the body meant someone was hermaphroditic. Another theorist in this decade, British obstetrician James Young Simpson, soon expanded these ideas to argue that there were not multiple hermaphroditisms but two: "spurious hermaphrodites" and "true hermaphrodites." Spurious hermaphrodites were limited to those with genitals thought to approximate the "opposite" gender, whereas the bodies of "true hermaphrodites" included a range of gendered characteristics.

Under these broad definitions, by the mid-nineteenth century, increasing numbers of Europeans were identified as "hermaphrodites": "Indeed, there seemed to be shocking numbers of anatomical "hermaphrodites" turning up in the general populace. One French medical man lamented that "hermaphrodites" seemed to 'literally run about on the streets.' . . . So, while deeply fascinated by cases of human hermaphroditism, many medical and scientific men simultaneously expressed disgust at the very idea and resentment at the confusion 'hermaphrodites' caused" (Dreger 1998, 27). The growing numbers of those diagnosed as "hermaphrodites" under theories with widespread acceptance created anxiety and confusion among Europeans who tasked themselves with policing gender dimorphism. As the social magnitude of multiple hermaphroditisms and the implicit challenges posed to gender binaries continued to trouble European scientists and doctors, cases of "doubtful" or "mistaken" sex evoked intense disagreements among professionals who could not agree on criteria for gender assignments. Physicians and scientists began to replace the generalized term *hermaphrodite* with dozens of diagnoses of the gendered body, and the word *intersexual*—first defined in the *Oxford English Dictionary* in 1866 as "existing between the sexes, pertaining to both sexes"— gradually began to serve as umbrella term.

But as colonial strictures tightened in the second half of the nineteenth century, scientists would aim to create consensus by substantially limiting hermaphroditic diagnoses in Europe and the United States.[32] Like Simpson, German-Swiss scientist Theodor Albrecht Edwin Klebs contrasted "true" hermaphrodites and those he called "pseudo hermaphrodites." Importantly, Klebs restricted his focus to gonads. This shift had importance that cannot be overstated and that lasted for well over a century. In 1876 Klebs redefined "true hermaphrodites" to include only those who could be proved to have both ovarian and testicular tissue. As a result, from this point on, gonadal anatomy dominated gender diagnoses, harkening the advent of what Alice Dreger famously identified as "The Age of Gonads" (1870–1915).[33] Klebs's definition was widely adopted in theory and clinical practice and would endure for the following 150 years. This fixation with gonads meant that "true hermaphrodites" could only be identified surgically or in death by autopsy.[34]

Many in intersex studies mark this redefinition as a critical moment that effectively obliterated "true hermaphrodites."[35] When medical and scientific professionals came to a consensus that gonads were diagnostically fundamental, it became nearly impossible to diagnose a person as a "true hermaphrodite." Poor techniques and uncontrollable infections meant that most patients did not survive surgeries. Given that biopsies were not performed to diagnose intersex until the 1910s, the new standardized rules of gonadal precedence meant that "the only possible true hermaphrodite was a dead and dissected hermaphrodite or, at best, a castrated one," and the only way to prove "true hermaphroditism was by removing, slicing, and microscopically examining the whole gonad" (Dreger 1998, 149). This reclassification created medical and social anguish for Europeans deemed ambiguous. A new invasive doctrine allowed doctors to dictate gender assignment (using criteria they referred to as "that sex which prevaileth") as they forced patients into rigid gender dimorphism.[36] In short, Europeans who did not clearly fit the gender binary posed a threat that was addressed first by undefining "true hermaphrodites" and later through surgical interventions.

The European extinction of "true hermaphroditism" paralleled a renewed focus on discovery in the colonies, and the search for so-called true hermaphrodites intensified in the Global South. Cleansing colonial powers of the threat that true hermaphroditism posed to gender binaries allowed, in Hil Malatino's words, "sexual monstrosity to be abjected from the Western metropolitan interior to the colonial periphery" (2009, 91). In colonial contexts, bodies were subjected to a new kind of quest to prove primitivity and inferiority through true hermaphroditism diagnoses. This widened the divide between the colonies and colonized, with those medically designated as hermaphroditic in the Global North and Global South subjected to overlapping but often different kinds of violence.

The erasure of true hermaphroditism among those in Europe and the United States was also entwined with the reification of primitiveness. Comparative taxonomies categorized Africans as animalistic and temporally regressive in ways intertwined with hermaphroditism. During the late 1800s, scientists classifying plants, animals, and humans argued that hermaphroditism was predominant in organisms that were low on the evolutionary scale. For instance, in *The Evolution of Sex* (1889), biologists Patrick Geddes and J. Arthur Thompson argue that "sluggish and fixed animals," such as parasites, typify hermaphroditism as "the primitive condition" (1890, 77–79). They viewed reproduction that required a sperm and an egg as evolutionarily successful and dominant, while hermaphroditic organisms were judged as inherently undifferentiated and inferior. Lawson Tait (1876) similarly relied on Darwin's theories of evolution to denigrate human hermaphroditism. He argues that hermaphroditism is common, and "unisexuality is the rule," in beings classified as lower organisms, but the frequency of the "malformation" diminishes as one goes up the hierarchy of beings until in "man," at the top of this hierarchy, it is found very rarely (322).[37] Scientists of this time held the belief that the higher beings were in the evolutionary hierarchy, the stronger the differentiation between "males" and "females," and they asserted that rigid gender differentiation evidenced colonialists' biological superiority.

Africa was already positioned at the bottom of this hierarchy in the citational chain of explorers and scientists' imaginings about the "Hottentot apron" traced earlier in this chapter. Following Klebs's 1876 redefinition, scientists became even more eager to valorize the bodies of Europeans. Toward this end, they engaged in revisionist history to expunge existing records of true hermaphroditism in the Global North, and scientific representations of European hermaphroditism prior to the "Age of Gonads" were intentionally erased from history and memory. British physicians George Blacker and William Lawrence (1896) were among those most instrumental in this effort: "In Orwellian fashion, they cleansed past medical records of accounts of hermaphroditism, claiming they did not meet modern scientific standards" (Fausto-Sterling 2000, 39). These and other authors justified these exercises by bemoaning prior diagnoses as lax and erroneous. In their views, failures to classify Europeans as clearly men or women had created a crisis of gender confusion that had to be remedied.

By instantiating new strict criteria about the presence of both ovarian and testicular tissue, those previously diagnosed were overwhelmingly reclassified as "false" or "spurious hermaphrocites" (not "true hermaphrodites"). But Dreger exposes these scientists' "confident, reverberating declarations" about so-called true hermaphroditism and gender dimorphism as "the frantic painting of a house falling down. Medical men triumphantly reconstructed and constricted the true hermaphrodite even while—perhaps because—they witnessed and were forced to confess serious doubts about sex" (1998, 154). These frenetic efforts to shore up gender binaries had wide ideological effects. For instance, in an influential textbook on obstetrics published in 1886, American Theophilus Parvin expressed the common sentiment of the time that in Europe, "In almost all cases of alleged hermaphroditism this condition is *apparent*, not *real*" (quoted in Dreger 1998, 83–84). With consensus about this extinction/erased existence in Europe, proof of "true hermaphroditism" was increasingly sought out by researchers in the Global South, and especially in Africa. Efforts to pathologize genitals turned to colonial quests to discover "true hermaphrodites" as coveted rarities, deemed extinct yet fetishized.

Medical Ocularization: *Bantu Gynaecology* and Plasticity

Meanwhile, allopathic medicine gained a strong foothold in South Africa in the late 1800s with the national establishment of professional organizations and publications such as the *South African Medical Journal* (1884) and the *South*

African Medical Record (1903), which were precursors to the books mentioned to introduce this chapter. In these journals, medical images were positioned as visual records of pathology, and images with evidentiary and quantitative cachet were publicly circulated in them. The relation between visual technologies and colonial governance established ways of seeing as fundamental to acquiring knowledge. South African medical journals were intended for a wide readership, and frequent topics addressed included racial degeneration, eugenics, mental hygiene, and sterilization of the unfit. Doctors were not merely benevolent but conceptualized themselves as part of the imperial mission, responsible for promoting values considered civilized as well as the latest scientific thinking (Dubow 1995, 141). A constellation of new fields, including phrenology, craniometry, and physiognomy, focused on racial sciences and compared skulls and facial expressions. Doctors relied on observation and measurement as the basis for comparative anatomy.

The "Hottentot apron" was a continued preoccupation within this growing medical literature. Publications included visual representations and detailed descriptions of external genitals in drawings and photographs. In South Africa, this analysis was increasingly accompanied by anthropometric measurements of pelvic size. The term *pelvimetry* was coined in the 1860s to quantify pelvic bones and vaginal canals as evolutionarily significant and predictive of cultural and behavioral difference (Burns 1995). Various contradictory and politicized interpretations depicted Africans' pelvises as alternately too small or too large when these contentions served different political purposes. For instance, Schiebinger explains, "In Africans, the female pelvis, by contrast with the male, was said to be light and delicate; the male pelvis was said to be so dense that it resembled the pelvis of a wild beast" (2013, 157). When comparing pelvises from Africa to those found in those in Europe, however, "the African woman's was described as entirely destitute of the transparent delicacy characteristic of the female European" (157–58). These inconsistencies were not incidental but critical to colonial ideologies, as gendered bodily data were created to support racialized social policy.[38]

In South Africa, the turn of the century also brought colonially motivated reproductive control and more theories comparing humans and animals on an evolutionary scale. Eugenics was "explicitly designed as a scientific solution to the perceived needs of society, namely, the need to promote racial 'vigour' and prevent 'deterioration'" (Dubow 1995, 10). European scientists were focused on so-called race improvement and reproductive success among the "fit" while curbing it among the "unfit." In Europe and the United States, the treatment of impotence in the early 1900s often made use of animals' transplanted body parts, including the testicles of apes imported from West Africa, that enforced racist conceptions of virility (Petit 2013). The medical focus on shoring up male bodies in the Global North capitalized on the exotic as feared yet restorative.[39]

Jules Gill-Peterson identifies this as a moment when racialized and gendered bodies were bound together in eugenics and endocrinology. These fields jointly relied on conceptions of "plasticity"—the mutability of the human body—as shaped through environmental and biomedical interventions. Gill-Peterson theorizes that the idea of a child absorbing their environment or being plastic, changeable, was imagined to allow the enhancement of the racial stock of America and generations of children to come (2018a, 53). Theories of plasticity fit well within colonial scientific ideologies that sought to foster comparative human hierarchies developmentally and evolutionarily.

In South Africa, eugenics manifested explicitly in attempts to control Africans' reproduction. This focus was fundamental to the eventual creation of what came to be termed Bantu Gynaecology.[40] Dr. J. Marion Sims is credited with originating the field of gynecology in the United States in the 1800s, developing instruments and practices through experiments on enslaved Black women's bodies undertaken without anesthesia under the horrific supposition that these patients would not feel pain (Washington 2006; Judd 2014; Snorton 2017; Owens 2017).[41] C. Riley Snorton surmises that Sims's conceptualizations of the field reflected "what he must have learned in medical school about the *nègre* and Hottentots whose nates [buttocks] and pelvises were dissected and copiously referred to in sexological and anatomical literature as 'sufficiently well marked to distinguish [them] . . . from those of any of the ordinary varieties of the human species' [Flower and Murie 1867]" (2017, 23). By the time Bantu Gynaecology was conceptualized as a field, the barbaric origins of gynecology were thinly veiled under generic assertions about "women" versus "men" that endeavored to mask racist ideologies and practices.

Bantu Gynaecology baldly reasserted that Bantu/black women's bodies in southern Africa were anatomically deficient and not fully "female." Interest in pelvic capacity and birthing practices were growing in concert with paranoia about South African population growth. Within this framework, what Catherine Burns describes as the "perceived characteristics of African women's bodies" were scrutinized in research dedicated to proving evolutionary inferiority of southern Africans (1995, 398–99). Political efforts to institutionalize racial segregation and eugenic policies relied heavily on gynecologic pelvimetric research, which began around the turn of the century. Ideologies and practices developed as part of scientific efforts to pathologize the bodies of those designated as

"Native" (and later Bantu) and to control their reproductive and productive labor. Patients were subjected to pelvic bone and vaginal canal measurements, as well as to investigations of birthing practices, as their bodies were photographed and scrutinized.[42]

Bantu Gynaecology was institutionalized in the 1950s with the inception of apartheid.[43] The official origin of apartheid in 1948—following the election of the National Party and the enactment of its policies of violent racial segregation—coincided with a substantial ideological shift that influenced international perceptions of South Africa. In the mid-1940s, South Africa's reputation and leadership were globally celebrated, but by the end of the decade, international condemnation of apartheid had grown strong. The genocide of World War II incited a reckoning with scientific racism, and white supremacy in science was increasingly problematized. In 1950, the United Nations Educational, Scientific and Cultural Organization (UNESCO) issued a widely influential statement on "the concept of race," which was collaboratively authored by scholars from various fields and parts of the world. The statement condemned the role of science in racial genocide, confronting long-held beliefs in the biological bases of race and innate difference to argue instead for the "plasticity" and mutability of race.

While this landmark collaboration was hailed by many as the end of racism, it is more accurate to understand it as reordering racism. Instead of categorizing "ideal types," scientists' theories shifted to populations and genetics. Eugenic and racist efforts to control groups of people were not eliminated but replaced. Ladelle McWhorter explains how this manifested disciplinarily: "In 1954 the British *Annals of Eugenics* was renamed *Annals of Human Genetics*. In 1969 the *Eugenics Quarterly* became the *Journal of Social Biology*. In 1972 the American Eugenics Society changed its name to the Society for the Study of Social Biology. Eugenicists began to call themselves 'population scientists' and 'human geneticists'" (2009, 249). The shift was similarly reflected in language, as researchers began to discuss not "race" but ethnicity, heredity, and blood types, and a new form of comparative anatomy emerged.

In South Africa, despite global changes following the UNESCO statement, the rise of apartheid marked a resurgence of scientific racism in changing forms. Under the auspices of genetics instead of eugenics, South African scientists were leaders among those who continued to cling to arguments about race as innate. Their new focus on "knowledge in the blood" (Jansen 2009) positioned South Africa as a global defender of white colonial civilization. Local scientists continued to provide biological justifications for violence in direct opposition to UNESCO's emphasis on plasticity.[44]

How did these shifting ideas about race affect perceptions of Africans' bodies and perceptions of intersex? Theories of racial plasticity in the 1950s, including the UNESCO statement, proved fundamental to the development of medical treatments of intersex. Scholarly thinking about gender plasticity began to emerge in the early 1900s as the possibilities of a range of bodily morphologies and of gender "reversal" (grounded in Darwin's conception of "reversion") were increasingly commonplace. As Gill-Peterson points out, intersex bodies were increasingly framed as exemplary of plasticity and the medical alterability of the human body (2018b, 610).[45]

By the 1950s, gendered theories of plasticity were codified by Dr. John Money of Johns Hopkins University, whose conceptions of intersex and protocols for treating gender and sexuality "disorders" garnered him worldwide renown.[46] As South Africa was reeling from the brutal violence of apartheid, Money's gendered theories attained almost hegemonic dominance, and his protocols overrode all others. Money's arguments rested on the assertion that babies' genders are mutable in the first eighteen months of life. He advocated altering intersex infants' bodies surgically and hormonally, contending that humans do not have a "true sex" but that their gender identifications would follow medical interventions (Money 1952). Money and his colleagues argued for the importance of interventionist approaches to intersex built on theories that gender is not something innate but is developed cumulatively over time (Money, Hampson, and Hampson 1955). In comparison to definitions of true hermaphroditism and the long-standing focus on gonads that began in the 1870s, Money's scholarship shifted focus from one aspect of the body to a wide range of physical, behavioral, and psychological factors as determining gender.

Iain Morland argues that Money's theories were a direct outcome of the UNESCO statement on race, as this statement created broad acceptance of the idea that "the most evolutionarily important characteristic of *Homo sapiens* is 'plasticity'" (2015, 75). While notions of plasticity had already been ideologically significant for decades, the widespread intellectual acceptance of racial plasticity in this era was the catalyst for the swift adoption and dominance of Money's views of intersex as medically "correctible." The UNESCO statement also obscured the racial normativity that underpinned gender plasticity. Gill-Peterson argues that the racialization of gender plasticity was even more damaging in the postwar era than previously because the abandonment of explicitly eugenic science and medicine made racial normativity more difficult to see (2018a, 122).

Both race and political geography are inseparable from perceptions of plasticity and intersex. In early intersex and trans medicine in the United States, "black and brown bodies were consistently read as less plastic, as less evolved sexually, and thereby less worthy of medical care," whereas "the capacity to remake the white body into a binary form" was embraced (Gill-Peterson 2018b, 610). This led to what Gill-Peterson refers to as an "abstract whiteness of medicalized plasticity" (2018a, 101).[47] The eugenic impetus to protect whiteness and concerns about shoring up racial superiority justified brutal medical treatment of white intersex children in the United States and western Europe. But elsewhere, in locations including Africa, the Dominican Republic, and Papua New Guinea, intersex was seen as disproportionately common, and these sites were rife with racialized medical experimentation.[48] From the 1970s to the present, scientists conducted barbaric research on people in such locations to prove their colonially based theories of raced and gendered inferiority. Meanwhile famous scientists and physicians at institutions like Johns Hopkins University in the United States conducted their own violently "corrective" surgeries to make it seem like white intersex did not exist (Eckert 2017; Gill-Peterson 2018a).

It should come as no surprise that South African scientists continued their centuries-old efforts to discover African genitals and intersex, and especially true hermaphroditism. But now they emphasized an emerging intersex genetics and developed techniques to apply Money's theories. For geneticists such as J. D. J. Hofmeyr, South Africa continued to offer a "great laboratory" that could "put to the test diverse social and political theories as to the relations between white and coloured races" (quoted in Dubow 2006, 213). After the brutality of the Sharpeville massacre of 1960 revealed the atrocities of apartheid to the world, the South African government commanded the development of medical, engineering, architectural, and other nationalist efforts to strengthen white supremacy. This focus on technological innovation, scientific racism, and South African superiority set the groundwork for strengthened efforts to discover so-called true hermaphroditism and gendered inferiority.[49]

The 1950s and 1960s were the same periods in which the ascendance of Bantu Gynaecology as a field inspired the publication of the text by the same name that haunted Keguro Macharia in the recollection that began this chapter. Bantu Gynaecology fundamentally relied on the theory that gynecology in southern Africa required specific knowledge to address so-called Bantu women's embodied racialized inferiority (Burns 1995). The text quintessentially representing this field—simply titled *Bantu Gynaecology*—emerged under the auspices of the Medical School at the University of the Witwatersrand in 1956.[50] In its preface, G. P. Charlewood argued, "The composite picture of Bantu gynaecology whether seen in general practice or hospital wards is vastly different from that seen in the European" (1556). As discussed earlier in this chapter, this book is full of photographs intended to support his thesis.

Bantu Gynaecology articulated scientific racism with gender ambiguity from its first substantive chapter on "Congenital Malformations" and hermaphroditism to its final chapter on "Masculinisation of the Female" (Charlewood 1956). In this text, "Bantu" is defined by O. S. Heyns as representing "Negroid peoples" speaking dialects of the Bantu language and with phenotypic characteristics including "a black skin, woolly hair, a flat broad nose, thick, often everted, lips" and hair "which is in the form of 'pepper-corns'" (Heyns 1956, 3). Throughout this volume, authors claim that bodily distinctions as well as cultural practices (e.g., cannibalism) support their contentions of inferiority.

Like other scientific and popular representations of the time, the field of Bantu Gynaecology also assumed that the genitals of those in southern Africa were disproportionately ambiguous. *Bantu Gynaecology* rests on proclamations that, "congenital abnormalities of all kinds are seen in much greater numbers in Negros and related races" (Charlewood 1956, 12), though conceding that this frequency has not been proved. The representations and assertions of texts like this one enabled physicians' practices and reinforced discourses of bodily abnormality affecting those like Macharia who interacted with the text itself. The text attempts to codify contentions of disproportionate true hermaphroditism and other bodily "abnormality" in explicit photographs of unacknowledged people. And such photographs inspired strong emotions or desires that led to pages being ripped from the book itself.

Three notable studies published in the 1960s paralleled the rise of Bantu Gynaecology to merge centuries-old assertions of African genital difference with efforts to establish South Africa as a site for intersex discovery. The first of these is Sarah Klempman's (1964) report on patients designated as intersex in the Cytogenetics Unit of the South African Institute for Medical Research in Johannesburg from 1962 to 1963.[51] Among twenty-three patients under consideration, eleven patients are described as white and twelve as Bantu. Based on this small study and diagnoses of seven patients, Klempman claims that true hermaphroditism—by this time widely accepted as the surgically determined presence of ovarian and testicular tissue—is the commonest form of intersex among the Bantu (1964, 236).[52] A second study is similarly concerned with the global rarity of "true hermaphroditism" and fascinated by its supposed frequency in southern Africa. In "Intersex among Africans in Rhodesia," authors J. I. Forbes and B. Hammar (1966) reference eight prior cases of true hermaphroditism in South Africa and add discussion of three additional cases; they provide no mention of or comparison to white intersex patients, who are implicitly positioned as normative.[53] The third study, also based in the Cytogenetics Unit of the South African Institute for Medical Research, claims that forty-six "true hermaphrodites" were diagnosed and that all were Bantu. Geneticist E. Wilton explicates, "In our series no true hermaphrodites were diagnosed in the Caucasian. This is the most common intersex state in the Bantu population" (1969, 47). But Wilton also admits that though his unit has investigated 238 patients with anomalous sexual development, "these cases form a selected sample referred from the major hospitals on the Witwatersrand, and do not give a true reflection of the incidence of intersex states in the population" (1969, 47).[54] Not only are the claims cited in all three publications without substantive foundation, they undermine and contradict themselves and each other. Taken together, these studies formed an unsubstantiated basis for the medical association of "Bantuness" with true hermaphroditism that were the citational bases for the explosion of studies of intersex in the 1970s, which are the subject of the next chapter.

Continuations of Colonialism

At the beginning of this chapter, I contemplate the context for the photographs I found ripped from my loaned copies of both *Bantu Gynaecology* and Willem Van Niekerk's 1974 *True Hermaphroditism: Clinical, Morphologic and Cytogenetic Aspects*. Like many other authors, whose work I explore in the next chapter, Van Niekerk surmises that while it is almost nonexistent in the rest of the world, "true hermaphroditism is the most common type of intersexuality occurring among the Bantu" (1974, 83). He compares so-called true hermaphroditism—he labels it "the most uncommon variant" in the world except among so-called Bantu—in South Africa and the United States. On the basis of a literature review for which he provides no citations, Van Niekerk concludes that there is also an increased prevalence of true hermaphroditism among "American Negroes" (83). Van Niekerk's generalizations from Bantu to a diaspora outside Africa assume a biological continuity built on scientific racism. Despite his bibliography of 382 sources, he provides no references for his assertions about the United States, and his generalizations about African continental intersex among Bantu are similarly lacking in support. Instead, he extensively cites his own work in Pretoria—especially referencing his own gaze as authoritative (e.g., "I have seen this for myself")—and makes other unverifiable pronouncements that he is personally aware of unpublished data.

More than four hundred years of claims to "see" genital ambiguity in Africans, like Van Niekerk's, demonstrate that the colonies were not just testing grounds for gendered and raced theories. They were also essential to the mutually constitutive creation of fallacies of inferiority that centered on gender dimorphism. Zine Magubane asserts, "One thing that South African, US, and European medical texts from the seventeenth century through the twentieth seem to agree on was the fact that malformed or ambiguous genitalia (especially an enlarged clitoris or overdeveloped labia) were particularly common among women of African descent—a 'fixed peculiarity of race' [Waitz 1863, 107]" (2014, 769). Efforts to enforce the myth of the "Hottentot apron" and the categorical extinction of true hermaphroditism from the Global North together heralded the explosion of intersex research in the Global South that emerged in the 1970s.

The reiterated assertion in medical journals unpacked in the next chapter—that intersex and true hermaphroditism are disproportionately common in southern Africa—underpins a final example I share here. In 1974, R. H. Johnson, a surgeon at Princess Mariana Hospital in Gaborone, Botswana, published about his discovery of true hermaphroditism in the *South African Medical Journal* to mark a case that he "believed to be the first reported in a Motswanan" (1974, 1540).[55] After reiterating the common claims that "True hermaphroditism is the commonest intersex state in the Black population of South Africa"—citing two references with scant and problematic data—Johnson's short article scrutinizes the body of an unnamed patient referred to him because of an undescended testicle and inguinal hernia (1540). Details of this patient's life and consent are not discussed. But Johnson performs surgery on this patient, and "the organs removed were sent for histological examination [to] the Royal Army Medical College, London, as there was no pathologist in Botswana" (1540).[56] After further consultation, "a specimen of peripheral blood, a skin biopsy specimen and a buccal smear" were taken from the patient for karyotype analysis in an effort to attain "the diagnosis of true hermaphroditism" (1540). Johnson was the only surgeon in the three hundred–bed Princess Mariana Hospital at this time, and he operated on patients with a wide range of life-threatening afflictions, including cancer, bowel obstructions, ruptured appendixes, and ectopic pregnancies (Ward, Ward, and Johnson 1973; Johnson 1975a, 1975b). It is notable that he would take such a surgical interest in a patient with an undescended testicle in this situation, performing medically unnecessary surgeries and rare lab work just to try to diagnose true hermaphroditism, while he also discloses that fatal illnesses such as cancer often remained undiagnosed because of the lack of capacity to send specimens outside of the country (1975b, 260).[57]

This article is remarkable for its emphasis on discovery and because, in the interest of finding the first case of true hermaphroditism in the region, an unknown Motswanan's body parts are transported from southern Africa to England. The trajectory of this patient's bodily organs recalls the well-known export route from Africa to Europe for the transnational exploitation of so many Africans, including Baartman, and the dissection and display of countless genitals deemed pathological. In this and innumerable other contexts, bodies are dismembered to substantiate colonial claims of pathological African intersex. The next chapter exposes how erroneous claims of disproportionate intersex and true hermaphroditism came to dominate scientific and public imaginings about Africa in even more concrete ways.

2. "Intersex in Four South African Racial Groups in Durban"
Visualizing Scientific Racism and Gendered Medicine

A commonly expressed belief is that hermaphroditism is the commonest form of intersexuality among the Bantu races of South Africa and Rhodesia, and that intersexuality on the whole is more prevalent in the Bantu than other races.
—H. J. GRACE, "Intersex in Four South African Racial Groups in Durban"

· · ·

Why do white South African doctors assert that intersex and "true hermaphroditism" are more common among black South Africans than among white South Africans? And what have been the effects of these declarations? This chapter takes up these questions through an examination of five decades of South African medical literature, focusing on a remarkably influential master's thesis written in 1970 by Dr. H. J. Grace. By unpacking this thesis, and by reviewing the citational chain that continues to rely on its claims to the present, I demonstrate how and why these falsehoods become widely accepted as truths. In this work that begins in the 1970s, intersex medicine remains inseparable from colonial ideologies. The visual science of raced intersex continues to circulate between scientific and popular contexts with devastating impact on those diagnosed as intersex.

In this chapter, I argue that intersex in South Africa and in the Global South more broadly materializes through a particular set of linked strategies: *definition, scrutiny, repetition,* and *justification.* When taken together, these strategies collectively create perceptions of solid scientific truths where there are none. The first strategy is to provide a *definition* for an abstraction, a scientific explanation to make gender complexity seem simple. For instance, *true hermaphrodites* have been defined paradoxically at different times as having various combinations of bodily characteristics or as having both ovarian and testicular tissue ("ovotesticular DSD"), often only knowable through the surgical removal and microscopic examination of the contents of the body. The realities behind these definitions are politicized and never simple or consistent.

The raced science of intersex also relies on visual evidence, and *scrutiny* substantiates its claims. The medical gaze takes many forms—looking directly at the body but also looking into the body through exploratory surgeries and the removal of tissues and bodily substances for microscopic examination. Photographs of bodies are compared and manipulated to create norms. Medical imaging includes X-rays that test and create visual representations. Charts document and quantify doctors' gender categories. The documentation of this scrutiny is used as visual data to create illusions of truth.

Repetition of findings and ideas, however biased and flawed they may be, creates iterative power. Hearing a claim again and again enables its acceptance. Eventually the origins and basis become irrelevant and unknown. In the case of raced intersex science in South Africa, this repetition regularly links intersex to blackness. Citational practices and repetition contribute to an illusion of consensus, and circulation becomes a truth-creation strategy. Photographs are the most obvious technology enabling this—medical photographs and infographics are reproduced and distributed through publications, online, and in media as purportedly objective proof. Claims of raced intersex frequency have interdisciplinary and transnational audiences, far exceeding the academy and reinforced by media and popular portrayals, and create knowledge and meaning with wide reach.

Finally, raced intersex science relies on *justification* to explain inconsistencies or inaccuracies. Throughout medical literature reviewed here, those deemed intersex are blamed for bodily difference; they are accused, for example, of inbreeding or secretly using traditional medicine. Local acceptance of intersex also frustrates researchers who blame their unproven racist hypotheses on communities they represent as unevolved and uncivilized. Those in these communities are portrayed as deceptive (unwilling to talk honestly to researchers) and non-compliant (unwilling to submit bodies fully to science or surgery). Deception and noncompliance are then used to justify research failures and inaccurate hypotheses.

Definition, scrutiny, repetition, and justification are not always directly correlated or intentional. Instead, they form an overlapping set of strategies as claims and images are interwoven to create accepted truths without foundation. These strategies operate in H. J. Grace's seminal work and the citational chain that builds from it. While Grace spearheads a citational chain of troubling literature linking blackness and intersex (with origins in the 1600s), by his own standards his research actually proves that black South Africans are *not* disproportionately intersex. The conditions of this massive contradiction and its implications for contemporary medicine are explored here.

This chapter begins by exposing the inception of medical diagnoses labeled "intersex" in South Africa as predicated on scientific racism. I then expose how claims are codified through repetition in medical journals and popular media with global reach. Finally, I analyze visual representations, arguing that medical gazes—and especially medical photography—produce ideas of raced inferiority through broadly circulating images. Throughout this chapter, I expose how assertions of black people as disproportionately intersex are fundamentally flawed truth claims built on unsubstantiated evidence with catastrophic effects for those under medical scrutiny.

The Untoward Reach of One Master's Thesis

The creation of gender normality has deep ties to colonialism and apartheid. But it was not until 1970 and the publication of Grace's influential master's thesis—"Intersex in Four South African Racial Groups in Durban"—that the links between intersex and racist science were cemented in South African medical literature. Hatherley James Grace was trained in the Departments of Zoology and Animal Biology at the University of KwaZulu-Natal (then University of Natal) and pursued a prolific career through the Genetics Department at the Natal Institute of Immunology. Grace endeavored to map gender onto bodies through medical subfields including genetics and obstetrics/gynecology, publishing dozens of articles on his South African research in medical journals based in the Global North as well as in Africa-based medical publications. The content of these inquires varied, but the majority of Grace's work was concerned with intersex, particularly as congruent with apartheid's racial categories. His research on intersex paralleled and sometimes overlapped with his scholarly efforts to find other physical bases for racial categories in the body through studies of hands and fingerprints (dermatoglyphics) and "mental retardation" (see Grace and Ally 1972, 1973; Grace 1974, 1975a, 1975b, 1976; Grace et al. 1979; Ally and Grace 1979).[1] Citations of Grace's thesis, and three articles Grace published in the *South African Medical Journal* that drew from its data (Grace, Quantock, and Vinik 1970; Grace and Schonland 1970; Grace and Edge 1973), codified the assertion that intersex is more common among black South Africans than white South Africans.

Given the subsequent reach and longevity of this work, H. J. Grace might be likened to John Money. While less known on a global scale, Grace likely had an equivalent influence on the racialized treatment of intersex patients. Money and Grace also represent important scientific relationships between the Global North and South.[2] Their collaborations span the three sites discussed in the introduction—South Africa, the Dominican Republic, and Papua New Guinea—with scientists from Europe and North America tacking among them.[3] As part of these transnational discourses, Grace cited Money's work, while Grace's scholarship on black intersex frequency in South Africa was published and cited in journals across the Global North. Grace influenced scientists conceptualizing gender diagnoses and treatments in the United States. Money's and Grace's parallel work disrupts expectations of transnational flows of theory and knowledge as exported from the Global North to the Global South, demonstrating that the global creation of raced gender binarism emanated from and always relied on comparisons to the Global South.

What were the specific claims of Grace's work, and how do they hold up to contemporary scrutiny? The stated intention of his master's thesis was to prove the commonality of intersex among black South Africans. Grace's thesis begins by citing three specific studies in South African medical literature in the 1960s, discussed in chapter 1, that assert true hermaphroditism as the most common form of intersex among the "Bantu races of South Africa and Rhodesia."[4] Despite their contradictions and data deficits, these three studies form the shaky and tenuous basis for Grace's assertion that "over several years it has been claimed by authors and clinicians . . . that intersexuality is more prevalent among the Bantu of the subcontinent than in other race groups; and that in the Bantu hermaphroditism is the commonest form of intersex" (1970, 7). For African patients deemed intersex, the rare diagnosis of "true hermaphroditism" was embraced as part of efforts to position black intersex as the epitome of abnormality.

Grace is intent on defining intersex and differentiating among various syndromes and diagnoses focused on anatomy, hormones, and especially chromosomes.[5] He takes great care in introducing his reader to his detailed definitions in sections titled, among others, "The Differential Diagnosis of Intersex," "Classification of Intersex," and "Pathogenesis of Intersex." In addition to discussions of intersex in nature, history, religion, and mythology, Grace devotes a full six chapters of the thesis to categorical descriptions of conditions he believes fall under the rubric of intersex.[6] The rest of the document is devoted to thirty-four "case reports" focused on individuals diagnosed with these conditions. I return to these case reports in more detail below.

The other stated focus of this study is on "four racial groups." Grace's detailed taxonomy of intersex recalls scientific racism and extensive colonial efforts to categorize those in southern Africa. Yet in this entire thesis, which is 272 pages long, Grace devotes only three sentences to defining race because, to him, race is simple and needs minimal explanation. His description perfectly and uncritically follows apartheid logic with corresponding labels and statistics.[7] Intersex requires hundreds of pages of explanation, whereas "South Africa has four well-defined population groups, caucascids, negroids, Asiatics, and a mixed race of all three, the Coloureds, and is therefore an ideal area for studies of inter-racial variation; even more so than the west indies where miscegenation has obscured the true racial identity of the individual" (1970, 216).[8] These assumptions about apartheid racial categories are not confined to Grace's scholarship and were replicated in most medical literature in this period, reflecting a matrix of race, tribe, nation, ethnicity, language, and population, and these categorizations are rife with contradictions even within the same author's work.[9]

When I read about Grace's thesis, I was surprised at the longevity and breadth of citations based on it. How could a mere master's thesis that is decades old and makes such troubling declarations still have such a strong impact in medical literature? But when I closely analyzed the thesis itself, I found that not only is this study the penultimate source for the claim that black South Africans are disproportionately intersex, it argues the inverse: black South Africans are *not* disproportionately intersex. Remarkably, in this thesis, Grace is quite *unsuccessful* in finding proof of corporeal racial difference. Of the 20,690 live births included in his year-long study, which included four maternity wards in Durban in 1969, only 7 births of babies with supposed genital anomalies, including four with simple penile hypospadias and three diagnosed with "possible" intersex, were recorded (1970, 197–200).[10] The number of black intersex patients Grace cited was too low to allow for accurate statistical analysis and thus disproved his thesis.

In his conclusion, a disappointed Grace admits, "The overall impression gained from this work is that there is little difference between the frequency of intersex in whites and Bantu" (1970, 218). Regardless of his statements that link intersex to blackness throughout the text, his admission of failure throughout the conclusion to this thesis is direct and emphatic. Grace tries to prop up his failing hypothesis through cytogenetics, dermatoglyphics, and other more technically advanced and invasive forms of imaging and testing—shifting from examinations of external genitals to looking inside the body for sources of racial difference—but this proves unfeasible due to lack of resources. He is not easily dissuaded and shares suggestions for continuing the search.[11] But Grace eventually concedes that his "preconception of intersexuality being rampant in South Africa was incorrect" (1970, 218).[12]

Gendered medicine is historically dependent on confused and conflated concepts. Grace was interested in proving the commonality of both "intersex" and "hermaphroditism" among black South Africans. The difference in medicine at the time was that *hermaphroditism* referred to the concurrent presence of ovarian and testicular tissue (with *true hermaphroditism* sometimes used synonymously), while *intersex* served as an umbrella term for a wide range of conditions. Other researchers used these terms interchangeably. Grace, seeking order, proof, and clarity, bemoans these authors' classifications of intersex as incorrect, extensively citing publications of his peers to demonstrate that "in describing clinical cases it is regrettable that authors do not use the popularly accepted names for syndromes, instead of conjuring up synonyms . . . or failing to use a term when a suitable one exists" (1970, 9).

Given these inconsistencies, hypotheses about intersex and race cannot be supported and quantified. Grace himself points out that medical publications regularly misdiagnose intersex patients, complaining, "Some authors appear to be diletantes [*sic*] as far as the terminology of intersexual states is concerned" (1970, 9). This causes statistical confusion and inconsistency when trying, as he and other apartheid-era scientists tended to do, to quantify and classify people. In Grace's own words: "Calculation of figures for the national, or even regional prevalence of intersex is virtually impossible at present" (4). Nevertheless, from the point of Grace's thesis publication onward, researchers did indeed make quantitative assertions that true hermaphroditism is most common among black South Africans.

The statistics presented by Grace are inherently flawed yet rationalized. For instance, Grace claims that intersex patients are inconsistently motivated to seek medical attention due to various "geographic, economic and domestic conditions" (1970, 201). Grace justifies his failed research by blaming intersex people themselves, and especially black people, for the lack of statistics to support his hypothesis. He couches this in the language of "racial idiosyncrasies": "None of the races are particularly eager to present themselves for investigation of intersexual problems, but this is complicated by racial idiosyncrasies: for instance, the Bantu male does not seem unduly perturbed by gynecomastia unless there is some concomitant pain. These racial characteristics must have some influence on the apparent distribution of intersex amongst the four communities" (199). Grace and other scientists and physicians are unsettled when those in the Global South (here "Bantu") are unbothered by gendered conditions like gynecomastia (chest tissue growth) or hirsutism (hair growth). Their studies reflect this biased expectation. Not being "unduly perturbed" is taken as evidence of disproportionate intersex frequency and as a rationale for lack of statistical data. Nevertheless, while those researching intersex bemoan their colleagues' shortcomings and patients' racial idiosyncrasies and seem paradoxically resigned to the impossibility of statistical accuracy, they continue to rely on positivist research and statistics about intersex and to make sweeping false assertions.

Codifying a Citational Chain and Reifying Black Intersex Frequency

Since 1970, Grace's work and the scholarship of those who cite him have had amazing tenacity. They continue to be referenced in medical studies of intersex in South Africa and in those that slip into generalizations about Africa more broadly, creating a complex scientific façade. Oddly, even Grace himself continued to make his disproven claim of raced intersex in articles that drew on the same data and photos represented in his 1970 master's thesis. For instance, in 1973 he and co-author Edge asserted, "Hermaphrodites have frequently been found among the Negro peoples of Africa and their descendants in the West Indies, and also in mixed races who share Negro ancestry. In caucasoid races, however, hermaphroditism is rare and has hitherto not been described in a White South African" (Grace and Edge 1973, 1553). This article repeated data from "Case 29" in Grace's thesis (1970, 185, plate 17) and made unsupported assertions that became canonical.[13]

Grace's scholarship and its quick acceptance occurred at the height of apartheid. Rigid classification systems and violent control of bodies lay at the core of apartheid's project, mirrored in Grace's ongoing obsessions with racial purity, reproduction, and gender norms. But resistance to these restrictive policies was strong. In the 1970s, racialized pathologization of intersex was institutionalized at the same time that revolts over centuries of colonial rule erupted in violent conflicts. These conflicts were concurrent with tightening controls over bodies deemed intersex, particularly through the medical interventions of Grace and his South African colleagues.

I have already examined the flaws in the three publications that preceded and influenced Grace's thesis (Klempman 1964; Forbes and Hammar 1966;

Wilton 1969) in chapter 1. To construct the citational chain that followed his research and the purposes it serves, assessing a few examples proves instructive. These and countless other studies demonstrate the power of repetition of the unproven racial assertion that continued over the following five decades:

R. H. Johnson: *South African Medical Journal*, 1974
"True hermaphroditism is the commonest intersex state in the Black population of South Africa, with an estimated incidence of 1/10,000 live births" (cites Wilton 1969 and Grace and Edge 1973)

Howard W. Jones Jr.: *American Journal of Obstetrics and Gynecology*, 1976
"Professor van Niekerk lives in a part of the world [South Africa] where true hermaphroditism is relatively more common than elsewhere due to environmental or, more likely, genetic influences. In fact, he lives in an area where true hermaphroditism is the most likely diagnosis when a patient is encountered with ambiguous genitals" (cites Grace and Edge 1973)

J. J. L. de Souza et al.: *South African Medical Journal*, 1984
"True hermaphroditism is highly prevalent in the indigenous black population of South Africa" (cites Grace and Edge 1973)

I. A. Aaronson: *British Journal of Urology*, 1985
"True hermaphroditism is a rare cause of intersexuality in Western Europe and North America, but on the African continent is among the most common" (no citation, later reference to Van Niekerk 1974)

R. Wiersma: *Journal of Pediatric Surgery*, 2001
"A disproportionately high incidence of true hermaphroditism has been reported among South African black people, the cause of which has not yet been elucidated" (citations include Grace 1977; Van Niekerk 1976; and Aaronson 1985)

R. Wiersma: *Journal of Pediatric Surgery*, 2008
"With an unusually high incidence of this condition among South African patients investigated for ambiguous genitalia (51%), several authors have shown that true hermaphroditism in Southern Africa is different in several respects [primarily due to a 'unique histological pattern of ovotestes']" (cites Van Niekerk 1977 [*sic*, 1976]; Aaronson 1985; and himself)

Ganie et al.: *Hormone Research in Paediatrics*, 2017
"The prevalence of OT DSD [true hermaphroditism] is particularly high in black South Africans [and] . . . disproportionately high compared to

other centres worldwide" (cites Van Niekerk 1976; Wiersma and Ramdial 2009; and Wiersma 2004, 2011).

In these examples, scholars collaborate and cite each other, referencing scholarship repetitively and citing decades-old research with presentist assumptions. Note, for instance, the historical present assumed in Ganie's 2017 citation of research published forty-one years prior (in 1976). References with scant evidentiary bases become codified through citation without substantive engagement with the original publications. They begin to create norms about Africans' bodies, deriving power through their repetition. The sources in which these articles are published are notable. Of the seven articles cited here, only two are published in Africa-based journals, and the rest are published in journals based in the Global North. This reflects the broad reach and engagements among scientists and physicians worldwide. This consistent repetition and wide circulation create notions about black intersex frequency, especially in the Global South, as integral to broader theories of gender ambiguity.

In this citational chain and related medical literature, terms with varied meanings are used synonymously. In medical vernacular from the 1970s onward, *intersex* usually refers to a range of conditions of gender ambiguity, while *true hermaphroditism* is a specific diagnosis indicating the presence of both ovarian and testicular tissue. But slippages are the norm, and conflations of terms describing gender and race are found throughout these publications. Even Grace's own description of intersex among "Bantu" becomes "Negro" becomes "South African" becomes "Black" in his writings. Tribe, ethnicity, geography, and phenotype merge under the ahistorical and abiological rubric of race.[14]

Dr. Michèle Ramsay, who might be considered Grace's successor in medical literature, also provides links in South Africa's citational chain, but with an explicit influence on popular culture. Ramsay has similarly devoted much of her career to finding a cause for black intersex frequency. Like Grace, Ramsay authored numerous studies on race and intersex, looking to her own field of specialization: genetics.[15] But Ramsay's research is similarly unsuccessful. For instance, in a co-authored study published in 1988, Ramsay and colleagues repeat Grace's oft-cited claim that "a high incidence of 46,xx true hermaphroditism exists among southern African blacks"; however, the study again proves futile (4). In this research, conducted from 1976 to 1988, and in subsequent studies, Ramsay concedes that she can find no genetic or environmental rationale for the assumed frequency of black intersex in southern Africa. Ramsay's most recent analysis of intersex and race, published thirty-three years after the start of her original study, in 1976, continues her career-long attempt to find cause for disproportionate prevalence of true hermaphroditism but is again unsuccessful. The failed results are blamed on patients not providing blood samples for molecular analysis (Ramsay et al. 2009) in work that cites the same the citational chain just examined. Researchers including Ramsay repeat the same question from slightly different (albeit unsuccessful) angles: Why are black people more likely to be intersex? A more instructive question might be Why is the unproven high prevalence of black intersex the subject of such intense scrutiny and interest?[16]

The longue durée of intersex and race is furthered by the strong interplay between science and popular culture, as depicted in films such as *The Third Sex* (Roberts 2004).[17] This film, produced by the BBC and the US-based Learning Channel, features expert commentary from Ramsay and is, unfortunately, one among dozens designed to titillate and educate a popular audience into accepting troubling understandings of gender binaries and medical science. While human displays and photographs were historically sites for reiterating myths of raced intersex, from the 1990s to the present, film has supplemented these public claims. But what makes *The Third Sex* unusual is its focus on three sites: the United Kingdom (where otherwise "normal" families are affected and then cured in hospitals), the community of Salinas in the Dominican Republic (investigated by Imperato-McGinley and here represented anonymously as a pointedly secret location in the Caribbean), and South Africa.

In the segment on South Africa, filmmakers interview Ramsay at length as she reiterates the assertion that she has not proved, extending its popular impact. The narration begins with the recitation of unfounded and somewhat confounding statistics and allusions to normality/abnormality; the narrator states, "Whereas cases of hermaphroditism might normally be 1 in 1,000,000 births, here in South Africa the rate is as high as 1 in 8,000, possibly higher."[18] This narration is accompanied by footage of a South African landscape (likely Johannesburg and Soweto) taken from a car as the camera pans over self-constructed township homes and children sitting in the street. Slow drum beats mix with spooky violin music to evoke feelings of drama and unresolved mystery. The narrator introduces the expert for this segment as Dr. Ramsay of the South African Institute for Medical Research, who has worked in Johannesburg for the past twelve years.

Ramsay is interviewed while she drives through township streets, where random people are shown walking in groups in slow motion, and she details her interest in intersex this way: "I first became interested in hermaphroditism when one of my colleagues pointed out that this was something that occurs quite commonly in South Africa, particularly in the black population. And I think it is such an enormous puzzle to us why people can have both male and female parts. And it would be really interesting to find out why it happens, and particularly why it's so common in one population group and not in others." Ramsay's description not only demonstrates her interest, it also complicates understandings of intersex for the viewer. Colonial histories are echoed in confusing generalizations of various intersex and hermaphroditic conditions as "both male and female parts." If Ramsay is defining "parts" as the visible presence of a penis and a vulva/vagina, this is an exceptionally rare occurrence. Or maybe her euphemistic use of "parts" refers to internal organs. But so-called true hermaphroditism (or, in current medical vernacular, ovotesticular DSD) is based on the presence of ovarian and testicular tissue, usually undetectable except under microscopic examination. In either case, here, as throughout the film, definitions of *intersex* and *true hermaphroditism* are imprecise and conflated.

The narrator continues this segment of *The Third Sex*, still punctuated with spooky instrumental music and generic tribal drumbeats, by explaining the extent of the mystery Ramsay was trying to solve: "Dr. Ramsay began her work with little previous evidence to go on. In her search for clues, she knew that every possibility had to be considered." Ramsay then codifies her declaration— intersex/hermaphroditism is more common among black people—and introduces the possibility of traditional healing, an element of culture and spirituality that many researchers find fascinating yet "primitive," as a possible cause for this enigma. She states: "When we started this research we knew that it occurred more commonly in the black population than in the white or other populations. And we didn't know whether it was environmental or whether it had some kind of genetic basis. One of the things we looked at was whether the mothers, during their pregnancy, had been to see traditional healers, because they may have given them something, say, the first three months of pregnancy, that might have influenced the gender, like some plant that contained a hormone or something that would influence the gender of the fetus." This comment explicates Ramsay's research trajectory, seeking to discover an explanation, here alluding to something that mothers or traditional healers did to cause so-called gender abnormalities. The narrator then discloses, however, that "the environmental possibilities, in the end, drew a blank. No clear line of connection could be found." So the specter of traditional healing is raised in the film with no clear purpose other than to speculate on the causes of this "problem" in black South African communities.

Still fostering the sense of mystery, the narrator continues: "Dr. Ramsay began to believe that the answer lay somewhere in the genes. That the abnormality was passing through the chromosomes from one generation to another. Exploring this meant speaking not just to the patients, but to their extended families." But, Ramsay suggests, research participants themselves thwarted successful and definitive research into genetic causes for the supposed prevalence of intersex in their communities:

> People don't want to talk about it. They're reluctant to, sort of, say too much. And in some of our earlier studies, we thought it was very important to look at the families to find out if there was more than one individual affected within a family. And we're not always sure when they say that there isn't that there really isn't. Because it may be hidden and even, sort of like, cousins or aunts or uncles might not know about it. So it's been an enormous problem from the research point of view. But you can understand that individuals want to protect their privacy, and that they don't necessarily want people to know that they're different.

Ramsay recounts a few reasons she believes that patients and their families may not speak honestly to researchers. Her explanations are focused on their confusion (they "might not know about it") and efforts to protect their privacy ("we're not always sure when they say that there isn't [intersex] that there really isn't"). This kind of tautological reasoning is impossible to disprove. But Ramsay posits that the failure of her own inquiries do not undermine her claim of black intersex frequency. Instead, inability to determine the cause of this connection is blamed on patients and families who may deceive researchers or do not understand their own bodies and histories.[19]

The final portion of the film segment focused on South Africa shifts from fear-inducing instrumentals to upbeat African-style drumming and wordless choral vocals. The camera pans over black South Africans in silhouette, playing basketball on an outdoor court in slow motion, while the narrator attempts to educate the viewer on genetics:

> What makes a hermaphrodite different is the pattern of their sex chromosomes. In a normal male, every cell in the body will carry male genes. A female carries only female genes. In hermaphrodites, some cells carry male genes, others female. Some think the presence of the male genes in some cells is linked to the growth of testes in hermaphrodites, but how and why, no one knows. The mystery remains. But for the people in these South African communities, it's an everyday reality. The problem for them isn't understanding why they are intersexuals, but to be accepted as intersex person in wider society. The first step here is self-acceptance, and that process starts at birth.

This is a simple explanation of a complicated reality, within which hermaphroditism = genes, and it contradicts Ramsay's earlier definition—hermaphroditism

= male and female parts. Intersex and (true) hermaphroditism continue to be fused as confusingly synonymous. The resolution to this segment of the film is similarly reductionist. The narrator suggests that South Africans don't need to or cannot understand their supposed medical condition; instead, they need individualistic self-acceptance. Overall, the filmmakers consistently assert that intersex is common in remote and primitive communities in the Global South, including South Africa and the Dominican Republic, and that people may cause or facilitate intersex themselves through traditional practices or dishonesty with researchers. The viewer is urged to accept the complications of gender and the authority of (white) researchers and doctors to intervene and solve this crisis through the power of modern medicine.

Visualizing Violence: Creating Truths through Medical Photography

Visual representations in *The Third Sex* and other films recall the photographs of those labeled as "hermaphrodites" and "true hermaphrodites" ripped from the pages of the South African medical books detailed in chapter 1. In the colonial record, images of raced gender difference are framed through sexual fetishization, clinical gazing, and panoptic surveillance. In South African medical literature beginning in the 1970s, photographs in intersex scholarship thinly veil violence. These photographs rarely conceal patients' identities but usually picture them naked with their faces and bodies revealed, often looking at the floor and away from the photographic gaze. They also represent very poor outcomes of surgeons' efforts at genital construction. The images are accompanied with captions often expressing overt condescension or disdain for individual patients.

How can these haunting photographs be understood in ways that honor and value those exploited by their capture? My first answer to this question was to exclude the images themselves from this book. The tendency toward spectacularization is why this book intentionally excludes photographs even while it focuses on ways of seeing. Images are not inert objects that convey an objective truth but play a powerful role, holding power and emotion that go far beyond their physical replication.[20] Ariella Azoulay (2008) suggests the importance of *watching*, rather than looking at, photographs, and Fred Moten (2002) and Tina Campt (2017) give us methodologies to *listen* to images. These approaches interrogate multiple temporalities of images—including their capture, reproduction, and circulation—and the necessary refusal to accept them as reflecting objective truth.[21] I analyze the images in Grace's work with these approaches and histories of African colonial photography and its refusal in mind.

Grace's master's thesis includes sixty-four images, and taken together, they convey the interplay of racism, objectification, and sanctioned violence. We don't know who took these photographs—doctors, nurses, medical photographers, or other hospital staff—nor do we know their intentions. Given the context and questionable consent, patients' agency is very difficult to assess. But one cannot help but notice facial expressions and body language. Some patients stand awkwardly spread-eagled, while others stand with their arms and legs clenched tightly to their sides. Their gazes at the camera (or the person taking the photographs) might be variously interpreted as irritated, resigned, pained, and sad. Grace's thirty-four case studies depict twenty-two patients classified as Bantu, seven as white, and five as Indian, and their ages range from newborn to sixty years old. The reasons they were seen by doctors varied. Some patients' bodies were subjected to treatment because of their supposedly ambiguous genitals or menstrual problems, and some patients sought treatment themselves.[22] But many patients facing intense diagnostic testing and treatment came to doctors for unrelated conditions, including a swollen leg, an earache, and dysentery. And several patients analyzed in Grace's case studies were seen for supposed psychiatric conditions; different individuals were described as "catatonic," "manic," and "mentally slow," while one patient's history of conviction for fraud was presented as related to his intersex diagnosis.

Predictably, given colonial and apartheid foci, Grace's thesis includes eighteen photographs of patients' genitals.[23] But perhaps more notably, these genital photos are often shown with hands on them, purportedly exposing their size, structure, and abnormality but also indicating violent objectification in the moment they were captured.[24] These anonymous hands expose patients' bodies to the photographers' gaze and documentation. A useful point of comparison comes in the work of South African visual anthropologist Rory Du Plessis, whose analyses of photographs of patients at the Grahamstown mental asylum taken between 1890 and 1907 lay bare the violence faced by black patients in residence. Du Plessis examines the hands that hold black mental patients in place, gripping their necks and bodies as they are forced to submit to intake photographs, and he details patients' movement as they resist restraint by staff members. He surmises that patients' efforts to writhe away and refuse photography make the asylum's staff's bodies part of the images: "This failure of the authorities to remain hidden leads the viewer to meditate on the intrusions, discipline and conditions under which the photographs were produced" (2014, 27). For Du Plessis, such images "underscore the point that the taking of a photograph is never neutral" (27) and is often a violent act.[25]

A hand holding genitals is also notable in a photograph of Eugénie Rémy circulated among French medical professionals in the late 1880s, largely considered the first photograph of a person deemed intersex. Hil Malatino points out the underlying power of the hand on Rémy's genitals: "The hand that directs the scenography here while remaining otherwise disembodied—we follow it to the wrist, which the border of the images severs, invisibilizing the physician, diffusing medical authority, rendering it part of the miasmic milieu while sterilizing its violence" (2019, 138). Like Du Plessis, Malatino foregrounds the violence of the moment the photograph was taken and the absent physician or photographer. Alice Dreger, analyzing the same photograph of Rémy, provides historical context about hands in both medical photographs and sketches of the time, when the stated intent was scientific control, and never wanting the viewer to "forget that there is a 'hand guiding the given image" (1998, 48). Hands on genitals in medical photography not only displayed external genital structures, but in some medical photos, hands were "inserted in the patient, ostensibly documenting 'insufficient' vaginal depth" (Malatino 2019, 141). Malatino submits that doctors' gazes of dominance coupled with their own invisibility made a physician photographer a "modest witness" in philosopher Donna Haraway's (1997) terms. Haraway's modest witness is one who serves as an objective and legitimized authority and entrée to scientific truth, self-invisibilized yet omnipresent in his gaze. He is modest in the depiction of his hand, but not his face or body, inviting observers to overlook the violence and subjectification of the moment.

Photographed hands have had another significant meaning in photography: as a means of identification and racialization. Tina Campt's analysis of what she refers to as compulsory and compelled photos—photos that are forcibly taken without consent—considers criminal identification photos taken at Breakwater Prison in Cape Town around 1893. These photos show prisoners' faces with their hands positioned as part of the portraits, held against the shoulders of their uniforms: "The positioning of these hands is more than purposeful—it is both prescribed as well as literally transcribed onto the uniforms themselves, where we see painted white marks that seem to indicate exactly where these hands should be placed" (Campt 2017, 81). In Campt's view, hands are as significant as faces in photographs of prisoners, scrutinized for distinguishing features and carefully documented to identify them for possible recapture. Grace's photographs also include some hands of patients themselves, forced to spread their own genitals for the gaze of the camera, compelled into the photographs as subjects and assistants in their own visual capture.

Grace was obsessed with hands. In addition to his work on intersex, which continued throughout his career, he pursued another focus of research in genetics: racialized dermatoglyphics. This research analyzed handprints as a site of anatomical difference. Grace's publications on the subject number almost a dozen and include titles such as "Dermatoglyphs of the South African Negro" (Grace and Ally 1973), "Palmar Dermatoglyphs of South African Negroes and Coloureds" (Grace 1974), and "Concentrations of Similar Finger Print Patterns in Four Race Groups" (Grace 1976).[26] Indeed, Grace's master's thesis includes three chapters dedicated to dermatoglyphics as a branch of inquiry that merged scientific racism with intersex genetics.[27]

Contemporary fingerprinting grew from efforts to predict and control criminality under British colonialism. Fingerprinting was popularized in India in 1888 through the work of Francis Galton, a half cousin of Charles Darwin's and the founder of eugenics, who believed that criminality was biologically determined. Galton and his contemporaries were concerned about the "treachery of the native population and the impenetrability of their languages," and he approached "fingerprints as images that could end the cycle of presumed deception" (Waits 2016, 20). Fingerprinting was a precursor to dermatoglyphics, both claiming hands as racially distinct and continuing to combine colonial surveillance and racialized science.[28] Grace's work merged his own research into dermatoglyphics with intersex conditions such as Turner's and Kleinfelter's syndromes, genetic quests that continue today.[29]

Faces are as significant as genitals and hands in medical photographs of those deemed intersex, both when obscured and when revealed. Photographs taken of those considered "hermaphroditic" in the late 1800s in Europe initially revealed faces of patients and even printed their full names in publications, but around the turn of the twentieth century, "some investigators began to photograph subjects after placing a black bag over their head . . . the precursor to the practice of placing a black bar across a subject's eyes in later medical photographic representations" (Dreger 1998, 49). Images of intersex patients' heads covered with black bags evoke images of bags tied over people's heads for executions. Such strategies are not intended to protect the privacy of those enveloped in the bags, who will soon be killed, but to create distance to shield those engaging in violent gazing from a returned intimate gaze in the moments before and after death.[30] Black bags concealing patients' faces in medical photography were soon replaced with conventions of altering photos to include blurred or whited-out faces or bars over the eyes—sometimes referred to as black bars, white bars, or censor bars—imposed after the photograph was taken. Malatino suggests, "While the pragmatic function of this trope is to ensure the anonymity of the patient, it works to further stigmatize intersex bodies through entrenching the idea that the visibly intersex body must remain secret, covered, socially and politically invisible—it cannot be attached to a person" (2019, 122). This move toward what Malatino calls "dispassionate detachment" is facilitated by medical photographs that show exposed genitals before and after surgeries juxtaposed with covered faces, disallowing the patient to gaze back but allowing gratuitous imaging of bodies.[31]

Viewers do not know how Grace's patients felt about the photographs taken for his case studies, but traumatic consequences of clinical photography can be expected, as intersex patients already experience intense ostracism and medicalized violence. In the only clinical article on intersex medical photography of which I am aware, from the *British Journal of Urology*, patients from two adult intersex clinics in the UK describe long-term psychological damage attributable to clinical photography (Creighton et al. 2002, 67). Creighton and colleagues spoke to intersex patients who, as adults, found photos of themselves taken when they were children in their medical files. One patient reflects on this experience: "They made me be naked in a room and take pictures of me and they took pieces of my skin and left two marks one on each arm and nobody said to me why they were doing it. Those marks are still there, and I look at them and I think 'Why did they do that?' You know, why did they make me stand in a room and have pictures taken with no clothes on and humiliate me like that without saying anything to me. Why, what was wrong with me?" (Creighton et al., 2002, 69). The photographic trauma expressed by this patient is disturbingly common, and it is echoed by intersex South African activists in chapter 5.

Alice Dreger, as part of her work with intersex activists in the United States, decided to include a nude photograph of herself with a black bar over her eyes on the cover of her 1999 anthology of intersex adults' stories, *Intersex in the Age of Ethics*. Her intention was to show that this kind of imagery is pathologizing.[32] Dreger recounts, "I learned from contriving this 'medical' photo of myself that intersex activist Cheryl Chase was absolutely right when she told me that the only thing the black band over the eyes accomplishes is saving the viewer from having the subject stare back. Even with blackened eyes and blurred parts, those who know me can recognize me in that picture" (2000, 162).[33] The photos of Grace's patients are also fully recognizable; eighteen patients, including children, are clearly identifiable by pictures of their faces and bodies. The kinds of photographs included in Grace's thesis are also troublingly gratuitous, their bodies shown with little explicit medical rationale.

In the early days of photographic technologies, researchers were enthralled with the possibilities of photography to record the "lifeless bodies" of those considered primitive (Pinney 2011, 36). Christopher Pinney recounts that in 1893, anthropologist Im Thurn argued that corpses were photographically preferable to live humans, as bodies would "be more accurately measured and photographed for such purposes dead than alive, could they be conveniently obtained when in that state" (quoted in Pinney 2011, 36). In parallel course in nineteenth-century Europe, medical diagnoses of "true hermaphroditism" necessitated dissection or death. In both contexts, dehumanization and categorization motivated visual documentation. Corpses and gendered body parts were displayed, measured, and dissected in necropolitical quests to prove gender and racial binaries.

Perhaps the most disturbing photographs in Grace's thesis are of deceased infants. Grace's case studies include four patients who died while under his medical care. For instance, one infant ("Case 25"), who lived for only forty-six hours due to severe breathing difficulties, was subjected to blood draws, oral buccal mucosal smears, and hand-printing during their few hours of life because of persistent efforts to diagnose the patient's intersex condition.[34] Grace continued to photograph the infant's body in death. In other case reports, patients are subjected to unnecessary surgeries that may indeed have contributed to their demise, and their cadavers are dismembered and photographed. Two photographs focus on the genitals of the deceased patients—a neonate ("Case 1") and a sixty-year-old ("Case 5") who died under medical care—and their genitals were removed and dissected after their death.[35] Postmortem photography has a long and complicated history in medical literature, including in the examination, removal, and photography of genitals and reproductive organs to "prove" gender.[36] In these ways, the visual violence described here doesn't merely mirror but ultimately works to control and produce notions of raced gender binaries.

The Intractability of Racing Intersex

While this chapter focuses on a fifty-year-old unpublished document, it is a document with powerful contemporary significance. A Google search of "Intersex South Africa" in 2020 quickly linked me to the digital library of the University of KwaZulu-Natal and the description of Grace's thesis. Indeed, Grace's entire thesis is provided as a free PDF, widely available on the open web. Contemporary readers continue to find and cite this troubling study, adding links to the citational chain I critique here. I recently questioned my own possible role and unintended complicity in this chain of intersex literature. During my dissertation research over twenty years ago, I requested Grace's thesis via interlibrary loan from the University of Minnesota libraries. As this request preceded digitization, librarians at my alma mater and at the University of KwaZulu-Natal went to significant trouble to provide me with this document. I still have five plastic sheets of Grace's thesis on microfiche in an envelope sent to me on December 2, 2002. Could my request for a then-obscure document have played a part in the current online access provided to Grace's racist research? Reproductions sometimes work idiosyncratically to create "truths," and the stakes of practices that create data are thus matters of intense import.

I want to return to the strategies of raced intersex science that begin this chapter—*definition, scrutiny, repetition,* and *justification*—to briefly consider their application. Complicated and contradictory *definitions* and language pepper this chapter. Various authors inconsistently define *intersex, hermaphrodite,* and *true hermaphrodite.* The slippage among these terms, and quantitative reliance on them to create statistical evidence, dovetails with problematic assertions about race. Ellison and de Wet's survey of 668 articles in South African medical literature for "any categories that might have been used or interpreted as measures of genetically determined 'racial' differences (including 'racial,' ethnic and sociopolitical 'population group' categories)" (1997, 1671) finds that that the use of racial categories in health research in South Africa has been similarly "ill-conceived, misleading and divisive" (1672). This elision gives the appearance of racial solidity and is used as contrived proof of innate and genetic behavioral differences.[37] As the authors demonstrate, there was little evidence of decline in the use of historical or contemporary "racial" labels published in the *South African Medical Journal* between 1950 and 1990. In this chapter, similar trends in racialized and gendered language mask their inaccuracy and longevity.

Scrutiny is paramount in the creation of raced intersex, as demonstrated in visually dependent medical practices, film, and photos. These representations, like Imperato-McGinley's medical photographs of residents of Salinas, still freely available on the website of the Urological Sciences Research Foundation, form a taxonomy of intersex difference that transcends its origins. Visual representations in Grace's work are analogous to the South African Museum's "Casting Project" of racial types in their broad public impact. Grace's work is far from alone in these efforts. For instance, in this same period Willem A. Van Niekerk's exhaustive effort, *True Hermaphroditism: Clinical, Morphologic and Cytogenetic Aspects* (1974), extended his work in the field of Bantu Gynaecology, pathologizing gender and genitals through raced categories of apartheid. Like Grace, Van Niekerk includes charts, graphs, and extensive ledgers that form part of the classification and scrutiny of science. He photographically depicts patients' faces, bodies, and genitals as well as dissected organs categorized as "operative specimens" (body parts displayed on white backgrounds) and "laparotomy findings" (internal organs photographed during surgical procedures). He publishes X-rays, slides of dissected body parts, and diagrams of their locations in patients' bodies. I mentioned this book earlier, as a photograph from it had been torn from my library-loaned copy, presumably for individual consumption. Van Niekerk's exhaustive imaging and documentation was characteristic of the violence of apartheid. The scrutiny of visual representations didn't merely reflect classificatory systems of apartheid; it created classification.

Citational chains in which Grace's and Van Niekerk's works are prominent exemplify the power of *repetition* as a strategy for creating ideas of raced gender binarism. Judith Butler's discussions of citationality help explain this scholarship in historical and geographic context. Analogizing a judge's role in the law, Butler (invoking Lacan) explains that "the judge does not originate the law or its authority; rather, he 'cites' the law, consults and reinvokes the law, and, in that reinvocation, reconstitutes the law. The judge is thus installed in the midst of a signifying chain, receiving and reciting the law and, in the reciting, echoing forth the authority of the law" (1993, 107). Compare Grace to the judge in Butler's example. Citation and recitation/repetition of his work (and his own reinvocation of centuries of this colonial assertion) do not simply restate the claim of disproportionate intersex frequency in Africa. Grace's and his successors' citations rework and reinforce the claim itself, thus building its power.

This citational power is global, as the myth of black intersex frequency far exceeds South African national borders. The intersection of Grace and Van Niekerk's work in the United States demonstrates its wide-reaching authority. In 1976, Van Niekerk was invited to present an updated summation of *True Hermaphroditism* to the 96th meeting of the American Gynecological Society in Virginia, and his remarks and comments from United States–based colleagues were published as an article in the *American Journal of Obstetrics and Gynecology*. In this article, Van Niekerk cites all three of Grace's publications of "case studies" that replicate Grace's master's thesis findings (Grace, Quantock, and Vinik 1970; Grace and Schonland 1970; Grace and Edge 1973), repeating the assertion that "it is interesting that true hermaphroditism is so common among black races" (Van Niekerk 1976, 907). Again, the citation both precedes and exceeds each author and their respective reconstitutions of the body.

The claim of disproportionate raced intersex is also uncritically affirmed by the paper's prominent discussants. Dr. Howard W. Jones of Johns Hopkins University in Baltimore was John Money's contemporary and the surgeon who put Money's psychological theories into practice as he treated intersex patients. Jones is also credited as the innovating pioneer of in-vitro fertilization.

He even personally cared for Henrietta Lacks at Johns Hopkins Hospital (R. H. Epstein 2010).[38] Reflecting on Van Niekerk's work on intersex and race, the influential Jones surmises, "There is little to be added to such an authoritative and comprehensive review," and, he continues, "Professor van Niekerk lives in a part of the world where true hermaphroditism is relatively more common than elsewhere due to environmental or, more likely, genetic influences" (in Van Niekerk 1976, 905). Like so many others, Jones parrots the problematic assertions of the citational chain without critique or even minimal vetting.

With these claims and transnational connections in mind, it is perhaps even more notable that the reference tool Web of Science documents consistent reference to Van Niekerk's article on "True Hermaphroditism" for the past four decades. As with Grace's thesis, contemporary references to this work are startling, given the age and overtly racist bases of the publication. Web of Science also provides information on the "countries/regions enhanced" by this publication; researchers citing Van Niekerk's article were based most often in the United States (36 percent), South Africa (17 percent), and France and England (11 percent each), with further citations from researchers in Mexico, the Netherlands, Turkey, Algeria, Belgium, Brazil, Iran, Switzerland, Yugoslavia, Australia, Bulgaria, Canada, Chile, Germany, India, Indonesia, Israel, Jamaica, Poland, Scotland, and South Korea (listed from most to least frequent). These citations again demonstrate the power of repetition across geographies and historical periods, showing how this biased claim traveled and garnered unquestioned acceptance.

The final strategy under consideration—*justification*—allows truth creation in the face of inconsistencies and demonstrable flaws in research. I return here to Grace's counterpart, Money, and his most famous failed case. Money was known for his influential theories of the mutability of gender and his prescription to surgically alter intersex infants' bodies to fit norms he created. His theories and practices largely rested on the case of the Reimer twins. The Reimer children were assigned "male" at birth, and both were born with penises; but one child's penis was severely injured during circumcision. Money surgically and hormonally reassigned the injured baby as "female," unbeknownst to the child. He widely touted this treatment as a success that proved his theories about childhood gender development and intersex infants' plasticity.[39] But David Reimer eventually learned the truth of his own history and demanded to be reassigned as male again at age fourteen. His experiences became widely known when he told his story publicly and exposed Money's failings at age thirty-two. But a few years later, in 2004, bearing the stress of medical and psychological treatments and global public attention, Reimer tragically committed suicide.[40] Money, rather than admitting his fallacies and the flaws in his theory's underpinnings, justified the errors of his own research. And his assertions that rested on Reimer's failed treatment remain the dominant standard for intersex infant treatment today.[41]

In this chapter, erroneous medical claims are regularly cited as scholars continue to assert that intersex (and true hermaphroditism) is more common among black than white South Africans. Perhaps the most bizarre component of Grace's work provides a fitting conclusion to this chapter, reflecting his deep efforts to ground black inferiority in the body. In trying to understand the scope of Grace's work, I read everything he ever published, including dozens of articles that initially seemed irrelevant to this inquiry. Imagine my surprise when I went beyond the titles of two articles he coauthored on snails—"On the Haemagglutinin of the Snail *Achatina Granulata*" and "The Agglutination of A_{bantu} and Other Human Erythrocytes by Reagents from Snails"—to discover that these works represented further efforts to scientifically locate inferiority in black bodies. The intention of this element of Grace's research was to prove that racial difference affects immunity. Grace used snails found regionally only in South Africa. He drowned them, dissected them, and ground up their albumin glands to mix them first with the blood of animals (oxen, pigs, rabbits, sheep, and goats) and then with the blood and saliva of so-called Bantu, European, and Indian donors. Co-authors Brain and Grace assert that "there is a substance in some human salivas . . . [that] appears to be present in significantly greater quantity in the saliva of Bantu than it is in that of Europeans" and claim this as evidence of "quantitative differences" between races (1968, 298; see also Grace and Uhlenbruck 1969).

This final example reiterates why Grace's claims about black intersex are not only unsound but connected to broader racial comparisons with deeply troubling roots. Grace's career centered on trying to locate racial difference and black inferiority in the body. Taken together, his widely accepted assertions about genitals, reproductive organs, and chromosomes—and even saliva—are inseparable from histories of scientific racism and African pathologization. This pathologization and its effects on those deemed intersex would be the focus of South African intersex activism beginning in the 1990s, where the next chapter begins.

PART II
Recovering
Decolonial Intersex Interventions

3. Defying Medical Violence and Social Death

Sally Gross and the Inception of South African
Intersex Activism

Sally Gross was perhaps the most influential intersex activist in African history. But despite her global precedent-setting influence, she has received scant attention for her visionary work. As an anti-apartheid organizer and the founder of the first intersex organization on the African continent, Gross created a sophisticated body of writing and thinking on intersex in the Global South. Her self-representation in news media, online discussions, and TV/film contexts strongly confronted dominant representations of intersex. Theorizing complex precarities, Gross exposed the violence she and innumerable South Africans experienced to develop a decolonial critique of the science of intersex. In opposition to the medical objectification discussed in part one, this chapter explores Gross's pointed interventions into gendered scientific theories and medical protocols.

Perhaps the most visible of Gross's public challenges to colonially based science can be seen in the documentary *The 3rd Sex* (van Huyssteen 2003), initially shown on South African television as a three-part documentary series.[1] In it, black and white photographs from medical journals form a startling backdrop to a vivid critique of doctors' protocols. Unlike in their initial context, these photos are intentionally blurred by the movement of the filmmaker's camera as it zooms in to focus on intersex patients' faces, staring back at the camera and preventing the viewer from scrutinizing their bodies. Discussions with doctors are juxtaposed with personal experiences of two intersex South Africans—Gross and Nombulelo Soldaat—and interviews with a few medical professionals working to shift conceptions of intersex. This film reverses the scientific gaze to reframe the taxonomies imposed on intersex people.

This chapter follows *The 3rd Sex* and a wide range of Gross's work centered on the concurrence of racism and poverty with intersex to detail her liberatory vision and politic. It draws on Gross's published and unpublished writings, archival material held by GALA Queer Archive at the University of the Witwatersrand, and videos and interviews with Gross from various media and activist sources.[2] This is also a deeply personal chapter for me. I first met Gross just as she returned to South Africa from her years of exile. In March 2000, during the third year of my dissertation research in South Africa, I learned that Gross planned to start an intersex support group in Cape Town through the offices of the Triangle Project.[3] I emailed her to express interest in learning more about her emerging activism, and she immediately called me and initiated the first of many long conversations to come. I was conducting interviews jointly with my partner at the time, Sam Bullington; he was analyzing the impact of the new constitution while I explored how apartheid's architects policed gender ambiguity. Gross was eager to talk to us about personal and intellectual subjects and about her new initiatives, so we set up a time to meet. We started our relationship with a long life-historical interview and initiated a friendship that continued until her untimely death. These interviews and personal communications from 2000 to 2014 supplement this chapter.

Gross's personal and political goals hinged not on conformity or assimilation but on radical ideological change. This chapter begins with a brief discussion of her anti-apartheid activism and its influence on Intersex South Africa. I explore how she challenged the theories of prominent scientists like John Money and H. J. Grace and confronted the spectacularization of intersex. This chapter also builds on Gross's positionality and activism to locate whiteness and class in South African intersex history. The pillars of her interventions include conceptions of intersex social death and challenges to teratology, the branch of medicine that since the 1860s has positioned intersex people as monstrous. Taken as a whole, Gross's work connects colonialisms and apartheid to medical theories and damaging protocols to reframe ways of thinking about intersex for the future.

Working against Apartheid and Initiating Intersex Activism

Gross was born in Wynberg, South Africa, in 1953, just after the official start of apartheid, and she studied to be a rabbi in her youth. But she increasingly felt alienated by the response of official South African Jewish institutions to apartheid. She explains, "There was a policy of tacitly going along with apartheid. People from the Jewish community who challenged apartheid found themselves marginalised: the Joe Slovos, the Ronnie Kasrils and so on'" (quoted in Coan 2000).[4] Her commitment to justice motivated her to become deeply involved in anti-apartheid struggles as an active member of the African National Congress (ANC). The strong resistance to apartheid in the 1970s, and especially the Soweto uprising in 1976, led to violent backlash against ANC activists. This just strengthened Gross's political commitments. In 1977, her immersion in the liberation struggle became the catalyst for her decades-long exile: "'I wrote a draft programme which included an armed struggle clause—I had seen children being shot at on the streets of Cape Town—and it included a clause on co-operation with the ANC.' When a copy of the document disappeared under mysterious circumstances Gross was instructed to flee the country by her comrades. 'I skipped the country in May '77'" (Coan 2000). In exile, Gross remained an active member of the ANC and served as a member of the ANC delegation to Dakar, Senegal, in 1987 that was headed by former president Thabo Mbeki. Her movement from country to country seeking refuge eventually led Gross to England, where she continued her engagement with liberation theologies. She studied Catholicism and was ordained as a Dominican priest with Blackfriars in Oxford.

This was a critical time for Gross's exploration of tensions between what she referred to as her "aggressive Jewish identity and being a Christian" (van Huyssteen 2003).[5] Not coincidentally, it was also during exile and her priesthood that Gross finally chose to explore the gender ambiguity she had struggled to suppress her whole life:

> The decision to confront the issue of my bodiliness was a decision to confront what I feared the most, and what I had tried to run from in many different ways. . . . It became clear that the issue of gender—gender-identity— was much more prominent as a driving force in my life than I had realised and it was something I had to confront if it wasn't to pull my life to bits. . . . At that stage I rather naively thought I'd see someone with some expertise in this area and after a couple of sessions I could get on with the rest of my priestly life, full stop. . . . It wasn't as simple as that. (quoted in Coan 2000)

Intersex conditions were largely unfamiliar to her doctors, and Gross was unaware of her personal history. So her efforts initially led to a diagnosis of gender dysphoria and medical treatment as a transsexual. She felt as though she had "lifted the lid on a kind of Pandora's box" (van Huyssteen 2003). A doctor required her to follow the Harry Benjamin Standards of Care, a common medical protocol that involved cutting off contact with those who knew her, and her religious superior grudgingly allowed her to undertake the process known as a "real life test."[6] Gross had to move to an area of England where she did not know anyone; she was forbidden to talk to friends, coworkers, and family and was denied employment contacts. She was ostracized by church leaders and required to present herself as a woman. In the film *Intersexion* (Lahood 2012), she reflects on this period of her life, explaining, "I didn't like the process of having to learn to put on makeup, you know; wearing the clothing, well okay. In a sense, presenting as female did less violence to me than did presenting as male, but the truth is I'm a person, I'm me." During this time that came to function as a second kind of exile, Gross was denied moral and material support.

As this painful period progressed, bloodwork revealed that Gross's testosterone levels were much lower than expected and in the middle of what was described as a "normal female range." Given these test results, and in light of her genital ambiguity, Gross was rediagnosed as intersex. She described her diagnosis as knowledge for which she paid "a considerable personal price" ([Gross and Nicodemus] 1999), and she labeled this period as "the biggest trauma of my life" (quoted in Coan 2000). She was expelled from the Catholic priesthood under great duress.[7] These experiences of secrecy, stigma, and isolation would shape her emerging activist strategies and theories of intersex.

Gross began to seek support and get involved in what little intersex activism she could find at the time, mostly in the United States. Paralleling her strong history of anti-apartheid activism, she developed close connections with activists who started the influential Intersex Society of North America (ISNA) in 1993, including Cheryl Chase and Martha Coventry.[8] She explains the importance of the connections: "Something which helped me to cope, and to realise that I was not the only such creature in the world, was making contact with other people who are intersexed. . . . Many people who are intersexed are kept largely in the dark about their bodiliness and well away from information, access to their medical records, and from peer support" ([Gross and Nicodemus] 1999). As Gross notes, this invisibility and secrecy—including hiding medical histories from patients and from their families—was standard medical practice that had devastating personal outcomes. This made her even more determined to create a different reality for others deemed intersex.

Inspired by the promise of the formal end of apartheid, Gross returned to South Africa to establish Intersex South Africa. Her intent was to work for a "new South Africa" (as it was often called then) that went beyond gender binaries. Gross summarizes her trajectory this way: "I encountered ISNA, hit a stone wall in trying to raise the general issue of IS [intersex] in Britain, got an offer of work in South Africa, came back home to Cape Town, and it seemed natural to seek to start something out here. I was looking for an opportunity to do so for a long time" (Gross 2000). In August 1999 she sought out a reporter from the *Mail and Guardian* newspaper to announce her intention to form Intersex South Africa.[9] The resulting article explains: "While there are some support groups in countries like the United States and Britain, there is currently no network for intersexed people in South Africa, says Gross. She hopes that publicity about intersexuality will bring the issue out into the open, help to remove the stigma attached to it, and help intersexed South Africans to make contact with one another for mutual support" ([Gross and Nicodemus] 1999).[10] Goals for the new group included offering advice and psychological support to its members, educational outreach in schools, and legislative advocacy.[11] Intersex South Africa was initially affiliated with the health-oriented Triangle Project; Gross thought this partnership would help intersex people like herself seeking to discover their own medical histories and navigating treatment protocols.[12] In South Africa, speaking back to medical professionals was (and remains) a key activist strategy, and this included engagement with the ideas of prominent scientists and doctors.

Confronting Intersex Medicine: Dominant Theorists and Eugenic Traces

MONEY AND *MUTI*

When Gross was born at the beginning of apartheid, John Money's gender theories were not yet popular. In the 1950s, surgeries on infants with genitals deemed ambiguous had not yet been widely instituted. As the narrator in *The 3rd Sex* explains, "Sally was spared surgery because she grew up in an age where surgery was not yet standard procedure in South Africa" (van Huyssteen 2003). From childhood onward, however, Gross "had a sense of things being awry, being different. . . . Anatomically my body is exceedingly ambiguous and was clearly so when I was born" (quoted in Coan 2000). While she was not subjected to early medical treatment, a religious circumcision left scar tissue, "and something my father said to me about difficulties with the circumcision attest to an awkwardness about that" (quoted in Coan 2000).[13] Gross's articulation of a South

African intersex analytic reflected the contrast between her experiences of living without "corrective" surgery and the invasive medical theories that would quickly become dominant.

Gross was poignantly aware of the South African impact of Money's theories and popular protocols. From the first time we met, she routinely discussed Money's work at length, including the failed treatment of David Reimer.[14] She described Reimer's experience as the basis for Money's theories and for protocols adopted by physicians worldwide presuming that infants are born "sexually neutral" (Gross 2000). As detailed in chapter 2, Gross explains that Reimer (referred to in medical literature with pseudonyms of John/Joan) was one of two identical twins whose penis was severely injured by medical circumcision via cauterization in 1966. Money theorized that a child with an injured penis was a "blank slate." Gross explained how doctors proceeded thusly:

> They turned John into Joan by means of genital surgery. John Money, who now had a pair of identical twins to play with, was obviously very fascinated by this and followed up and wrote these very optimistic reports. [The reports described] how, just as his theories predicted, little Joan, as John—having been caught at the right time within the window of opportunity—had developed a robust unequivocally female gender identity. Very happy, bouncing pretty little girl, typically . . . very feminine.
>
> Except that it was bollocks. Because actually little Joan had resisted dresses and was kind of tomboyish and isolated and confused and [a] very unhappy little child. At the age of 14 . . . tried to resist taking estrogen, feminizing puberty, it was forced on the child. But after a while the child, John/Joan, put her foot down and said "no." And she bludgeoned Daddy into coming out with what had actually happened. And father in tears describes what had actually happened. And the child says, not shaken by this, "Well, I knew there was something the matter. I'm not living as a girl anymore, I'm living as a boy." [He] had phalloplasty later in life, is married now, adopted children, and is as well-adjusted as anyone who was subjected to that kind of trauma can actually be. (Gross 2000)

Gross humanizes the medical violence that David Reimer faced. She articulates how Money dictated the standard protocol of treatment for intersex patients based on conceptions of gender plasticity. Money, and physicians who then followed his recommendations globally, glorified this one case as validation of his theories until David Reimer's traumatic experiences were publicly revealed. After my initial conversation about this case with Gross, Money's high-stakes human experiment turned even more tragic when Reimer committed suicide in 2004.[15]

Not only did this medical intervention by Money ruin Reimer's life, Money's recommendations became the worldwide standard protocol for decades to come. Beginning in the 1960s, South African surgeons and endocrinologists implemented theories of gender plasticity. Perhaps most analogous to Reimer's penile injury are South African cases that occur due to circumcision accidents and through *muti*, a rare practice of ritual kidnapping of young male infants in which their penises are amputated by traditional healers for medicinal use in witchcraft.[16] While documentation of *muti* penile mutilations are rare and largely absent from medical literature, they have been sensationalized in the media and are widely known by the general public in South Africa. Anecdotal reports of medical treatments of children injured through *muti* demonstrate South African applications of Money's theories.

For instance, in 1992 the Afrikaans newspaper *Beeld* published a story entitled "Sex Change Is a Boy's Only Hope" (Van der Westhuizen 1992). According to this account, eighteen-month-old Nhlanhla Mkhwanazi was captured from his house by a "*Muti*-man" (traditional healer) and his thumbs and penis were mutilated.[17] Nhlanhla was apparently left for dead in a trash dump in Soweto, and according to the *Beeld* article, he almost perished from blood loss, strangulation, and exposure. The baby was discovered and taken to Chris Hani Baragwanath Hospital in Soweto, the largest hospital in Africa, where pediatrician Joao da Fonseca advised Nhlanhla's parents that the only way for the child to live a normal life was for him to be surgically reassigned as a girl. His parents were twenty-two years old and unemployed, and the baby's mother, Triphinia, worried, "I don't know what to say that my only son will change into a daughter. I am very upset and it is going to take a lot of accepting." The newspaper account cites a social worker who suggests that the parents "should undergo extensive therapy to be able to accept him as a little girl." She reiterates Money's discredited theories about the necessity of gender reassignments and vaginoplasties to surgically "normalize" infants' genitals after penile injuries.

Despite this article's title claims, gender reassignment was not the "only hope" for baby Nhlanhla. Rather than helping his genitals to heal, Nhlanhla was likely treated with hormones and multiple surgeries at least into his adolescence. Dr. Fonnseca claimed that operations like those facing Nhlanhla were being performed on approximately twelve babies at Chris Hani Baragwanath Hospital each year (Van der Westhuizen 1992; SALC 1995). He asserted that when Nhlanhla reached adolescence and underwent the vaginoplasty planned for him, he would be able to have sexual intercourse with men. Fonseca assumes Nhlanhla's heterosexuality and omits discussion of physical and psychological risks altogether. Nhlanhla's Sowetan parents, described as poor and young, express distress about the transition and procedures Fonnseca is performing on their child.

Gross and Nicodemus recount another South African application of Money's disproven protocols seven years later. Responses to a *muti* injury of another baby parallel Reimer's infamous treatment even more vividly. Gross explains,

> Faced with a baby boy whose penis had been cut off in a *muti* attack, doctors at Chris Hani Baragwanath Hospital evidently recalled Money's textbook-paradigm claims about the outcome of the "John/Joan" case. They decided to perform gender-reassignment surgery on him. It soon became evident that the new gender didn't "take" in the way Money's theory predicted. The toddler refused to wear dresses or to play with other girls. His mother told the *Sunday Times*: "We thought we could change him after the operation, but he is more like a boy than ever." Doctors conceded failure, and may consider reconstructive surgery—to try to build a new penis—when he turns 18. The boy's case suggests that a similar sea change is badly needed in South Africa. The apparent invisibility of intersexuality and of intersexed people, and the coyness of the medical establishment about the issue despite the debate elsewhere, also make it clear that intersex advocacy and support groups are needed here to encourage the necessary changes. ([Gross and Nicodemus] 1999)

In this case, the baby ironically referred to in media reports as Lucky is subjected to surgery with catastrophic ramifications. Like Reimer, Lucky eventually refuses his gender reassignment. Gross compared Reimer and Lucky in our life-historical interview in 2000, stating, "The consequences of imposing surgery on infants who have been mutilated for *muti* reasons and what have you, as in the case of the child Lucky, are disastrous. I mean it's going over the John/Joan case again" (Gross 2000). She also details the international ramifications: "I believe that John Money's misleading reports about the outcome of the 'John/Joan' case, which became standard text-book fodder, provided a model for the interventions in these *muti*-mutilation-related surgeries. Since John Money used the 'John/Joan' case and its alleged outcome to provide 'empirical' support for his theories about the treatment of intersexed infants and children, the issue of surgery on babies and children who were victims of *muti*-related mutilation is related to the treatment of intersexed infants and children" (pers. comm. 2000). South African applications of Money's theories had irreparable effects on babies like Nhlanhla and Lucky. Gross observes that these interventions were not predicated on saving infants' lives but on responding to social threats to gender binaries in the absence of subjectively "good enough" penises.[18]

Gross brought her critique of Money's disproven theories to the public eye in *The 3rd Sex*, using the film to help viewers understand the violence of existing protocols.[19] In this film, psychologist Gareth Hunt and the film narrator take turns summarizing Money's gender theories and then exposing their failures. The narrator explains how these theories have had local impact: "In South Africa a similar case played off in 1996. A boy nicknamed Little Lucky lost his penis during a *muti* attack at age two. Doctors at Baragawanth Hospital decided that the best thing to do was to turn him into a girl. But as early as age four, Lucky refuse to live as such. Doctors had to concede that they wrongfully forced the gender assignment onto the boy. Penile constructive surgery will be performed on Lucky once he reaches the age of eighteen" (van Huyssteen 2003). In this film, viewers see a public articulation of the problems of Money's protocols. They also learn of the personal and painful impact of abstract gender theories. Utilizing strategies such as film and news media allowed Gross and other activists to challenge dominant medical protocols with wide public influence.

WHITENESS AND SOUTH AFRICAN INTERSEX

Patients like Nhlanhla and Lucky were publicly scrutinized in newspaper and film accounts, but white South African intersex patients were more hidden and unacknowledged. While H. J. Grace and other physicians were spectacularizing intersex blackness, they were shrouding white intersex in South Africa in secrecy. Gross engaged with intersex medicine and the complexities of whiteness thorough her work with South African patients and parents who sought support from Intersex South Africa. The experiences of those reaching out to Gross underscore the inextricability of whiteness from ethnicity and class as well as the deep influence of eugenics in South Africa.

For centuries, South African politics turned on tensions between Anglo and Afrikaner colonial settlers, reflected in distinctions between British and Boer settler populations. Whiteness was far from monolithic, and people referred to as "poor whites"—mostly Afrikaans-speaking descendants of Boers—emerged during the uneven development of capitalism, as rural livelihoods were supplanted by commercial agriculture and mining.[20] Growing white poverty was represented as "anomalous and unacceptable" within the colonial façade of white dominance (Dubow 1995, 171). As the numbers of "poor whites" grew with the rise of the Great Depression, they constituted a highly visible underclass in impoverished urban centers (Klausen 2001, 56; 2017, 295). White poverty was increasingly considered a problematic indicator of white racial degeneration and fragility.

In what Saul Dubow refers to as a "reassertion of scientific racism," scientists argued that "poor whiteism" was caused by defects of the body (2015, 242).[21]

So-called poor whites were represented as innately criminal, ignorant, and deviant. Scientists argued that in addition to exhibiting a range of mental and physical inferiorities, their bodies were inherently incapable of successful reproduction yet highly fertile.[22] These assertions came to a head when the Carnegie Commission of Inquiry into the Poor White Problem (1929–1932) convinced the Department of Public Health that poor whiteism was a problem to be solved with birth control and sterilization. Medical experts asserted that protecting South Africa from the proliferation of innately inferior "poor whites" and the threat they posed to the monolith of white supremacy would require widespread eugenic methods.[23]

The corporeal surveillance that accompanied eugenic fears was to shape the development of intersex medicine. Before the increased interest in "poor white" reproduction, births usually took place alone or with just the support of family members. This intimate context often protected infants with genitals that might have been considered ambiguous from judgmental medical gazes. But as medical services grew, albeit racially segregated and uneven, reproductive control of so-called poor whites intensified in parallel with Bantu Gynaecology.[24] While Bantu Gynaecology was premised on broadcasting false ideas of black South Africans' physical deficiencies, growing anxieties about "poor whites" as innately inadequate were shrouded in secrecy. Eugenicists endeavored to curtail their procreation, asserting that those with physical differences should be genetically exterminated. As fears about inferior white bodies intensified, so did policies about white children with "birth defects." For instance, one of the only legally permitted rationales for abortion under apartheid was to prevent births of children considered disabled (Klausen 2017, 304). Children pathologized as defective included those born with intersex conditions, who might be subjected to secrecy about their bodies or to surgical "correction." The mere existence of white infants characterized as abnormal was perceived as a threat to the myth of white physical superiority.

Gross's work with Intersex South Africa personified the secrecy that surrounded white intersex in South Africa. For example, she recounts the experiences of Angie, a pseudonym for a white woman she met through Intersex South Africa, who encountered a culture of concealment when her child was diagnosed as intersex in the 1990s. "Angie felt that it would be very helpful to be in touch with other parents and for her child to be playing with other children who are affected by [intersex] or by things that are relatively similar. She was stonewalled—absolutely stonewalled.... One parent who she actually came across by happenstance rebuffed her by saying, 'Well we don't talk about this. We have little boys. We don't talk about this'" (Gross 2000). Parents' refusal to acknowledge their children's bodies followed their doctors' orders. And doctors followed accepted protocols at the time, overtly demanding secrecy from patients and their families. Gross continues her account of Angie's experiences:

> The doctors said [*whispering her impression of doctors' reactions*]: "You don't want to get mixed up in this [with] all sorts of types . . . people with skins that are darker than yours. . . . You know, you're going to get mixed up with the hoi polloi! And you really don't want that. We don't want that to happen. It is not in everyone's interest!" So, you get this kind of stonewalling. That's been her experience. . . . I think that that's fairly typical of the white sector, with most parents that just be given straightforward . . . lies. And the children who grow up in isolation and with a sense of dark, undefined shameful secrets. (Gross 2000)

Gross shared many similar accounts of white conformity. In her perception, the illusion of innate superiority exacerbated secrecy around intersex children. In this example, doctors suggest that Angie shouldn't talk about intersex, and she should maintain separation from the "hoi polloi"—a well-known phrase used to refer to the "common masses"—people who have "skins that are darker." White parents and patients in contact with Intersex South Africa were routinely encouraged to maintain the fallacy that white intersex did not exist, a fallacy mirrored in the claims of H. J. Grace and other scientists (e.g., Grace and Edge 1973).

As Gross was born before the inception of regularized "corrective" surgeries, she avoided intense medical scrutiny. She talked about how both timing and privilege kept her from being forced to undergo surgical procedures against her will. But from the 1970s onward, refusals by white intersex patients were less possible as Money's protocols became more widespread. Increasingly, white patients were subjected to nonconsensual surgical interventions. These experiences were not widely discussed by scientists and doctors but were compounded by commands to silence and hide their experiences. This treatment recalls secrecy around white gay and lesbian conscripts under apartheid, who were subjected to "conversion therapy" and even forced "sex reassignment" surgery to compel the illusion of monolithic white heterosexuality.[25]

The racially segregated history of public and private healthcare in South Africa is also significant to intersex medicine. Under colonialism, black South Africans obtained allopathic medical care from missionaries and then from community-based healthcare centers. When apartheid was instituted in 1948, racist policies led to the formation of Bantustans, quasi-independent "homelands" with severely underfunded health departments, known for poor medical care and maintained by the apartheid government. By contrast, unlike in most British colonies, healthcare for white South Africans relied on private insurance programs, referred to as medical schemes, which began in 1889 to care for white mine workers. These medical schemes grew over the twentieth century, leading to the massive expansion of private for-profit hospitals in the 1980s; by the end of the 1990s, 60 percent of South African physicians were working in the private sector (Coovadia et al. 2009). These histories of South Africa's racialized healthcare deeply informed the development of intersex medicine along separate but linked paths in public and private contexts.

One of the first things I asked Gross about when we met in 2000 was H. J. Grace's assertions of disproportionate black intersex frequency, the claim in medical literature that occupied my thinking. Gross responded with her own theory about the role of race and class in shaping South African intersex. She speculated that because childbirth among white South Africans historically took place in private medical settings, segregated according to apartheid's racial categories and less beholden to apartheid oversight, white intersex had been "covered up." Gross theorized that white intersex was underrepresented in public records and medical scholarship in accordance with apartheid's broader objectives. In her view, black babies diagnosed as intersex would be spectacularized to support perceptions of black South Africans as inferior and less than human, especially as they were often born in public hospitals, where gender difference was viewed as a racialized curiosity.

There are parallels and divergences between racialized treatments of intersex children in South Africa and elsewhere. A growing body of scholarship points out that "corrective" surgeries targeting white intersex children were a particular focus of early intersex medicine in the United States (e.g., Malatino 2019; Gill-Peterson 2018a; Magubane 2014). Gill-Peterson points to the "abstract whiteness of medicalized plasticity" (2018a, 101) that propelled surgical interventions on white intersex children to "correct" bodies to fit the supposed superior monolith of binary whiteness. By contrast, archival work reveals that black and brown trans and intersex people in the United States were routinely denied consensual medical care. But in South Africa, surgical interventions seem to have focused on "poor whites" and on black South Africans of all ages. Black patients were sought out for treatment and spectacularized as disproportionately intersex on the pages of academic journals and in popular culture.[26] While black South Africans faced medical experimentation intended to demonstrate racist theories of apartheid science, white South African children were subjected to "corrective" surgeries shrouded in secrecy,

Another lesser-known connection between intersex health and racism in South Africa preoccupied Gross. In the years just before her death, Gross made me aware of a small body of scientific literature in South Africa on the effects of the insecticide dichlorodiphenyltrichloroethane (DDT) on "urogenital malformations" and similar conditions diagnosed under the broad rubric of intersex (e.g., Bornman et al. 2009, 405). The chemical was first used to control mosquitos that caused malaria during World War II, and its use as a pesticide was continued after the war. But while it was banned in the Global North in the early 1970s because of evidence that it caused infertility and cancers (Carson 1962), DDT is still used in the Global South to control malaria.[27] Highly efficient mosquitos and particularly deadly strains of malaria have become predominant in South Africa, in part due to decades of clinical drug testing and scarce resources.

The connection between intersex and endocrine-disrupting chemicals (EDCs) has been documented among a broad range of animals—"from polar bears to people"—in all parts of the world (Langston 2008, 41).[28] The class of chemicals that includes DDT, EDCs are widely known to be both carcinogenic and estrogenic, leading to gendered effects on the body referred to using terminology such as "birth defects" and "reproductive alterations." The embryonic influences of environmental toxins is scientifically labeled as *teratogenesis* (loosely translated as "monster making").[29] This terminology recalls the discussion in chapter 1 about the inception of the science of *teratology*, a term coined by Isidore Geoffroy Saint-Hilaire in the 1830s to pathologize certain bodies, including those of "hermaphrodites."

Since 2004, a growing body of literature has documented so-called intersex effects of EDC exposure among fish and mammals in South Africa (Horak, Horn, and Peters 2021).[30] Gross was in conversation with a few South African scientists working to connect DDT to intersex incidence in humans, as well, though the connection has been minimally studied. The scant publications by these scientists trace DDT to what they label "external urogenital birth defects" and "diseases of sex development" in humans exposed to DDT in malarial-affected areas of South Africa (e.g., Bornman et al. 2009; Bornman and Bouwman 2012).[31] Though preliminary, these studies argue that intersex births may be more common in rural areas with high malarial infestations.

Initial research on the gendered effects of DDT in South Africa was published around 2009, coincidentally concurring with the international scrutiny of Caster Semenya's body, explored in the next chapter. A few news articles featured interviews with scientists conducting research in rural Limpopo, natal home to Semenya, known to have the highest rates of malaria and DDT-related indoor residual spray in South Africa. These scientists speculated that efforts to prevent malaria through the use of DDT may result in increased prevalence of intersex in this region. For instance, one reporter interviewed Tiaan de Jager, professor of environmental health at the University of Pretoria, who stated that DDT is passed on to infants through breast milk, resulting in "a 33 percent higher chance of 'congenital abnormalities'" (Graham 2016).[32] He also recounts that a study by the Water Research Commission in South Africa found "'disturbingly high' levels of DDT in water, soil, vegetables, chicken and fish in the Vhembe district near the village of Ga-Masehlong, where Semenya was born" (Graham 2016; Bornman, Barnhoorn, and Genthe 2010).

But public discussions and research have been truncated by intense controversy about the continued use of DDT. In 1996 the South African government stopped using DDT because of concerns about its risks and effects, but from 1996 to 2000 malaria cases rose from fewer than ten thousand to sixty-five thousand annually. Malaria-related deaths that had rarely exceeded 30 a year spiked to 456 in 2000 (Groenwald 2009). Thus, DDT was reintroduced in 2001, and deaths drastically and immediately declined again. Long-term effects of DDT on rates of cancer and "birth defects" are known globally but difficult to quantify. South African government officials have denied any toxic effects of DDT whatsoever, despite overwhelming scientific evidence to the contrary amassed since the 1960s.[33] When Semenya's public exploitation raised issues of intersex in the media, debates about public health became so controversial that some scientists interviewed in press coverage about DDT and intersex in rural areas chose to remain anonymous (e.g., Tempelhoff 2009).

As activists including Gross have argued for decades, intersex is not a medical problem but a social one. Eli Clare (2017, 56) attests that ableist arguments about "birth defects" position so-called teratogenic effects as tragic and in need of prevention and eradication. This perspective demeans those living with such diagnoses and, as Clare poetically expresses, "It ignores the brilliant imperfection of our lives" (56). Instead of problematically declaring bodies deemed intersex as bellwethers of pathology, analyses of the gendered, raced, and classed effects of EDCs in the Global South could form part of an emerging intersex critique of environmental racism that embraces all bodies. Scholars including Julie Sze (2006) and Donna Haraway (1991) remind us that no bodies are "pure," as we are all constantly exposed to environmental pollutants; the effects of EDCs on bodies can "illuminate how we are already hybrid and that there is no nature or body that is not shaped by culture, technology, or medicine, no purity that we can stand upon to define concepts of nature, race, gender, or humanity itself" (Sze 2006, 793). While advocating for more research on environmental racism, disability and intersex activists demand that bodies deemed intersex, including those exposed to DDT, not be perceived as defective and assert that they challenge impossible ideas of normativity.

Toward Decolonial Intersex Critique: Teratology and Social Death

Like many other Africans whose intense experiences with texts addressing intersex punctuate *Envisioning African Intersex*, Gross was strongly influenced by books. One book in particular was paramount in shaping Gross's activism. She recounted to me that in her youth, "A weighty tome that I read years ago informed me that . . . there is no such thing as hermaphroditism among human beings" (2000). The author and title of Gross's tome remain unknown. But a familiar theme emerges again here, as she explains that its strong influence made her question the existence of intersex. Indeed, this "tome" affected her experience of her own body and prevented her from discovering her own intersex identification. For Gross, this published denial of human intersex undermined her own ability to live between the rigid binaries of gender. This book continued to inform her thinking years later, as she developed a critique of taxonomies and centuries-old claims.

One of Gross's most important contributions was to expose the colonial thinking that motivates contemporary medical theories. As early as medieval times, gender binaries and sexual difference were seen as key indicators of humanness. Gross was acutely aware of the roots of these pathological taxonomies and their continued effects on intersex people. She critiqued notions of monstrosity that plagued her.

> Remember also that the branch of medicine that studies people who are intersexed. You know what that's called? It's called "teratology." And that's a label from the Victorian [era]. You know what teratology means? It derived from a Greek term *teratos*, and *teratos* means monster. So it's that area of medicine, of medicine or science, which studies monstrosities. Terms which are used to describe people who are intersexed include monsters; it's the domain of the teratological, sports and nature, freaks. You're into freak show territory. So acknowledging people who are intersexed . . . acknowledging that they're in-betweens, acknowledging that dichotomous taxonomy . . . for an awful lot of people it also raises questions about their own identity. (Gross 2000)

In this interview, Gross identifies the origins of medicalized pathologies. She critiques them as foundations for condemnations of intersex that remain fundamental to South African science and medicine.[34]

In *The 3rd Sex*, Gross goes on to explain how she internalized this perception at the heart of teratology, comparing herself to the character ET, the lovable extraterrestrial in the popular (1982) film of the same name. "You know, you feel really at a certain point that I'm like ET. I'm the only one of a kind. And you do feel a little bit like a monster. You're alone and desperately desperately alone. And actually knowing that there are other people who are like you, you're not alone and it's not kind of [the line from the movie] 'ET phone home' is actually really a lifesaver. It was for me" (van Huyssteen 2003). Gross links this alienation to the inception of her activism. She explains that she first connected with intersex activists from the United States and then started Intersex South Africa to combat the effects of theories of monstrosity.

Gross's work, premised on arguing for the inherent normality of intersex, strove to undermine authoritative medical voices that perpetuate these theories. In *The 3rd Sex*, Dr. Christie Steinman expresses a perspective shared by many physicians: "You're either male or you're female. Definitely so. And that's the norm, and that's the acceptable way" (van Huyssteen 2003). Steinman is a white South African urologist dedicated to "correcting" intersex patients surgically.[35] He holds fast to his pathologization of intersex, suggesting that it should be eradicated surgically: "Look, I'm sure that there are patients all over the world maybe that 'have' intersex that may live their whole lives like that. They are satisfied, and maybe they don't know better, and they haven't [sought] medical advice, so they're happy to live the way that they do. But I don't think that it's normal, and I think you should function as a boy or a girl" (van Huyssteen 2003). Steinman's equation of intersex with abnormality is a viewpoint that has been ubiquitous for decades.

But *The 3rd Sex* reframes this perspective by positioning intersex as a normal human variant, not as a disease or illness. In the film and in her corpus of work, Gross opposes surgery unless required for preservation of health. She explicates: "What I and other intersex activists argue is that the lived experience of adults who had such essentially cosmetic surgery imposed shows it leads to physical and psychological problems later in life. . . . What we oppose, and view as mutilation, is the imposition of such essentially cosmetic surgery without the personal choice of the patient, and which perhaps irrevocably closes certain significant future choices to that person" (quoted in Coan 2000). Gross is clear that nonconsensual surgical procedures cause deep harms. She flips derogatory terminology on its head, unsettling *teratology* and *monstrosity* to instead critique doctors' interventions as *mutilations*.

Gross also reverses the objectifying medical gaze. In *The 3rd Sex*, photographs of intersex patients from South African medical literature are reframed as a critique of visual science. As Gross, Soldaat, and supportive medical professionals rebut Steinman and his contemporaries, photographs flashing across the screen offer an implicit commentary on the violence of the moment they were captured. Gross directly connects teratology to the alienation of intersex photography: "Perhaps before the operation you get a whole cluster of doctors and medical students and what have you coming and peering at the genitalia as well. And the message which actually gets across is, you know, I'm ET [extraterrestrial]. These photographs are an icon of the propensity to pathologize the treatment of human beings as specimens, laboratory rats" (van Huyssteen 2003).

Gross explained to me that when she was diagnosed as intersex, she refused surgical and photographic impositions. She describes doctors' pressures to surgically examine her internal organs for diagnostic purposes and her response: "I wasn't prepared to be cut, as if I were some kind of specimen or lab rat. You know there was pressure to be photographed and dah, dah, dah. And I said, 'To hell with it! No!'" (2000). As a respected white adult at the time of her diagnosis, Gross was thankfully able to reject surgery and efforts to photograph her body to satisfy doctors' curiosity. But the pathological surveillance at the heart of medicine—expressed in its most vehement form through diagnostic surgery and imaging—is too often violently imposed on patients deemed intersex across race, class, and location.

The last piece of writing that Gross authored, a year before her death, was perhaps her most direct response to the degradation of teratology and pathologization. In 2013, she presented a paper—"Not in God's Image: Intersex, Social Death, and Infanticide"—via Skype at the Intersex, Theology and the Bible conference at the University of Manchester in England.[36] In it, Gross began to conceptualize an intersex theory of "social death" that tied together many of her theoretical contributions with a decidedly South African grounding. The concept of social death was first introduced by Orlando Patterson (1982) to explain enslavement in the United States as characterized by the powerlessness and denial of humanity, reducing enslaved people to property and alienating them from connective relationships. Patterson's concept of social death has since been applied in many geographic and historical contexts. Perhaps most famously, Daniel Goldhagen's (1996) application of social death to the Holocaust described how ideologies of antisemitism were enabled not just by murderous leaders but by ordinary Germans who facilitated the atrocities of genocide.[37]

The development of social death to explain Black and Jewish experiences of violence was compelling to Gross. Indeed, her anti-apartheid activism and identification as Jewish initially sparked her interest in this concept as correlating racial, ethnic, national, and religious violence. She writes, "In his book *Hitler's Willing Executioners*, Daniel Goldhagen argues that Jews in the German-controlled territories were seen as socially dead. He makes use of a model developed by Orlando Patterson in analytical work on slavery in the southern states of the United States of America, and which has been applied to slavery at large" (Gross 2013). Gross goes on to explain how genocidal social control operates both through force and through the quotidian, typified by apartheid and the Holocaust.[38] Framing intersex through theories of social death allowed her space to wrestle with these tensions of everyday violence, while she simultaneously developed theories to explain intersex resistance in the face of the impossibility of existence. Varied reconceptualizations of social death explore lives under violent duress and the denial of humanness.[39] Perhaps most notably, in C. Riley Snorton's (2017) pivotal work on histories of Black trans identity, he extends notions of social death as a denial of personhood at the core of "thingification."[40] Snorton's discussion of Black trans thingification as not-quite-human liminality recalls Gross's articulation of becoming extraterrestrial.[41] For Gross, social death is a framework to theorize the dehumanization, alienation, and monstrosity of intersex.

Exclusion from societal personhood and the entanglement of life and death in intersex experiences strongly influenced Gross's later activist strategies. "Not in God's Image: Intersex, Social Death, and Infanticide" explains that two experiences following her intersex diagnosis most shaped her thinking on intersex social death. First, when Gross was diagnosed with an intersex condition while serving as a Dominican priest, Catholic religious authorities responded by expressing their categorical denial of her existence and by encouraging her to commit suicide. In her unpublished paper, she details the impacts of these powerful dictates. Following Goldhagen, Gross compares religious authorities to everyday people perpetuating social and literal death for those who were Jewish and/or intersex:

> Listening to the narrative [of religious leaders' projections of my death], a comrade of mine described it as "Holocaust-level stuff," and it struck me that this was apt at a level which went beyond travails and victimhood. In the Holocaust of European Jewry, many of the perpetrators of terrible actions were decent, ordinary people who loved their spouses, their children and their pets but were driven by overwhelmingly powerful social pressures and archetypes. This led them to deny the humanity of Jews. More specifically, it involved a denial that Jews were truly co-inhabitants of the social and moral world which so-called "Aryans" inhabited. (Gross 2013)

When Gross revealed her intersex diagnosis, the Catholic Church refused to allow her to exist outside the male/female binary.[42] Gross experienced this as a denial of humanness: "Treating someone or a class of people as socially dead implies the denial that the person or class of people belong to the world of human beings" (2013).[43] In the context of Catholic teachings that defined her priesthood, Gross was deemed unworthy of living.

This experience was the beginning of what Gross called her "shadow-existence," her way to describe the simultaneous denial of her ways of living and encouragement of her material death. Frantz Fanon ([1952] 2008) argues that in the colonial world of white superiority and black inferiority, he confronted dominant logic to accept himself as pathological and to inhabit blackness "under the shadow of social death" (Sexton 2011, 27).[44] Fanon's self-acceptance in the face of pathology parallels Gross's embrace of her own categorical inhumanity. Gross also uses shadows metaphorically to explain that within the Catholic Church, she had "fallen off the edge of the socio-moral world": "In this shadow-existence, the conventional reciprocity of rights and duties broke down. As one who was socially dead, I had no moral rights—least of all to life—but was deemed to have duties. It was acceptable to seek to push me to suicide, and had the legal order permitted, it would have been deemed acceptable to have taken my life more directly" (2013). In Gross's assessment, her "shadow-existence" reflected her threat to the Church and society, so, in her words, Church leaders wanted to "protect others from the highly infectious miasma which I was held to embody" (2013). Social death and the encouragement toward her suicide had grave implications on Gross's shadow-existence, while also motivating her to create intersex community.[45]

The second experience that prompted Gross's theory of intersex social death was the denial of her legal personhood. Societal belonging authorized by gendered state documents enables tasks as workaday as driving, entering a building, and using a bank; these gendered state documents also confer citizenship and enable movement across national borders.[46] By contrast, legal denial engenders liminality. Lisa Marie Cacho's analysis of the experiences of undocumented immigrants and the racialized poor—*Social Death: Racialized Rightlessness and the Criminalization of the Unprotected*—reworks Patterson's theories to demonstrate how citizenship is intentionally manipulated by those in power (2012, 6). Denial and criminalization renders certain groups of people legally ineligible for personhood as rightless nonbeings.

Gross theorizes intersex social death to expose strategies of administrative denial and their effects. After the unbanning of the ANC in the 1990s, Gross wanted to return home to South Africa. But this would prove far more difficult than anticipated. As a long-term committed member of the ANC, when apartheid officially ended and Nelson Mandela came into power, Gross was entitled to restore her South African citizenship and passport. As she explains, "[My South African passport still] described me as male and was due to expire in November 1996. But as I was living as female and all my other documentation stated that I was female I sought to explore the possibility of changing details in the passport. I was told this would not be an insuperable problem" (quoted in Coan 2000). Unfortunately, the change in Gross's documents created a conundrum for South African authorities, who demurred until her passport eventually expired, leaving her stranded in England. For Gross, the inability of the South African state to recognize her gendered existence created a crisis of exile, migration, and citizenship. She was then prohibited from reinstating her passport, and she recalled, "At one point the authorities decided they couldn't issue a document under any gender. 'I had ceased to exist in law as a person'" (Gross 2009b, 14–15).

Gross's passport file was referred to the Department of Health for adjudication. As in many contexts, proof of gender was a decision granted to medical professionals, here a manifestation of the collusion between medicine and law. To get her passport reinstated, it was suggested that she undergo what she referred to as "genital disambiguation"—surgical procedures to make her genitals less ambiguous.[47] Gross declares, "I considered this an immoral suggestion—to undergo dangerous and unnecessary surgery as a condition for having a legal identity" (quoted in Coan 2000). Eventually legal threats that she would invoke the new South African Constitution and Bill of Rights as well as the pro bono work of a prominent human rights lawyer convinced authorities in the Department of Home Affairs to take action. Gross was finally issued a new birth certificate and passport. She states, "the experience of finding myself denied personality and humanity in law was the biggest challenge of my identity I have ever encountered" (quoted in Coan 2000).[48] This experience was to shape her activist foci for the rest of her life.

When Gross began Intersex South Africa on her return to South Africa, she drew on her "struggle credentials"—her reputation built over years of commitment to the anti-apartheid movement and the ANC—to conceptualize strategies for change.

> I've been active in the ANC for years and years, I mean a long time before the ANC was legal and at a time when it could cost you many years in jail. I'm active in my local ANC branch. I was elected in my absence to the executive of my branch, and the contacts which followed from that. I have friends and comrades from ANC activities when I was in exile, and there are possibilities which followed from that. . . . So networking like

mad, and using [the] Constitution and law and all rest of it as an instrument . . . pointing out that this has implications . . . for attitudes about people who are intersexed. (Gross 2000)

Gross had established herself as an organizer through her decades of activism and the personal price she paid for her commitment to the ANC. Amid excitement about the new South Africa in the 1990s, Gross planned to raise awareness through the (then) new constitution. I quickly learned about the import of the constitution to Gross during our first conversation, when she went and retrieved her own well-worn copy of it. She waved the document in the air as she enthusiastically explained that the Bill of Rights was "an instrument of transformation" that "runs ahead of attitudes": "It's trailblazing, in one sense. It marks where we need to get at. There's a great deal here which has, it seems to me, direct implications for people who are intersexed" (2000). The South African Constitution was renowned as the first in the world to protect from discrimination on the basis of sexual orientation. Gross wanted to parlay this document to protect intersex South Africans.[49] In her view, doctors could be held accountable through the new Bill of Rights and its emphasis on patients' rights: "That revolution has still to come here, but it's gonna come because we've got the Bill of Rights. . . . Doctors' attitudes to patients are going to have to change," while recognizing that the change will not be easy, that "it's going to take advocacy work to bring about that change, not just in this domain but in other domains, but they will change" (2000).[50]

As Gross endeavored to get intersex "into the public eye and to drum up sympathy around it," she invoked the cliché of South Africa as the "rainbow nation" that was popular at the time, seeking to reframe it: "To use a rather hackneyed metaphor: we are a rainbow nation, and that rainbow quality, that diversity, is to be seen as a strength rather than as a weakness. And perhaps intersexuality shows also that we are a rainbow species: there is more diversity in physical types than people find it easy to concede" (quoted in Coan 2000). For Gross, the addition of intersex to South Africans' notions of their "rainbow nation" reflected the liberation struggle that led to the transition from apartheid to democracy. Though the language of intersex social death would come later, Gross explained strategies that foreshadowed her future theorizing "People like me had not had an unimpugnable right—even to life—before. Now, by statute, we are *bona fide* human beings in South African law, protected from discrimination on the grounds that we are intersexed" (Gross 2009a).[51]

Eventually, Gross and a few other dedicated activists successfully challenged the political logic of binary gender in South Africa. As a result of their work, significant legal changes in South Africa now explicitly protect intersex people under the law. The Alteration of Sex Description and Sex Status Act (2003) permits sex to be changed in birth registers (Republic of South Africa 2004). Activists demanded that such a change not require genital surgery and that medical opinions not be relevant. Further, in 2005 the Promotion of Equality and Prevention of Unfair Discrimination Act (known as PEPUDA or the Equality Act) became the first in the world to include "intersex" within the legal definition of "sex" as "a congenital sexual differentiation which is atypical, to whatever degree." This definition of intersex reflects activist work as it is almost identical to the recommendation submitted to the court by Intersex South Africa (Thoreson 2013, 653). In both cases, Gross and other activists worked to ensure that medical professionals held no authority. This revision of personhood under the law specifically includes those self-defined as intersex, an identification no longer reliant on medical oversight or surgical interventions.

Transnationally, activists working for intersex equity celebrated Gross's victories and touted them as pioneering on a global scale. Praise and appreciation recognized Gross as holding "the distinction of being the person who was responsible for the first intersex inclusion in anti-discrimination law and therefore the first national constitution in the world that is fully intersex inclusive" (Wilson 2011). But while Gross's efforts were widely recognized outside South Africa, she remained concerned that those who could benefit were unaware of their protections. "In South African law, one needs *locus standi*, the right to address the court, to mount a legal challenge. Since the intersexed did not fit workaday definitions of 'human beings' and '[natural] persons,' arguably they lacked the *locus standi* to challenge this or any other type of discrimination. It followed that the intersexed, because they were intersexed, had no secure rights—not even to dignity or to life itself" (Gross 2009a). To Gross, this lack of *locus standi* was a manifestation of intersex social death that legal changes could help to ameliorate.[52]

Social Life and Death in the Global South: A Requiem

Should I die in my bed tonight, be I remembered for it or not, my life and endeavours will have laid the legislative foundations in our law for the significant enhancement of the rights and prospects for people who [are] intersexed. Knowing this, when I go gently into that good night I can go proudly. —SALLY GROSS, "The Chronicle of an Intersexed Activist's Journey"

The timing of Gross's legal successes coincided with the most intense public attention to intersex in South African history. In August 2009, elite athlete Caster Semenya began to be subjected to public interrogation by international sporting authorities, and contestations over her ability to compete in women's sport took on global significance. As media frenzy surrounding Semenya rose to its initial fever pitch, the significance of these discussions for South Africans who self-identify as intersex was largely ignored; however, Gross took the opportunity to share information about intersex legal protections. In a discussion with Emi Koyama of the Intersex Initiative in the United States, Gross discussed her intentions: "Semenya's dignity and privacy have been ridden over roughshod, [it is] important to affirm her rights to privacy and dignity and to use this as an opportunity to note that this applies to all the intersexed" (2009c).[53] She also argued that this media attention was shifting popular perceptions concerning visibility and discrimination: "In direct consequence of the Caster Semenya saga, South Africans in general and the South African government in particular were forced to realize that there are in fact many intersexed people in South Africa and to acknowledge that there is a human rights issue" (Swarr, Gross, and Theron 2009, 660).

In 2009, Gross published a newspaper article entitled "Life in the Shadow of Gender" that anticipated her final reflections on her "shadow-existence" and intersex devaluation. Gross strongly identified with Semenya's medical interrogation and the questions she faced about her bodily existence. "Semenya's plight 'pushes buttons' for me. Some 15 years back, aged about 40, I discovered that I am intersexed and made a conscious decision to be honest and open about it. As a direct result, I was ostracised, stripped of status and even identity, and forbidden to exercise my vocation. . . . The unravelling of my life, standing, expectations and hopes was a witting and brutal display of power. The message: this is what happens to those with aberrant bodies" (2009b, 14). Just as Semenya was prevented from competing in professional sport by questions raised about her body, Gross was stripped of the priesthood and ostracized. Gross further compared the medical scrutiny of their bodies, sharing a poignant example of her own experience during a medical emergency.

> Perhaps three years back I was carted by ambulance to a hospital emergency room. Like Semenya, I do not have a curvaceous feminine figure and have a fairly deep voice. Unlike her, I can pass for a beached whale. Be that as it may, I'm classified in law as born female because of evidence about the nature of my anatomy at birth. The ambulance men knew I am classified as female, addressing me as "lovely lady" almost mockingly. Both they and medical personnel referred to me in my presence as "he" and "him" despite my requests that they not do this. I displayed my birth certificate and pointed out that in law I am female. This was ignored. Explaining that I am intersexed made it worse. The message was that they, the "experts,"

determined who and what I am, whatever the consequences, and would pull my life apart if it was expedient. . . .

The way in which Caster Semenya's sex is being questioned reminds me of my emergency room experience. A patriarchal sex-police claims the right to determine her very identity, regardless of the consequences for her. As I have pointed out elsewhere, the "gender verification" process is anything but objective and scientific. It is moot whether any intersex condition actually gives athletic advantage in the first place. (2009b, 14–15)

Gross's own experiences, like Semenya's travails, personify the consequences of intersex dehumanization.[54] Building on Semenya's visibility and popularity, she implores the South African people and government "to take up the plight of the intersexed no less vigorously than the cause of Caster Semenya" (2009b, 15). Gross hoped that Semenya's mistreatment might force a society-wide reckoning with intersex social death and abuses in medical and legal contexts, a hope which is explored in the next chapter.

The work that Gross undertook under the auspices of Intersex South Africa was purposeful. Gross wanted to normalize intersex and to unsettle gender binaries. Her activism rested on a "core-need": "to put the issue of intersex on the conceptual maps of people who influence and educate others, and to put information about intersex 'out there'—deep ignorance, in the gender community no less than anywhere else, being a major contributor to the stigmatisation and sense of miasma surrounding intersex in South Africa" (Swarr, Gross, and Theron 2009, 658). She wanted to increase visibility, stating, "Making intersex visible and workaday is fundamental to the bringing an end to the stigmatization" (Swarr, Gross, and Theron 2009, 658).

But despite—or more likely because of—the complex and time-consuming work that was Gross's life passion, poverty and medical issues undercut her ability to function. These challenges were heartbreakingly inseparable from the social alienation and poverty she challenged in her work for social change. When reflecting on the first decade of Intersex South Africa in 2009, Gross revealed,

That my body is failing looms large. Diminished mobility makes public transportation inaccessible, while eye-problems prevent driving. The expense of getting to and from work is unsustainable, so getting out and about is beyond my means. This is isolating. It isn't due to intersex. Highly pressured work and the deep wounds from the past have taken a toll. Several lifetimes' worth of experience are packed into 56 years, and perhaps my health problems reflect this. My body is like a car which bears the marks of heavy and productive use. (2009d)

The medicalized poverty Gross faced intensified, and her health worsened over the following years. Her limited funds were supporting Intersex South Africa at her own personal expense, and help was limited. Her dedication was contributing to her undoing.

On January 24, 2014, prominent New Zealand–based intersex activist Mani Bruce Mitchell posted a GoFundMe appeal for help on Gross's behalf. Mitchell prefaces Gross's words by explaining, "I have known Sally for over 15 years and consider h/er a friend, mentor, inspirational human of the highest order—fellow intersex activist. Sally needs our help." In Gross's own words, her work on behalf of Intersex South Africa had severely depleted her own limited resources and, as a result, her health:

> Since July 2012 in particular, I have subsidised Intersex South Africa (issa) heavily—by not taking any salary for three months back then so that other employees could be paid, and by taking a half-salary—significantly less than my monthly expenses—between October 2012 and last October. issa was hit very hard indeed by the funding crisis which was a consequence of global economic meltdown, and over the last few months this has been exacerbated greatly by the collapse of my health. As of October 2013, I have been without any salary at all, and such financial reserves as I had are exhausted.
>
> A larger issue which I believe that the activist community needs to tackle in the longer term "probably well beyond my life-time" is to look at ways, as a matter of urgency, in which activists in circumstances like mine, where commitment to activism and unanticipated illness take toll can be afforded help and support. I am neither the first nor the last activist to be in these straits and believe that this needs to involve approaches to international institutions, states and international donors and will require the setting up of a support-system. Our issue "intersex" is being taken up both at the level of states and at the international level, and I believe that safety-nets can be put in place for activists though it will require much lobbying, time and patience. (GoFundMe Appeal, 2014)[55]

Still thinking less of her own health and finances than of the broader issues at hand, Gross outlined ways to support intersex people in need. Facing homelessness and medical catastrophe, unable to afford a place to live or medication to keep her alive, Gross reluctantly appealed to her friends and supporters for assistance. In what became her final selfless strategic formulation of how and why health and financial well-being are central to intersex activism, Gross continued:

In summary: my immediate need is to get through the coming month-turn and as much longer as is feasible. Questions about sustainability are relevant only if this can be achieved. For the longer term, we need to think about seeking to get a support-system in place for intersex activists who find themselves in similar circumstances, and this will require more than the private resources of members of our intersex activist community and investment of energy, time and patience. This longer-term project would be unlikely to benefit me personally: it would be a matter of legacy and a project and resource for all of us.

All of this is complicated, and it embarrasses me to make these requests.

> With all my love.
> Sally (GoFundMe Appeal, 2014)

Gross passed away less than a month later, alone in her apartment. Her last communication had been with Mitchell on February 11, and her body was found on February 14, 2014.

Many obituaries followed her death, and one published by Organization Intersex International (OII) provides a small consolation: "Appeals were made through the intersex community, including a fund-raising project, the latter of which came to fruition too late for Sally to benefit from, unfortunately. However, early individual donations to Sally's account did mean that she was able to stay in her home, and continue communicating with her friends and family up to the end, and not die on the street, which is what she feared would happen" (OII 2014). In death, as in life, Gross faced isolation and challenges. Her friend gertrude fester-wicomb reflects on the trajectory and impact of Gross's life poignantly:

> She resigned from her secure government position at the Land Commission, and used her own money to set up this structure; such was her commitment to supporting and educating others. She was a pioneer in drafting national legislation and including the term "intersex" for the first time within the definition of sex in South Africa's anti-discrimination law [and] . . . she also worked on legislation related to the Alteration of Sex Discrimination and Sex Status Act 49 of 2003. The organisation Intersex South Africa was demanding in terms of energy and finances. Towards the end of her life, Sally was compelled to request financial aid from friends for rent and medical bills. As her health worsened, she became nearly paralysed before her death. It is ironic and tragic that this valiant fighter for marginalised people died alone (2021, 83).

Fester-wicomb knew Gross's advocacy and what she describes as her "pioneering spirit" well. She muses, "Her death shows the neglect that intersex people endure in a society that does not accommodate or understand" (2021, 79).

In one of the discussions of Gross's life and impact published and posted online in the months that followed, South African intersex activist Nthabiseng Mokoena (2015) similarly asserted that it is difficult to talk about intersex activism in South Africa without mentioning Gross's groundbreaking work: "Sally helped to secure the first known mention of intersex in national law, and also assisted in the drafting of the Alteration of Sex Description Act of 2003." Mokoena recounts Gross's dedication to intersex activism. She mentored other activists while Intersex South Africa was struggling to find any funding at all, in part because of the paternalism of international donors while her own health deteriorated.

> What was frustrating, and continues to be frustrating, is that activists like Sally Gross are expected to run NGOs with little to no money at all. It is a huge sacrifice to leave normal paying jobs in the pursuit of making a difference through the NGO sector. We are expected to stick to work plans, run and report on projects, travel to conferences, contribute to policies, while in reality we cannot even pay our rent or pay for healthcare, at the same time we are told to "take better care of ourselves" to ensure that "self-care" is part of our work, how do you take care of yourself when you can't even afford groceries? People see you travelling the world to conferences (sponsored by donors) and think that you are living well; in reality you sleep in fancy hotels and then go back home and sleep in an apartment you probably will not occupy the next month because of an eviction. After Sally passed away, the work of Intersex South Africa also disappeared, indicating another flaw in NGO politics, that our organisations are usually run by one or two people, and if one person leaves or passes away, the NGO itself dies. (Mokoena 2015)

Mokoena's frustrations about the devaluation of intersex activism dovetail with Gross's final words in Mitchell's GoFundMe posting. Such systemic analyses are not peripheral or incidental but integral to improving intersex futures.

Following Gross's death, from 2017 to 2020 the website of Intersex South Africa was pirated by an unknown person who falsely claimed credit for her writing. Gross's (2009b) biographical and very personal article, "Life in the Shadow of Gender," was posted and inaccurately listed "Rosemary Lennox" as its author.[56] Due to this online plagiarism, I have seen numerous erroneous citations of this work (2009b) as coauthored by Lennox. This years-long misattribution of Gross's work and biography is an affront to her memory and to the organization she worked to establish and maintain at such high personal cost. Activist websites may not have funding or technological capacity for long-term maintenance, or they may change formats and lose posts and actions that were previously archived.[57] They may also be stolen. Like pages torn out of books, ephemeral activist spaces can be manipulated or suddenly gone without explanation. The reasons Gross and ISSA were targeted are open to speculation, and at the time of this writing, the ISSA website has become defunct and the domain is for sale.[58] But the organization itself has been strongly revived by South African activists, and their recent work is discussed at length in chapter 5.

South African activist histories and strategies are integral to Gross's praxis, and her analyses embed intersex in anti-apartheid liberation struggles. Gross explains what makes her work "a uniquely South African contribution" grounded in "the possibilities opened by the impact of the struggle for liberation in South Africa":

> Something one learns through involvement in struggle over many years is that liberation is, like Jesus' garment, a seamless whole. Struggle against class-based oppression, against racial oppression, and against forms of oppression rooted in sex and gender, cannot really be teased completely apart; and, in a fundamental sense, liberation is not complete when any of these forms of oppression persists. . . . Given an awareness of inter-sexed, the liberation history and culture creates a moral obligation to take the issue up and to ensure that law and practice afford the intersex adequate recognition and protection in the context of a culture of rights and not of pathologization. In view of the holistic nature of liberation, failure to do so would be tantamount to betrayal of the spirit of the struggle against Apartheid itself. (Swarr, Gross, and Theron 2009, 661)

Gross contends that history, culture, and even morality are imperative to struggles against the theoretical vestiges of colonialism and extend "the spirit of the struggle" against apartheid. Gross's South African intersex analytic mobilizes self-representation and normalization to strategically undermine the forced secrecy and pathologizing taxonomies that characterized apartheid. Further, her lifelong insistence on acceptance of the body with which she was born formed a radical intervention. She leaves us with this assertion in her final unpublished work:

> When I was thought to fit the binary, I had a recognised identity and status. I was deemed to be a competent priest and preacher, and an able teacher, someone who had a powerful voice. When it became increasingly clear that what I am challenges the dichotomy, it is almost as if I was seen as threatening the very order of creation. I was no longer seen

as a legitimate inhabitant of a shared social and moral world. . . . I was not really human and my existence threatened the set of categories which were deemed to be constitutive of humanity and of the ordering of human life. (Gross 2013)

She ends her last writing with the assertion, "What is needed is to stop clinging to misleading categories and to false dualisms, accepting people and things as they are" (2013). For Gross, the future rests on challenging those who cleave to binary taxonomies and creating a new sense of order. She continually theorized and lived her own life in a "shadow-existence" while enacting new visions of liberation that continue to benefit intersex people today.

4. #HandsOffCaster

Caster Semenya's Refusals and the Decolonization
of Gender Testing

Black excellence must always be put under a microscope and made to jump
through rings of fire, to meet ridiculous standards just to prove its own worth.
#HandsOffCaster —KING SBU (@SBUISKING), Twitter, April 25, 2018

• • •

Caster Semenya has been thrust into the headlines as an elite runner and, most
famously, because of contentions about her body. In August 2009, she won a
gold medal in the 800-meter World Championships in Athletics. From this
time to the present, officials have subjected her to "gender verification" testing, and global debates have raged over her eligibility to compete as a woman.
Semenya has been repeatedly banned and unbanned from competition, and
her treatment has spurred outrage over the overt racism of the International
Association of Athletics Federations (IAAF)/World Athletics, her rivals, and
the media.[1] Despite innumerable barriers, Semenya continued to succeed in
sport, winning gold medals in the 2012 and 2016 Olympics and multiple world

championship races. But her career has been marred by authorities' fights over what it means to be a woman and a specific, long-standing desire to exclude her from sport.

The scrutiny of Semenya spans a decade and extends worldwide. Within academic contexts, she has been objectified in accounts that tokenize her as representative and that neglect analyses of race and colonialism to focus on efforts to "discover" her body.[2] She has been falsely portrayed as a victim to the whims of reporters, politicians, and sporting regulators, while her South African supporters have been characterized as ignorant nationalists eager to reinscribe gender binaries and uphold femininity. This chapter unseats these perceptions. I explore how Semenya and her supporters have mobilized social media to theorize the interplay of colonialism, race, and intersex. I articulate Semenya not as beholden to imposed femininity but as redefining what it means to be a woman. And I highlight how recent social media campaigns (such as Twitter's #HandsOffCaster) and Semenya's self-depiction form important challenges to racist claims of disproportionate intersex in the Global South.

This chapter engages Semenya's experiences and perspectives to argue for the decolonization of gender testing and medical treatment in sport.[3] The colonial histories of intersex explored in the previous chapters are integral to Semenya's exploitation over the past decade. And the citational chains and repeated medical claims interrogated throughout *Envisioning African Intersex* are explicitly linked to present-day gendered science in sport. Racist intersex science and medicine justify contemporary persecution of athletes from the Global South. Athletes including Semenya are regularly subjected to medically unnecessary and devastatingly invasive examinations and procedures—including clitoridectomy, gonadectomy, and life-threatening hormonal interventions—under the authority and medical supervision of sporting officials.

Racist Suspicion: Targeting "Hermaphrodites" and "Hybrids" in Sport

This is really a racial issue. White people have always been after us and they'll continue to hold us back with the power they have left. Fight for Caster Semenya because the fight is really for your own Black self, your kids and great grandkids #JustDoItForCaster —NOKUPHILA SHANGASE (@NokuPh), Twitter, May 2, 2019

There is nothing objective about gender testing and who it targets. When contestations over Semenya's ability to compete in sport began, suspicions were articulated in their rawest forms in comments made publicly by her competitors from the Global North:

Mariya Savinova (Russia): "Just look at her!"

Elisa Cusma (Italy): "These kind of people should not run with us. For me, she's not a woman. . . . It is useless to compete with this, and it is not fair."

Diane Cummins (Canada): "Even if she is a female, she's on the very fringe of the normal athlete female biological composition from what I understand of hormone testing. So, from that perspective, most of us just feel that we are literally running against a man."

These competitors' views were seized on by the media and added to the frenzy of speculations. Their comments were falsely represented as evidence of Semenya's ambiguity rather than as evidence of competitors' jealousy and inability to "see" Semenya clearly.[4]

Media further created visual images of Semenya as a suspect imposter with raced and colonial undertones.[5] The late South African feminist scholar Elaine Salo explains, "The media reports of these responses were juxtaposed with the visual images of Caster Semenya's muscular body and . . . her blackness and her dominance over her more experienced European counterparts that seemed to be so antithetical to acceptable femininity" (2016, 155). These images stigmatized Semenya's confidence, problematizing her masculinity and ease. For instance, one AP photo reproduced in many media accounts shows her relaxed at the finish line in the seconds following a race, raising her finger to indicate her victorious placement as "number one" while her competitors continue to strain behind her. In another popular photo, Semenya flexes her biceps with a serious look on her face. These visual representations were accompanied by headlines that questioned her gender—"Could This Women's World Champ Be a Man?" "Is She or Isn't He?" and "Woman, Man . . . or a Little Bit of Both"—as well as loaded descriptions of her body. Photos and text that dominated the media intentionally facilitated doubt about Semenya's gender and worked to create impressions of hypermasculinity in the ways they represented particular postures and expressions.[6]

The media was also quick to bring to bear falsehoods of disproportionate African intersex in relation to Semenya. For instance, just days after her public interrogation began, the *New York Times* reported on the controversy and asserted that, according to Dr. Maria New, an endocrinologist at Mount Sinai School of Medicine, "The indigenous South African Bantu-speaking people may be more predisposed to being hermaphrodites but they do not always have obvious male genitalia" (Clarey and Kolata 2009). The longue durée of intersex and race is clear in this casual iteration of a scientific untruth. Further, this copy was corrected because the original article "referred incorrectly to people in South Africa whose sex characteristics have been studied because of the prevalence of hermaphroditism among them. They are Bantu-speaking people, not 'Bantus,' a term considered offensive because it was used by those in power during apartheid in reference to black people" (Clarey and Kolata 2009). Not only was the original error (using the term "Bantus") significant for its highly problematic terminology, the correction itself restates New's citation of the centuries-old myth, factually asserting the "prevalence of hermaphroditism" among South Africans.

Bodily suspicions and gender testing in sport are modern extensions of colonial quests to prove hermaphroditism in Africa. When gender testing was instituted in 1913, it was publicly posited as a way to identify men pretending to be women for sporting success. In reality, the International Olympic Committee (IOC) has always conceptualized gender verification as a means to exclude those they classified outside the racialized category of "woman."[7] L. Dawn Bavington's careful historical work reveals that beginning in the 1930s, efforts targeting "abnormal women athletes" (the language used at the time) motivated officials to seek medical examinations for Olympic competition (2019, 185).[8] Not coincidentally, she explains, these initiatives emerged as African American women entered competitive track and field in the interwar years (1919–39). While gender testing is usually traced to the institutionalization of standardized tests in the 1960s, Vanessa Heggie (2010) similarly identifies systemic and medicalized gender testing as actually beginning in the 1940s, at the same time as perceived masculinity was racialized and pathologized in elite sport.[9]

Disdain for those seen as "too masculine" and disproportionately "hermaphroditic" or "hybrid" has always driven testing. In the 1950s, as black women came to dominate track and field, Olympic governing bodies considered eliminating several women's track and field events that they deemed insufficiently "feminine." Olympic official Norman Cox "sarcastically proposed that rather than ban women's events, the IOC should create a special category of competition for the unfairly advantaged 'hermaphrodites' who regularly defeated 'normal' women, those less-skilled 'child-bearing' types with 'largish breasts, wide hips, [and] knocked knees'" (Cahn 2015, 111). Cox's ideas about normality matched those of his contemporaries, and mandatory gender testing targeted athletes who were "presumed intersex."[10] The doctor in charge of testing in the 1960s, Jacques Thiébault of the French Olympic Committee, explicitly stated his intent to dissuade "hybrids" from competing. As Bavington writes, "Underpinned by the benevolence of Western medical intervention, Thiébault considered it his duty as a doctor to treat these *hybrid beings* and outlined a procedure of diagnosing them medically" (2019, 187).[11] Sporting authorities like Cox and Thiébault gave voice to common perceptions of black women's bodies as hermaphroditic that resonate throughout this book.

Concerns and rumors about intersex were further institutionalized in routinized gender testing in the 1950s and 1960s. Perceptions of black, Chinese, and Soviet women reveal the raced and classed geopolitics of such testing.[12] In the years following World War II, North American and western European capitalist nations demanded fragile femininity, whereas communist Soviet Union and eastern European countries encouraged women to be strong and muscular. Contrasting ideas about femininity, labor, and domesticity were integral to the development of gender testing.[13] Rising distrust of strong Soviet athletes in women's sport made them targets, and their success was stigmatized, while limited ideas about athleticism constrained US and western European white women's success in Olympic competition. These differences were material manifestations of ideas about gendered bodies and class, but they were represented as innate.

In the 1980s and 1990s, as China's influence and economic power grew, so too did the pathologization of Chinese women in athletics. Victorious athletes were represented as "fraudulent and unnatural," and their success was "cause for suspicion, not celebration" (Pieper 2016, 167). Doping tests and gender testing have been problematically conflated since the 1960s.[14] While testing relied on similar science, doping testing sought to prove intentional drug use and cheating, and gender testing was focused on natural processes in the body. But both have often been grounded in racist and geopolitically initiated claims about "masculine" women. As Lindsay Parks Pieper argues, "Although no Chinese woman failed the compulsory drug test, journalists voiced suspicions of steroid abuse as a tactic to protect the rightful claimants to athletic victories—white, hetero-feminine, Western women" (2016, 167–68).[15]

Athletes from the United States and western Europe have long histories of complaining about their competitors by framing them as intersex. Perhaps the most explicit and influential white complaint to date focused on Chinese athletes. In 1993, a group of women including elite athletes—dubbed the Heinonen Sixteen—demanded that the IAAF further institutionalize restrictive gender testing. Threatened by Chinese athletic successes and led by *Keeping Track* editor Janet Heinonen, the group made unfounded accusations of doping and argued that athletes from the Global North need "protection" from so-called male frauds.[16] This collective ignored the intensive training that propelled Chinese athletes' success, instead reviving the familiar trope of protecting women's sport from, in their words, "men trying to pass as women" (*Keeping Track* 1994, 2).[17] But the real intentions of the Heinonen Sixteen are peppered throughout their writings as they demand that authorities police "the grey area of sex" and especially athletes of color, "whose bodies are not unequivocally male or female" (2). The untoward influence of white women was similarly revealed at meetings about gender testing in Lausanne, Switzerland, hosted by the IOC in 2010. At this time, retired Alpine ski racers from Sweden and France "threatened to go on strike if something *was not done* about young, black, African runners" (Bavington 2019, 195).[18] In these and other instances, including recent social media battles, white athletes from the Global North have made false accusations and strongly influenced policies around gender testing. Sporting authorities have constituted white women as "more deserving of fairness, privacy, and protection from harm" (2019, 183).[19]

Throughout the rise and fall of political and raced rivalries, African and African American women have been disproportionately scrutinized by those jealous of their success.[20] Considered the ultimate expression of physicality and the most prestigious sport, running had been long argued by scientists to harm women's bodies, especially their reproductive organs. From the inception of women's Olympic sport, persistent ideologies of eugenics ensured that the reproduction of white women was cautiously guarded and overprotected, while African American and African women were pathologized for their athleticism.[21] This focus on Africa intensified in the 1990s. In 1992, after almost three decades of exclusion due to apartheid, South Africa was reinstated into the Olympics.[22] African women's growing dominance in track and field coincided with the fall of the Soviet Union and the end of eastern European dominance in women's sport and became a constant source of media discussions.

Semenya came into the public eye within this historical context, with questions about her body raised by complaints from her racist rivals and sporting officials' suggestions that her performance had improved too easily. Over the past decade, cooperative efforts to determine the boundaries of gender among the IAAF/World Athletics, IOC, gynecologists, endocrinologists, psychologists, and other experts demonstrate that gender is not natural but is decided by consensus. As Brenna Munro puts it, "categories of 'male' and 'female' are as man-made as the decathlon and the nation-state" (2010, 387), with Semenya's experience at the nexus of these debates.[23] Given this kind of disagreement, it is reasonable to label these debates as, in the words of Judith Butler, "a massive effort to socially negotiate the sex of Semenya, with the media included as a party to this deliberation" (2009).[24] Semenya described the personal torment this deliberation wreaked on her early on: "I have been subjected to unwarranted and invasive scrutiny of the most intimate and private details of my being" (Semenya 2010; see also Smith 2009).[25]

Troubling Comparisons: Semenya in Colonial Context

As women our bodies have always been subjected to public scrutiny. From the days of Sarah Baartman to today. "Your breasts are small, your hips are too wide . . . nywe" now it has elevated to changing our hormonal makeup. Aowa this is too much #CasterSemenya (Simphiwe (@Simphziy) April 26, 2018). —quoted in SESONA NGQAKAMBA, *"Semenya Ruling—South African Fans Are Furious"*

What makes Semenya different from other athletes, and why has her experience brought so much visibility to gender testing and intersex? Semenya's public declarations made her one of the first athletes to begin a trend of openly resisting the cacophony of experts who struggle to arbitrate the (raced) rules of who counts as male or female.[26] She has also been fearless and forthright. In 2019, Semenya revealed that she had taken medications to lower her testosterone when such measures became required by the IAAF/World Athletics, but that they made her feel continually sick. She spoke about the side effects, including night sweats, weight gain, fever, and abdominal pain. It was at this time that she publicly rejected sporting authorities' efforts to make her and other athletes, in her words, guinea pigs. As Semenya has explained, "It's taking the soul out of my body. . . . They want me to take my own system down. I'm not sick. I don't need drugs" (quoted in Brenner 2021). Following her lead, other affected athletes have increasingly shared their stories about the lived effects of gender restrictions.[27] The physical devastation of subjective testing and surgical and hormonal treatment have been largely hidden and unknown, but athletes are standing up to these practices.[28]

Semenya has also garnered global attention because of her South African backing.[29] While South Africans have been Semenya's strongest supporters, politicians' positions were particularly fraught. When Semenya's trials began in 2009, Leonard Chuene, founding president of Athletics South Africa, aptly alleged that gender testing was consistent with a history of "European imperialism," and he posited that "it would not be like that if it were some young girl from Europe" (quoted in Bryson 2009). The chairperson of a parliamentary sports committee, Butana Komphela, similarly opined, "just because she is black and she surpassed her European competitors, there is all this uproar" (quoted in Sawer and Berger 2009), while the South African minister of social development agreed that "these unfounded claims were perpetrated by fellow [European] women competitors who lost out in the race" (*Mail and Guardian* 2009). But this support was complicated when it was revealed that Semenya had been subjected to secret gender testing without her consent under the authorization of Chuene himself. Internal debates stating that Semenya was "a hermaphrodite" and "born a man" were leaked to the press (Sindane 2009; Levy 2009; Smith 2009). Chuene's initial inflammatory comments—including, "There's no scientific evidence. You can't say somebody's child is not a girl. You denounce my child as a boy when she's a girl? If you did that to my child, I'd shoot you" (Bearak 2009; Dixon 2009)—and his public outrage about the IAAF investigations of Semenya seemed hypocritical when his part in her scrutiny was exposed.[30]

Most elite athletes who have found themselves in similar positions historically have been shamed and rejected. But there are complicated contexts surrounding Semenya's support. Sport played a strong role in South Africa's transition to democracy and in political efforts at unity. This was exemplified in the ANC's strategy of encouraging sport boycotts to end apartheid and Nelson Mandela's 1995 transitional celebrations of national unity through World Cup rugby.[31] Thus it was not unexpected when politicians represented the stakes of Semenya's gender claims as significantly as Mandela had in the past, with responses drawing on South African sport histories. Many supporters initially rushed to cast Semenya as a traditional heterosexual woman and representative of the nation; when allegations began, politicians famously called Semenya "our first lady of sport." In 2009, she was subjected to a hyperfeminizing makeover in South African *You* magazine, which received global media attention (Dworkin, Swarr, and Cooky 2013). Early public responses positioned Semenya as a woman and not as intersex, as if these categories are necessarily mutually exclusive. But, as Semenya herself put it, "My organs may be different and I may have a deep voice, but I am a woman" (quoted in Brenner 2021). Over time, Semenya has redefined understandings of womanhood to include a range of bodies including hers.

Perhaps most significantly, South Africans frame Semenya's treatment in colonial context and as a racist imposition by the Global North. This has been most apparent through comparisons of Semenya to one of the most famous women in South African history—Sara Baartman. Dozens of academic publications, articles in countless media outlets, and postings on social media have connected the treatment of Baartman in the early 1800s to the treatment of Semenya in the early 2000s (Magubane 2014). As Carina Ray writes, both of their bodies have become public spectacles and are disrespected as anatomic curiosities: "Two centuries separate Baartman and Semenya, yet they are inextricably linked by the same fraught history that surrounds the West's fascination with and disregard for the Black body" (2009, 19). Baartman is a South African icon, and her experiences provide a tormenting reminder of colonial dehumanization and pathologization. Scientists and journalists used both of their bodies to convince colonial and contemporary observers alike of racist genital fallacies. Historian Pamela Scully recalls the histories that are brought into the present, as Semenya's treatment "brings up echoes of the horrible experience of Sara Baartman at the hands of the European press from 1810 to 1815. Journalists hounded Baartman determined to write about what they saw as a strange female body, linked to the strange because it was African. . . . [and scientists] who sought to establish 'truths' about links between sexuality and race studied Baartman's body, both in life, and in death" (2010).

But many South African activists argue that while representations of Baartman were out of their hands, contemporary representations of Semenya are not. When Semenya's genitals were repeatedly examined, tested, and photographed in efforts to verify her gender, academics and activists alike decried her exploitation and that of Baartman. After results of testing on Semenya's body were leaked, Neville Hoad reflected, "These details contain immense symbolic violence, evoking images of vivisection and willy-nilly the shameful history of Sarah Baartman, who was literally cut up and turned inside out for the world to see by [scientist Georges] Cuvier" (2010, 401–2). The Joint Working Group, a collaboration of South African activist organizations focused on gender and sexuality, similarly protested this comparative abuse, writing that while Baartman was promoted as a figure of curiosity in life and dissected after death two hundred years before, "Now Caster is likewise to be dissected; poked, prodded and tested by a panel of doctors who on the basis of their 'investigations' will pass judgement on who and what she is" (Craven 2009). In manifold ways, Semenya's supporters were determined to confront her mistreatment.

The leering gazes linked judgments of bodies deemed abnormal with monstrosity and Gross's discussion of teratology. Pumla Dineo Gqola argues that the IAAF's irresponsibility reduced "Semenya the outstanding athlete . . . to a freak, another curious body that does not fit categories we pretend are neutral. She is not even entitled to privacy from the leering eyes looking for the Adam's apple they claim to almost see, just like Baartman's mischievous 'Hottentot apron'" (Gqola 2009). The gazes that objectify them both seek signs of hermaphroditism with vision clouded by racist histories. Gqola points out that Semenya does not embody white idealized femininity in comparison to elite white athletes like British runner Jenny Meadows: "Semenya looks and sounds like many women we all know from across the world. Baartman looked like many African women. But she did not look like Jenny Meadow's foremothers" (Gqola 2009). Gqola reiterates how scrutinizing eyes look for white femininity as normativity. For Ray, this kind of visuality evokes a comparative caution: "Saartjie Baartman's short life came to a tragic end, in part, because her body was not strong enough to withstand the weight of the world's gaze" (2009, 19). Interrogating this gaze is critical to preventing the replication of the consequences of spectacularization.

Decolonial critiques of colonial histories and their impact on Baartman and Semenya extend to social media. Challenges to Semenya's visual objectification were exemplified by a meme circulating on Facebook, originating on August 23, 2016, by the South African anonymous and politically radical artistic collaboration Xcollektiv.[32] This meme is based on a French cartoon by Louis François Charon called *Les Curieux en Extase ou les Cordons de Souliers* (1814) and was intended to ridicule British fascination with Baartman.[33] In the original cartoon (figure 4.1), Baartman is displayed on a pedestal as the subject of different kinds of voyeurism, and her objectification is satirized in captions not replicated in the meme. Analyzing the 1814 cartoon, French scholar T. Denean Sharpley-Whiting explains:

> One soldier, behind Baartman, extends his hand as if to touch her buttocks and proclaims, "Oh, godem, que rosbif!" (Oh, goddamn, what roast beef!). The other soldier, looking directly into her genitalia, remarks: "Ah, que la nature est drôle!" (Ah, how amusing nature is!). The male civilian, peering through lorgnettes, declares: "Qu'elle etrange beauté!" (What strange beauty!), while the female civilian . . . looks through Baartman's legs and utters: "A quelque chose malheureux est bon" (From some points of view misfortune can be good). The woman is, however, looking not at the "Hottentot," but through the opening between her legs and up the kilt of the soldier behind Bartmann. (1999, 21)

In this analysis, Sharpley-Whiting suggests that the kneeling woman remarks on the exposed penis of the soldier in the kilt pictured behind Baartman. The dog, peeking up another soldier's kilt, represents the animality of voyeurism. The perspectives depicted represent ways in which Baartman and Semenya are commonly understood—as consumable meat (roast beef), as biological variants (amusing nature), and as exoticized (strong beauty).

In Xcollektiv's meme (figure 4.2), captions from the original cartoon are omitted, and the spectators are left wordless and mute. A fully clothed Semenya replaces Baartman on the pedestal, and her face and body language, with wide stance, hands on her hips, and eyes skyward, might indicate irritation. Xcollektiv

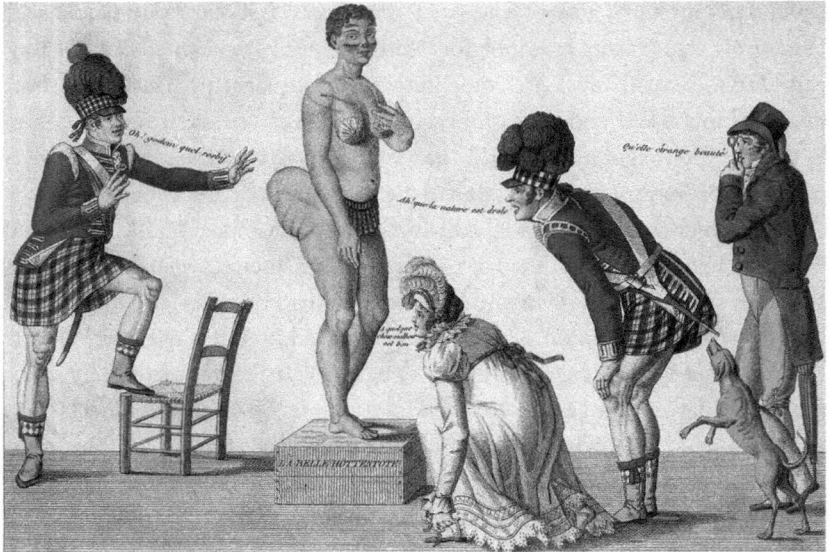

Figure 4.1. Louis François Charon, *Les Curieux en Extase ou les Cordons de Souliers* [The curious in ecstasy or bootstraps], 1814.

The unrelenting gaze. 1789 - 2016

Figure 4.2. Xcollektiv, *The Unrelenting Gaze, 1789–2016*, meme circulating on Facebook, 2016.

also adds a new title to this meme—*The Unrelenting Gaze, 1789–2016*—historically connecting Baartman to Semenya and to the countless other South Africans subjected to colonialist and racist visual regimes for those 227 years. Rather than accepting the spectacularizing gaze, Xcollektiv's meme pushes back against it through social media circulation, reversing this visual objectification.

Puppet Masters of Gender Verification and Their Racist Assumptions

What is happening to #CasterSemenya is so painful. They want her to take drugs to alter her to inferior level. They couldn't stand being defeated by a black woman so they force her take drugs. There must be something we can do to put an end to this racist rule. —ANDI MOTSEPE (@AndiswaMadikazi), Twitter, September 9, 2020

Underpinned by colonial logic, current regulations continue centuries of histories of policing gender binaries focused on African women. Perhaps most unsettling are the ways these regulations have specifically targeted Semenya with overt discrimination. In 2018, the IAAF decreed that it would only police testosterone levels in a handful of events in the entirety of the Olympics—track events from 400-meter to the mile—in which Semenya competes.[34] The current focus on Semenya and other successful athletes from the Global South exposes the long-term motives of sporting authorities. With the growing global expansion of sport, the IOC Medical Commission has increasingly created barriers to success from its geopolitical rivals, which increasingly include those in the Global South.

The parameters of gender in sport have been manipulated by powerful puppet masters who necessitate interrogation. One of the key orchestrators of gender testing was a spectacularly unqualified prince. Prince Alexandre de Mérode of Belgium served as the chair of the IOC's Medical Commission from 1967 until his death in 2002. This aristocrat was neither a doctor nor a scientist, and throughout his thirty-five-year tenure, de Mérode promoted unsubstantiated fearful fantasies about athletes in the Eastern Bloc, China, and the Global South.[35] Most of the time, the prince publicly claimed gender testing was necessary to protect women's sport from so-called male masqueraders, but occasionally, he would admit he was more motivated by a parallel savior narrative about intersex. In private correspondence, de Mérode explains:

> When we carried out the first tests in 1968, we simply wished to put a stop to the development of a particularly immoral form of cheating which

had been spreading insidiously within high-level competition sport. . . . [But] we were informed that in certain regions, a systematic search was taking place for young people presenting sexual anomalies, which were then knowingly aggravated instead of any attempt being made to correct them. This unspeakable approach permanently compromised their future lives, having irreversible traumatic effects. It therefore seemed to us imperative to put a stop to these shameful practices which flout the most elementary rules of medical ethics.[36]

Prince de Mérode repeatedly asserts the prevalence of "cheating" from "certain regions," echoing the false claims of sporting officials like Cox. But in this passage, he exacerbates this claim by suggesting the need to save athletes with "sexual anomalies." In de Mérode's imagination, such athletes were sought out and manipulated, thus leading to unfair competitive domination. In manifold correspondence, de Mérode parroted colonial tropes that justified violence under the guise of "saving" colonized women.

In this period, a global coalition of scientists rallied to bring attention to the grave inaccuracies of gender testing.[37] They documented athletes' suffering and even suicides that resulted from testing inaccuracies and sporting exclusions.[38] But despite these challenges, Prince de Mérode clung to his inconsistent and baseless arguments. One of de Mérode's primary detractors, Finnish geneticist and international expert on gender and chromosomes Albert de la Chapelle, lamented, "The Prince is quite concerned about what could happen in countries or clubs where unscrupulous sports coaches 'produce' unfairly competing 'females.' That, he says, is why gender verification was instituted in the first place; to prevent 'certain countries' from sending 'hermaphrodites' to compete as women."[39] The prince and his supporters chose to act in contempt of scientific consensus and with disregard for the sweeping condemnation of professional medical associations.[40] The political reasons for supporting gender testing as a tool of intimidation and influence outweighed the importance of their failings.

Since de Mérode's thirty-five-year reign ended in 2002, the orchestrators of gender testing and surgical and hormonal "treatments" have continued to exercise undue influence with the same biased roots.[41] Stéphane Bermon— director of health and science for the IAAF/World Athletics and lead physician in the development of testosterone regulation—has perhaps been most instrumental in conceptualizing and implementing such policies. Repeating the baseless racist assertion cited throughout this book, Bermon claims that intersex is most common in the Global South (Karkazis and Jordan-Young 2018, 20).[42] But Bermon combines this tired refrain with another narrative. Recall Prince de

Mérode's unsubstantiated claim that he began gender testing to stop what he called immoral cheating and his assertion that in certain regions, systematic searches took place for young people presenting "sexual anomalies." Bermon reiterates the unfounded claims of the prince more than two decades later, cautioning that nefarious and deceptive forces in the Global South are heavily recruiting intersex athletes. He warns not just of intersex frequency in the Global South but of dishonesty in Africa, South America, and Asia, where athletes "have a very clear advantage, they were pushed to compete at the highest level" (quoted in Karkazis and Jordan-Young 2018, 23). In Bermon's racist imaginings, ignorant doctors, oblivious athletes, and fraudulent nationalists conspire to steal victories in global athletic competitions from white women.

Gender verification rests on centuries of colonial fascination with the genitals of African women. Bermon routinely emphasizes the importance of gynecological examinations for women athletes from the Global South, and he asserts that doctors should focus on the size of the clitoris as indicative of pathology. To resolve what he represents as unfair advantages in global sport, he advocates that clitoridectomy and other medically unnecessary surgical procedures be performed by doctors supported by the IAAF (Fénichel et al. 2013, E1057). In Bermon's assessment, lack of medical intervention for intersex athletes—specifically failure to perform surgical and hormonal "corrections"—is ignorant and neglectful. There is irony in the deeply entrenched judgment of Africa as a site for locally initiated traditional genital cutting, while clitoridectomy is imposed by allopathic doctors from the Global North.[43] Africans are both condemned for performing traditional procedures and condemned for *not* performing these procedures under allopathic sporting auspices. Bermon and his allies argue that Africans are intentionally fostering the sporting performances of "uncorrected" intersex athletes so they can unfairly compete in sport.

The declarations of the prince and Bermon dovetail again in white savior narratives about preventing women from the Global South from competing. Sporting officials and doctors position themselves as benevolent. They claim that providing unwanted and nonconsensual medical interventions is helping athletes they condescendingly see as duped by those facilitating their athletic careers. This facade of protection belies their investment in fostering North American and European sporting success at any cost. Protecting white women from black and brown interlocutors is a familiar colonial trope used to justify violence. In a rare interview about current gender testing protocols in 2019, Bermon belligerently positions himself as an altruistic guardian, asserting that those who refuse his violent treatment prescriptions are therefore not "true" women.[44]

Cut by Consensus: False Promises and Medically Unnecessary "Treatments"

black women's bodies are regularly ground zero for barbarity masquerading as science for the benefit of white women. caster semenya is at risk of osteoporosis and infertility so that paula radcliffe and sharron davies can maintain their status quo —Daniellé DASH (@DanielleDASH), Twitter, May 3, 2019

The protection of white womanhood dominates contemporary sport. Not only are the problematic agendas of doctors like Bermon who promote elite athletes like Radcliffe and Davies increasingly apparent; they also promote damaging and unnecessary medical practices.[45] Such doctors' ethics are questioned, even by their peers, and they rely on the racist citational chain traced throughout this book. Of particular note is a published article from 2013 that has become so infamous it is commonly referred to as "the Fénichel paper," a paper for which Bermon is a co-author.

The Fénichel paper focuses on the medical "treatment" of four elite athletes ages eighteen to twenty-one years and identified as "from rural or mountainous regions of developing countries" (Fénichel et al. 2013, E1056).[46] These athletes were sent to the Nice and Montpellier University Hospitals in southern France after their national doctors and an antidoping officer reported them as having external genitals deemed suspicious or testosterone levels deemed too high.[47] Initial testing included interviews about family histories and sexual relationships, blood and urine collection, imaging (e.g., MRI, X-ray), and clinical exams of their labia, vaginal canals, and abdomens. The athletes were diagnosed with 5α-reductase deficiency and subjected to medically unnecessary surgeries.[48] As the authors explain,

> Although leaving male gonads in SDRD5A2 patients carries no health risk, each athlete was informed that gonadectomy would most likely decrease their performance level but would allow them to continue elite sport in the female category.[49] We thus proposed a partial clitoridectomy with a bilateral gonadectomy, followed by a deferred feminizing vaginoplasty and estrogen replacement therapy, to which the 4 athletes agreed after informed consent on surgical and medical procedures. Sports authorities then allowed them to continue to compete competitively in the female category 1 year after gonadectomy. (Fénichel et al. 2013, E1057)

Though couched in medical language, the implications of these statements are staggering. Doctors and policy makers acting on behalf of the IAAF report that they plan to remove functional and healthy clitorises from athletes—performing cosmetically motivated clitoridectomies—for no reason other than subjective perceptions. Obviously, this procedure would have no bearing on their athletic performance. Doctors also proposed surgically reshaping and "feminizing" their vaginal canals—performing vaginoplasties—though conceding that such procedures were also medically unnecessary.

These authors' recommendations disregard the significant side effects of testosterone-lowering medications and admittedly unnecessary surgical interventions that they performed, including bilateral gonadectomy.[50] Gonadectomy removes internal healthy organs and tissues and causes hypogonadism and often sterility. Hypogonadism brings about severe side effects, including decreased bone and muscle strength, and increased risk of chronic weakness, depression, sleep disturbance, decreased libido, and adverse effects on lipid profile, diabetes, and fatigue (Jordan-Young, Sönksen, and Karkazis 2014, 21). It is irreversible, and postoperative patients must stay on expensive hormone replacement therapy for their entire lives. The American Association of Clinical Endocrinologists does not recommend gonadectomy for treating high testosterone (HRW 2020, 52–53), and the World Medical Association and United Nations Human Rights Council critiques the harms of the regulations. But, following the leadership of Bermon and his counterparts, the IAAF/World Athletics requires surgical and/or hormonal interventions to lower testosterone for competition, claiming that "the changes wrought by lowering women's testosterone for athletes, among them reduced muscle and increased fat are 'gender-affirming'" (Jordan-Young and Karkazis 2019). In short, doctors in bed with elite sporting organizations engage in chemical experimentation and cut bodies into shapes that match the imaginations of their orchestrators.

Not incidentally, the Fénichel paper relies on other problematic racialized research on intersex. In the introduction, I highlight three locales in the Global South that have been the focus of intersex research since the 1970s: the Dominican Republic, Papua New Guinea, and South Africa. As detailed previously, Julianne Imperato-McGinley's scholarship pathologized and exploited Dominicans diagnosed with 5α-reductase deficiency in work that garnered global attention. Her research—including the objectifying photographs in her publications—incited academic and popular fixation with "discovering" disproportionate intersex in communities in the Dominican Republic that continues to the present. Scientists and physicians authoring current policies about international gender testing continue to rely on this medical literature from the 1970s.

When devising treatment plans for athletes brought to France, Fénichel and colleagues cite Imperato-McGinley and other researchers who heavily cite her scholarship. This work is dated in methodology and content and based on unethical research practices, yet it is referenced as current and accurate. Throughout this book, I have followed citational chains that allege disproportionate intersex among black people, especially in the Global South. These chains comprise not only bibliographical references but citations of ideas that gain authority and meaning through their reiteration. The citational chain linked to Imperato-McGinley's work in the Dominican Republic that began in the 1970s encompasses the following.

Fénichel et al. 2013:

> Imperato-McGinley et al. 1979 cited

> Thiele et al. 2005
> > Imperato-McGinley et al. 1991 cited

> Maimoun et al. 2011
> > Eight Imperato-McGinley co-authored articles cited:
> > 1974, 1979, 1986, 1991, 1992, 1992, 1996, 1997

> Houk et al. 2005
> > Fifteen Imperato-McGinley single and co-authored
> > articles cited: 1974, 1977, 1979, 1980, 1986, 1990, 1991,
> > 1992, 1994, 1994, 1995, 1996, 1997, 2002[51]

Claims of disproportionate intersex in the Global South take hold as they are cited, but they also derive power through the citations they compel (e.g., in this chain of references).[52] This citational chain defers to the authority of scholarship grounded in scientific racism, positioning the bodies of those in the Global South as inferior and "abnormal." It also shows how racialized and outdated work—going as far back as 1974—continues to be canonized. Decades later and with deep and multiple engagements, these authors' citational practices and the canon they create demonstrate how false beliefs about disproportionate intersex are constantly re-created.

Not only was the Fénichel paper troubling in its content and citations, its methodology and production were highly unethical. Since its publication, it has been widely critiqued for its deficiencies. Karkazis and Jordan-Young cite angry IAAF/World Athletics officials who denounce this publication as violating medical confidentiality, particularly for young and vulnerable athletes who are easily identifiable from the details shared. These officials declare that this paper absolutely should not have been published (Karkazis and Jordan-Young 2018, 5). The breaches of the Fénichel paper are so significant that it is currently under investigation by the French government (HRW 2020, 74–76).

Runner Annet Negesa, widely considered the best athlete in Uganda in 2012, believes she was likely one of the athletes under scrutiny in the Fénichel paper and that Bermon himself oversaw her treatment. The 2019 film *Gender Battle: The Abandoned Women of Sport* features Negesa and other athletes from the Global South who had unwanted surgeries that they did not understand because they were told this would allow them to keep competing (Sviridinko, Willison, and Seppelt 2019).[53] Her grief and broken spirit evident, Negesa explains that the results of her gender testing were never explained to her. Following invasive medical testing in France, she was coerced into having a procedure she was told would be "a simple surgery—like an injection" (Sviridinko, Willison, and Seppelt 2019); instead, she woke up with scars on her abdomen and later learned she had had a gonadectomy. While she was promised she could compete again, since surgery she has been physically debilitated and is unable to stand for long periods, let alone run competitively. Negesa shows official IAAF documents to the camera, indicating that Bermon and her surgeon collaboratively decided against using estrogen therapy postoperatively, a decision that left her with constant pain and weakness. In addition to her life and body being permanently altered, the public shame and threats that followed Negesa's experience led her to flee Uganda and obtain asylum in Germany.

This harrowing film supplements a report—"'They're Chasing Us Away from Sport': Human Rights Violations in Sex Testing of Elite Women Athletes"— based on interviews with thirteen similarly affected athletes from the Global South. Athletes all disclosed that they received partial or no information on testing processes and results, which were often withheld or shared in language they did not understand. The prices of gender testing and treatment consistently prove exorbitant; one athlete recounts that "her family made significant financial sacrifices for her, including selling some of their farmland to pay for a doctor's appointment following gender-stereotyped scrutiny of her body by a coach" (HRW 2020, 97). When athletes failed subjective gender tests, they were left with impossible choices, including public ruin and physically damaging surgeries and hormonal treatments.[54] Not one of the athletes interviewed for the HRW report had health problems or symptoms that bothered them prior to sporting interventions. But unwanted surgeries and the removal of functional body parts from their healthy bodies created hormonal imbalances that left them unable to function and without support or money for further treatment.[55]

Mental health tolls among affected athletes were also extreme: "Interviewees described intense self-questioning, shame, and a withdrawal from sport—even when it was their livelihood—and attempting suicide" (HRW 2020, 10).[56] As debates over gendered bodies continue, the highest costs are borne by the athletes themselves as their bodies become experimental testing grounds.

Semenya looms large in other athletes' accounts; she is the most famous exemplar of the public consequences of gender testing, and this is far from coincidental. Sporting regulators make public examples of successful athletes like Semenya as a deterrent. Gender regulations are a means of intentional intimidation, especially for athletes from (in the prince's words) "certain countries." They keep athletes in a constant state of enforced fear, augmented by the threat of suspicion.[57] The title of the HRW report—"They're Chasing Us Away from Sport"—references the intimidation and forced medical treatments that are, in the words of an affected athlete, "a way of disorganizing people . . . it can affect you physically and also mentally—so you cannot focus" (2020, 80). As the authors of the HRW report observe, since 2009 the most publicized investigations focus on athletes from the Global South, including those from India, South Africa, Uganda, Kenya, and Burundi. Bavington similarly documents that young athletes from the Global South have been subject to a disproportionately high rate of investigation, with most of the athletes who have faced "medical work-up" coming from Africa (2019, 196). The name and specter of Semenya continues to propel geographically focused and intentional threats to keep these athletes from competing.

#HandsOffCaster and #IAAFMustFall: Semenya's Past and Future

Stand Up Africa and fight! They are coming for all of us! It's a war. We can't celebrate freedom when our very blackness is challenged by those who stole our very being. Limpopo stand up. They hate her because she is a threat to their superiority over Africa. #HandsOffCaster. —ONICCA MOKGOBEDI (@tp1_moloi), Twitter, April 27, 2018

The hashtag #HandsOffCaster! and other expressions of support for Semenya slowly came to dominate social media for a time.[58] Semenya's understanding of herself, and South African social media campaigns on her behalf, theorize the interplay of colonial racism and gender binaries. Over the past decade, while Semenya has weathered constantly shifting judgments on her body, she has reclaimed her own representation. She has transformed from a shy unwitting participant in global discourses to a self-possessed leader of conversations about gender binaries and racist geopolitics in athletics. In 2009, her sudden rise as a household name necessitated protection from a bodyguard, and Semenya explained at the time: "People want to stare at me, to touch me. I don't think I like being famous so much" (quoted in McRae 2009). Commentators worried that Semenya would be rejected by her fans and might face violence, but instead, her successes and support multiplied. Semenya married her wife, Violet Raseboya, in December 2016. She graduated from the University of the North-West in Potchefstroom with a degree in sports science in 2018. She won gold in the Olympics in 2012 and 2016. She and her wife had two children. And she found self-directed visibility and voice on social media.

Semenya has been especially active on Twitter and Instagram since 2015, with more than four hundred thousand followers on Twitter and two hundred thousand followers on Instagram as of January 2022. She uses virtual spaces to speak back to her detractors and to inspire her supporters, using her own words, reposts, and memes. For instance, in a 2016 post on Instagram, Semenya wrote, "Dear Haters, I have so much more for you to be mad at. Just be patient," and journalists observed at this time that Semenya began "naming her critics on social media platforms, warning them that there will be no good news for them anytime soon" (Flanagan 2016). Semenya also uses virtual space to confront regulatory changes in sport directly. When a restrictive ruling on hyperandrogenism, limiting testosterone levels for women athletes in certain events, was announced in 2018, she responded, "I don't like talking about this new rule. I just want to run naturally, the way I was born. It is not fair that I am told I must change. It is not fair that people question who I am. I am Mokgadi Caster Semenya. I am a woman and I am fast" (quoted in Longman 2018).[59] This quotation was widely repeated and made into memes circulated on social media—"I am Mokgadi Caster Semenya. I am a woman and I am fast"—along with expressions of pride and assurance.

Support via social media helps Semenya face challenges to her gender. Seven years into the harms she has faced, the hashtag #HandsOffCaster took over the Twittersphere. Articles in *Sports Illustrated* and the *New Yorker* critiqued and lambasted Semenya, arguing that it was unfair for her to compete in the 2016 Olympics as a woman (Layden 2016; Gladwell and Thompson 2016). A conversation between reporters Malcolm Gladwell and Nicholas Thompson included Gladwell's opinions that Semenya should not be allowed to compete as a woman as she is "equipped with an extraordinary and anomalous genetic advantage" and was "born with the biological equivalent of a turbocharger" (2016). He went on to assert, "Semenya's difference put her outside the protected athletic category of 'woman'—and that makes it unfair to the other runners if she is allowed to compete" (2016).[60]

Expressions of anger and online petitions responded in solidarity with Semenya. In August 2016 more than seventeen thousand tweets made the hashtag #HandsOffCaster South Africa's top trend (BBC Trending 2016). The text of one such petition reads as follows:

> Attention to all sports players !!!! I believe we have all heard about the decision of the IAAF that has been taken, which is a disadvantage to some athletes like our very own Caster Semenya, who has high horme levels and now the IAAF has decided that Caster takes medication to reduce her hormone levels, because they claim she has a better advantage of winning. So we have created a movement which is ONLY GOING TO TAKE PLACE ON SOCIAL MEDIA. You can take part in the movement by either posting a video or a picture and use the hashtag #HANDSOFFCASTER or #IAAFMUSTFALL.

This support for Semenya represented a new kind of decolonial activism taking place exclusively on social media. South African supporters mobilize online to articulate gender policing and racist histories together, collectively protesting defamatory comments like Gladwell's and organizations like the IAAF. Semenya's supporters also amplify critiques of targeted gender regulations. For instance, in 2018 the Twittersphere exploded with appreciation following the resignation of University of Pretoria professor Steve Cornelius from the IAAF Disciplinary Tribunal in protest of new unscientific gender guidelines and their brutal effects.[61] South Africans tweeted support for Cornelius, sharing photos of his resignation letter widely. Such strategic and collective responses have had strong influence in garnering support for Semenya and retheorizing what it means to be a South African woman.

Other South African activism on social media overlaps with online support for Semenya, pushing back on the ongoing violence of colonialism and apartheid to mount substantive decolonial challenges.[62] Two campaigns emerged in 2015 that drew on South Africa's anti-apartheid history of student protest and current political dissatisfaction by strategically using Twitter in concert with traditional protest strategies.[63] The first of these was the #RhodesMustFall campaign begun at the University of Cape Town, symbolically focused on the statue of colonial figurehead Cecil John Rhodes but with far greater intent and impact. The second was the #FeesMustFall protest, which effectively curtailed fee increases at South African universities (Daniels 2016, 176).[64] On social media, the collective noun *fallism* emerged to unite these and other movements using the "Must Fall" hashtag, with #Fallist political movements demonstrating the power of online social movements.[65]

The "Must Fall" hashtag extended to explicitly feminist critiques, such as #PatriarchyMustFall and #RapeMustFall, exposing sexism and the erasure and silencing of women within these student movements (Hussen 2018; Maluleke and Moyer 2020). Desiree Lewis and Gabeba Baderoon describe the rising importance of these movements—and feminism within them—pointing out, "This period has seen calls to decolonise education, interrogate the trappings of post-apartheid democracy, and critique rainbow nation myth-making and its obsession with reclaiming cultural difference" (2021, 5). Within the same era, other significant hashtag movements led by young South African feminists—including #RapeAtAzania, #RUReferencelist, and #NakedProtest—similarly harnessed the power of Twitter to call out sexual violence within activist movements. These hashtags, as well as #RememberKhwezi, which called attention to former president Jacob Zuma's rape of Fezekile Ntsukela Kuzwayo, and #MenAreTrash, which trended following the brutal 2017 murder of Karabo Mokoena, expose silences and amplify abuses of the past. Taken together, these decolonial and feminist hashtag activist movements have fundamentally transformed political engagement in South Africa and demonstrate revolutionary approaches of a new generation.

Support of Semenya fits within this decolonial feminist activist framework. A quick scan of tweets posted with the hashtag #IAAFMustFall reveals a multiplicity of insights that echo other #Fallist movements. Trending in April 2018 was a comparison of Semenya and the Czech 1983 world record holder in the women's 800 meter, Jarmila Kratochvilova. Photos and memes stressed Kratochvilova's masculinity in concert with her race and nationality: "This is Jarmila Kratochvilova, the current holder of the women's 800m record, she has never had to endure half the criticism Caster has or have the IAAF force her to have her testosterone levels reduced. Ask yourselves why??" (Malume [@bozzie_t] 2018). This hashtag includes direct critiques of the IAAF, as well, for example, "The IAAF is a racist, sexist organization. I hope our athletes, sporting ministry, and bodies will throw their full weight behind the boycott of this trash organization" (Ntuli [@MsNtuli] 2018).

The hashtag #IAAFMustFall became a social media locus for analyzing racist gender discrimination originating in the Global North. Many tweets called for South African national unity, such as, "South Africans. Let us stand united against this sexist racism. #IAAFMustFall" (TaMphanyaTeam [@Tamphan-yos3] 2018). Others emphasized the body Semenya was born with as unproblematic; for instance, "What i like about her is that she's super natural deal with it #iaafmustfall #100%behindyousis" (Eunice [@Eunice_Kuhle] 2018). Social media trends on humor and political jokes provide another opportunity to challenge dominant thinking. One tweet hyperbolically suggested that the IAAF will soon tell Semenya to start running with her hands in her pockets. A funny video captioned "Caster vs everybody #HandsOffCaster" shows two people running in a close track race, one runner with the smiling head of Semenya superimposed onto it handily beating the other runner, who sports a globe for a head and IAAF emblazoned on their chest. Tweets like these and hundreds of similar expressions represent critiques of the IAAF and histories of discriminatory sporting regulations.

In response to the ongoing conflict, Semenya exhibited her characteristic calm confidence. She herself took to tweeting: "I love you Mzansi. Be happy in front of your haters. It kills them" (BBC Trending 2016).[66] Local news media noticed the shift; for example, in 2018 a headline in the South African newspaper the *Citizen* declared, "Caster Responds to IAAF Policy against Her with Awesome Tweets." The article explains that Semenya "has remained true to her style of not making grand statements, though she has been dropping a series of tweets and retweets." The article reprinted some quotations Semenya reposted on Twitter, including representations of her philosophies, such as: "I am 97% sure you don't like me, but I'm 100% sure I don't care" and "How beautiful it is to stay silent when someone expects you to be enraged" (@caster800m 2018). These kinds of tweets, in dialogue with Semenya's online posts of her daily life, marriage, and inspirational photos and text on Instagram and Twitter represent a complex picture of an athlete who has continued to thrive and succeed.

Semenya regularly posts photos of herself in opposition to exploitative visual representations of the past. These include Semenya's selfies and a wide range of other visual self-depictions that undermine media efforts to represent her as hypermasculine and cold. Photos on social media show her playfully having fun, exhibiting intense strength and discipline, endorsing products, and mentoring young athletes. Some are reposts of photos she likes that were taken by the media and corporate sponsors, this time self-curated. These visual images pose a strong contrast to those of a quiet eighteen-year-old famously subjected to a feminizing makeover in *You* magazine in 2009. Today's Semenya pictures herself, reflecting confidence and success.

Early online representations of Semenya on social media in South Africa were sometimes derogatory and at other times hyperfeminizing. But a growing respect characterizes most South African representations of Semenya. Derisive discussions of her masculinity are more rare. Many social critiques posted on Twitter are theoretically sophisticated and grounded in historical accuracies, advocating for her in no uncertain terms:

Caster Semenya is a natural Superwoman, but because her skin is black, her passport green & her partner a woman you think no one will fight for her. That you can create policies to exclude her despite precedent in your history. Think again @iaaforg #HandsOffCaster. (Du Plessis [@Zetsaid] 2018)

We must say [no] to western standards of femininity—what rubbish is that!!!! The IAAF hatred in Caster Semenya is sickening #CasterSemenya #HandsOffCaster. (Afrika [@SAYoungLion] 2018)

Unreasonable, unfair, unjustifiable, unscientific, racist and sexist—a "burn the witch" mentality that has no place in society. #HandsOffCaster. (Beningfield [@beningfield] 2018)

In 2016, Semenya supporter Sibongile Mafu observed in a tweet, "SA Twitter has grown up. The reaction to and treatment of Caster 2010 and Caster 2016 is vastly different. We're becoming better people" (@sboshmafu 2016) under the hashtag #IStandWithCaster. In the interceding years, South African acceptance has further shifted from debates about her claims to womanhood to representations of her as a complex person who challenges the medicalized strictures of gender and expands the meaning of "woman." A widely circulated meme with a photo of Semenya's face and the quotation—"God made me the way I am and I accept myself. I am who I am and I am proud of myself"—exemplifies support for Semenya and her opposition to changing her body through medical treatments.[67]

Many online representations of Semenya, including her own self-depictions, are decidedly commercial, and obviously social media platforms and athletic sponsors are motivated by profit.[68] Fears about her livelihood and corporate sponsorships have gone hand-in-hand with challenges to her eligibility to compete in global sport. But Semenya's athletic success has paralleled increasing corporate support for queer and gender nonconforming celebrities, including professional athletes. Take, for example, Semenya's role as a face of Nike in their popular "Just do it" campaign. In September 2018, Nike released an advertisement (they billed it as a one-minute "film") featuring Semenya that elicited a huge affective response.[69] The ad begins and ends with a brief depiction of a child actor playing Semenya in her youth in Limpopo, running along a rural road in profile. This image is quickly replaced by the profile of Semenya as an adult, racing to success, wearing Nike, in front of cheering crowds. A sports commentator is heard in the background: "And here's Semenya. She's pushing out again, and she's breaking away! She's going for something special here!" The footage then suddenly reverses with a focus on her Nike-clad foot, playing depictions of

Semenya's accomplishments in backward slow motion: her supporters cheering while watching her win on television, the South African flag unfurling, a medal now removed from her neck, her autograph unwritten, the training of her youth and even her first steps as a baby undone as reverse slow motion continues. Semenya herself narrates these scenes to slow piano music:

> Would it be easier for you if I wasn't so fast?
> Would it be simpler if I stopped winning?
> Would you be more comfortable if I was less proud?
> Would you prefer I hadn't worked so hard?
> Or just didn't run?
> Or chose a different sport?
> Or stopped at my first steps?
> That's too bad, because I was born to do this.[70]

The young Semenya then smiles, eyes closed with face raised to the sun, imagining the future, hearing the sports commentator and cheering crowds: "She does it again! Semenya takes the win!" The copy on the screen ends the advertisement: "When you're born to do it, just do it," with the trademark Nike swoosh.

Semenya narrates her own experiences and her defiance in this advertisement honoring her, but her voice is mediated through Nike's scripting and corporate decisions. While this representation was touching, it is not simply a film celebrating Semenya. It is an advertisement intended to increase Nike's sales with Semenya as one of its corporate representatives. Nike made $10 billion dollars in 2018 when this ad was released; it is neither a charity nor an activist organization. Nike is taking a calculated risk by foregrounding controversial politicized celebrities to boost the brand in its campaigns. Semenya's growing acceptance and strengthening voice are inseparable from a global shift in queer and trans (and perhaps intersex?) acceptance. Advertisements proclaiming Pride as a rainbow of queer positivity mask carefully calculated support from corporations, ranging from Pfizer to General Electric, that destroy communities and support homophobia, transphobia, and interphobia politically and financially.[71] Nike supports politically controversial athletes while producing its products in sweatshops. Facebook offers Pride flags as filters for social media postings while supporting white supremacist organizing. And, as explored in the next chapter, intersex people have been marginally included in these queer and gender-based politics when mentioned at all.[72]

But within the complex contexts of online activism, Semenya and her supporters continue to map new directions for social change. They challenge gender and undercut universalizations centered on the Global North. They generate new digital cultures and practices.[73] A new Twitter hashtag followed the Nike campaign featuring Semenya in 2018, complicating the idea that social media is simply revolutionary or counterrevolutionary. #JustDoItForCaster plays off the popular Nike slogan and has inspired tweets such as "We've always been a curiosity from our hair, skin color, body, culture and the way we are able to stand up no matter how many times they've tried to break us. From Sara Baartman, it bothers them that we are unique, special and yes different [*fist emoji*] we will still rise #JustDoItForCaster" (Mologadi [@Lebza_leo8] 2019). Activists are creating radical change, taking histories of African liberation, Pride, and social media limitations and possibilities into consideration simultaneously. On Instagram, Semenya reposted and reclaimed the muscular AP photograph of herself mentioned at the beginning of this chapter, this time with the caption "09 flex." Another post included an image of a rainbow fist raised in solidarity with the words of the Mozambican liberation movement that have resonated and been repeated for justice throughout Africa—"A luta Continua!"—the (complicated) struggle continues.

Not the End: White Athletes' Attacks and Semenya's Vindications

Chills my people, A man can change the rules but the very same man can not rule my life, What I'm saying is that I might have failed against them the truth is that I have won this battle long ago, Go back to my achievements then you will understand. Doors might be closed not locked. —CASTER SEMENYA (@caster800m), September 8, 2020

This chapter begins with a discussion of Semenya's vocal competitors and ends with her responses to and successes over them. Russian runner Mariya Savinova's flippant 2009 comment—"Just look at her!"—was but one indication of her rivalry with Semenya. Their competitions continued over the following years in high-profile races, and the most watched of these occurred during the 2012 Olympics. In the months leading up to the games, Semenya continued to weather accusations about her body, as commentators speculated, "If Semenya wins the gold, she is likely to be accused of having an unfair advantage. If she runs poorly, she is likely to be accused of sandbagging the race so as not to be accused of having an unfair advantage" (D. Epstein 2012). When Semenya earned silver to Savinova's gold in the 800 meter she was, indeed, subjected to suspicion that she had held back on her speed to purposely come in second, though she vehemently denied these accusations. But in 2017, it was revealed that fierce critic

Savinova actually held an unfair advantage, winning 2012 Olympic gold by taking hormones illegally to enhance her performance. Savinova was suspended from athletic competition for doping and forced to relinquish her gold medal win to Semenya.[74] As Savinova ridiculed Semenya's masculinity, she had been using oxandrolone, an anabolic steroid and synthetic androgen with masculinizing side effects (thought of as a synthetic form of testosterone). Savinova's public disdain for Semenya's body and suspicion about her gender had occurred as she secretly used a version of the substance she publicly claimed to abhor in Semenya.

When Semenya was retroactively granted the Olympic gold medal, and Savinova was disqualified, Semenya expressed humility and indifference.[75] White athletes have routinely lambasted Semenya for unproven advantage, even famously excluding her from an all-white athlete embrace on the track after her 2016 Olympic gold medal win. But Semenya did not even make a statement about her own belated vindication (Tshwaku 2017). On February 10, 2017, the day Semenya learned she was retroactively awarded 2012 Olympic gold, she posted a meme of boxer and Olympian Muhammad Ali on Instagram. Ali, widely recognized as an advocate for racial justice, was pictured with the quotation: "What you are thinking about, you are becoming." This subtle but pointed comment from the Olympic champion led one of Semenya's Instagram followers, nonny_gorgeous (Nonhlanhla Mngyni), to reply with a direct comment about Semenya's win and profile: "not Silver 12 please change your [profile] my lady it's OLYMPIC GOLD 12 [gold medal emoticons] Well deserved they tried to cheat you but Gold lifted you higher than the haters. . . . Our South African Pride." This comment ended with a rainbow of heart emoticons.

Another well-known athlete who has targeted Semenya and continues to make false claims about intersex in the Global South is British marathoner Paula Radcliffe. Radcliffe is known for her limited views of womanhood and her crusade to "safeguard women's sport," in her words, from brown and black women.[76] In an interview with BBC 5 Live in July 2016, Radcliffe articulated assumptions that have underpinned controversies about Semenya, fixating on her body and representing her winning as somehow unfair. Radcliffe made thinly veiled racist accusations of cheating, echoing decades of such indictments, including those from Prince de Mérode and Stéphane Bermon. Her discussion was also couched in disingenuous efforts to "save" women in the Global South: "I think what worries me is we know that there are certain communities where the condition of intersex, of hyperandrogenism, is more prevalent. We don't want to get into a situation where people are actively going to those communities to seek out girls who look like they're going to be able to go out and perform and to run fast and then take them away and train them. It becomes a manipulated situation where they are being manipulated and the ethics of fair sport and fair play are being manipulated" (Radcliffe 2016). Radcliffe parrots a now-familiar script. In this interview, she suggests that there are large groups of intersex people (whom she describes as hyperandrogenous) living in "certain communities" in the Global South.[77]

While Radcliffe does not indicate where her assumptions of disproportionate intersex frequency originate, she provides another link in the citational chain and reiterates the unsubstantiated opinions traced throughout this book. Radcliffe paternalistically claims to want to protect ignorant "girls" who would be "manipulated" into cheating. Her sensationalist narrative imagines intersex athletes, unaware of their supposed innate advantages, duped by nationalist trainers from the Global South. Radcliffe's fabricated fear provides a simplistic excuse for "saving" black and brown athletes. All the while, she endeavors to preserve what she labels "fair sport" to allow white athletes from the Global North to win more easily and with less competition.

Following Radcliffe's false warnings of cheating and abuse of disproportionate numbers of "girls" (i.e., intersex athletes), in 2016 thousands of South Africans rose to Semenya's defense and started a petition confronting Radcliffe's offensive comments ("Stop the Bullying of Caster Semenya," Petition on Amandla! Action for Mzanzi, 2016, https://awethu.amandla.mobi/petitions/stop-the-bullying-of-caster-semenya; Boykoff 2019). But Radcliffe's bullying continued. In 2019, she publicly condemned Semenya again, suggesting that allowing her to compete could be "the death of women's sport." Radcliffe's comments were met with a flurry of social media opposition in support of Semenya and other athletes. And, in a classic expression of white fragility, Radcliffe decried the opposition as "vicious" and "aggressive" (quoted in Morgan 2019). She positioned herself as a victim of those she labeled as "internet trolls" in a host of news interviews while continuing to proclaim her biased critiques. But Radcliffe herself continues to troll Semenya and to incite online debates. For instance, on June 3, 2019, she retweeted an article about Semenya with the assertion that those who support her discriminate against "99% of female athletes." Semenya's Twitter supporters refuse to tolerate Radcliffe's erroneous claims. Replies to a tweet by Radcliffe celebrating a victory of black UK runner Dina Asher Smith exemplify their ongoing critiques:

> Shocked to see you celebrate another black women. #CasterSemenya #HandsOffCasterSemenya [South African flag emoticon]. (Sigidi [@Mbali_Sigidi] 2019)

Will she have to get testosterone lowering injections? Like you did to Caster? I means she's a black woman too [*coffee emoticon*]. (StreamCaution [@joelkings80] 2019)

I invite you to South Africa to come celebrate with us #CasterSemenya win. #PaulaRadcliffe YOU WILL NEVER BE AS FAST AS #CasterSemenya. Not even in your next life. [*emoticons of dancers and the South African flag*] #JustDoItForCaster. (Miss_Barbara-B [@Eng_Precious] 2019)

Such tweets are not just offhanded responses but represent a shifting discourse about gender binarism and confrontation of Semenya's racist detractors.

In much the same way that white athletes' lies are meeting confrontation, the shoddy and racist science justifying gender regulations is also falling apart. In August 2021, just after the Tokyo summer Olympics, in which Semenya was prohibited from competing, the fundamental study that asserted that testosterone causes athletic success was "corrected" by the *British Journal of Sports Medicine*. Study authors Stéphane Bermon and Pierre-Yves Garnier admitted their work had been merely "exploratory" and that their data did not, in fact, allow them to "prove a causal inference" between testosterone and sporting performance (2021, e7).[78] But the damage had already been done, as the impact of this study following its 2017 publication cannot be overstated. As Laine Higgins explains, "In 2019, when she [Semenya] first challenged the IAAF rule in the Court of Arbitration of Sport, a three-judge panel cited the study from Bermon and Garnier in its 2–1 decision against Semenya. Specifically, the panel found that the 2017 study provided 'empirical data' that 'the physiological effects of increased testosterone levels translates, in a real-world competitive context, to a significant and often determinative performance advantage" (2021). Indeed, Bermon and Garnier's now discredited article was the *only* data and evidence provided to support the regulation of track events from the 400 meter to the one mile (Pielke, Tucker, and Boyer 2019).[79]

While some hoped this public correction would bring a change in gender regulations and a step forward for Semenya, the data in this study had actually been roundly invalidated years before (Pielke, Tucker, and Boyer 2019). The belated and suspect timing of the published correction six years later and mere days after the end of the Tokyo Olympics—the games ended on August 8, and the correction was published on August 17—was clearly and deliberately intended to exclude Semenya from competing. Global outrage followed. As Semenya's lawyer Greg Nott exclaimed, "The timing is shocking, reprehensible. Unfair, cynical, untoward . . . the consequences of not allowing her to run, and then post-Tokyo, to then say 'Oh, by the way, the evidence we relied upon was misleading'—by the director of World Athletics (Stéphane Bermon) is absolutely shocking" (quoted in Mohamed 2021). But, unsurprisingly, World Athletics downplayed the significance of the correction, and President Sebastian Coe said that the 2018 gender verification rules "are here to stay" (quoted in Mohamed 2021).

How long can regulations based on inaccurate claims and racist histories continue? As the bar on gender in sport keeps shifting, Semenya and her supporters keep taking notice and pushing back. Semenya responded to the most recent restriction from the IAAF/World Athletics that banned her from competition with a defiant statement about the pharmaceutical treatments and torment she has already endured:

> The IAAF used me in the past as a human guinea pig to experiment with how the medication they required me to take would affect my testosterone levels. Even though the hormonal drugs made me feel constantly sick, the IAAF now wants to enforce even stricter thresholds with unknown health consequences. I will not allow the IAAF to use me and my body again. But I am concerned that other female athletes will feel compelled to let the IAAF drug them and test the effectiveness and negative health effects of different hormonal drugs. This cannot be allowed to happen. (quoted in Said 2019)

Semenya rejects her medicalization and the conflation of her status as an athlete with that of unwilling patient, and she exposes the embodied and material consequences of intersex medicine. Her commitment to other athletes and to changing ideas about gender is integral to her motivation. Semenya persists in her fight for herself and her peers. As she has asserted, "It's like a war. You don't give up. You beat me today. I beat you tomorrow. But I am not doing this for me. I am a world champion. I have achieved everything I ever wanted. At the end of the day, I am doing this for those who can't fight for themselves" (quoted in Cherry 2019). In the reclamatory spaces carved out through social media, histories of intersex and flawed scientific claims are being exposed for the colonialism and racism that underpinned them all along. Semenya, her online supporters, and African intersex activists are forwarding new visions and envisioning alternate futures that form the subject of the next chapter.

5. Toward an "African Intersex Reference of Intelligence"
Directions in Intersex Organizing

We exist to amplify the voices of African Intersex people at the regional level. We offer ourselves as the African Intersex reference of intelligence for stakeholders and allies who are interested in strengthening the ongoing liberation work for intersex peoples' rights and autonomy. We affirm that intersex people are real, and we exist in all countries of Africa. As intersex people in Africa, we live in a society that perpetuates violence and killings of intersex people by cultural, religious, traditional and medical beliefs and practices. —African Intersex Movement, statement on July 3, 2019

● ● ●

African activists have confronted the visual exploitation and racist histories that have been integral to intersex science and medicine for decades. Intersex activism on the continent began in the late 1990s and initially relied on a few individuals who were open about their experiences. Ugandan Julius Kaggwa's frank autobiography (1997) and Sally Gross's early organizing were two of these crucial interventions. Today, intersex activists have harnessed the power of social media in all forms, including videos, to publicly challenge Africa's past and present. Their self-representation stands in stark contrast to the anonymity and medical objectification discussed in previous chapters. The final chapter of this book explores contemporary activists' priorities and strategies, deferring to their authority as an "African intersex reference of intelligence."[1]

South African activists argue that the widespread stigma around and suppression of intersex means that "the need for research is dire" (*National Dialogue* 2018, 27). This is the charge that motivated me to write this book. They are also clear in their instruction to "put people with intersex variations and intersex-led organisations front and centre when talking about issues related to intersex" (30). Their directives guide the three foci of this chapter. First, I highlight activists' analyses of ways of seeing: exposing invisibility, hypervisibility, and violent medical scrutiny. Second, I explore how activists confront standard medical protocols and publicly call for accountability and retribution. Finally, I articulate how activists collectively theorize new ways of thinking about gender and their demand for new policy and protocols.

Paradoxes of Invisibility and Hypervisibility

In 2009, Sally Gross, Liesl Theron, and I wrote together about a critical question: How has the public attention paid to Caster Semenya affected intersex South Africans? Chapter 3 explores Gross's early reflections on Semenya's treatment, and chapter 4 considers Semenya's own views and online campaigns supporting her. This chapter revisits our question by exploring the contemporary work of intersex activists based especially in South Africa. When global attention to Semenya's body began, Gross, Theron, and I were concerned with how both invisibility and hypervisibility were affecting intersex South Africans. Public visibility was a critical component in activist agendas at the time, as was preventing backlash and increased violence. Theron, founder of Gender DynamiX, the first organization on the African continent focused solely on trans and gender diverse communities, considered the widespread conversations that had been initiated, musing, "I think this was the first time that we as a country—every person on the streets—spoke about and grappled with gender" (Swarr, Gross, and Theron 2009, 660). But, as Gross also pointed out at the time, "In a curious way, the sudden visibility of intersex as an issue because of the Caster Semenya saga highlights the invisibility of the vast majority of intersexed South Africans in the past and their continued invisibility despite the media focus on the issue" (662).

In the ensuing decade, intersex activists in South Africa worked to increase awareness and challenge this invisibility. They collectively argue, "The Caster

Semenya story is but one moment in the ongoing political issues around intersexuality and race" and challenge the racialized history of gender testing in sport more broadly (*National Dialogue* 2018, 25). After a Swiss court upheld a 2020 ruling targeting Semenya and other intersex women in athletics, a joint activist statement proclaimed their condemnation:

> We condemn this ruling in the strongest possible terms as indecent, indefensible and inhumane. How anybody can rule that fairness in sport can be upheld under a system which unfairly targets black African women for their innate physiology quite simply beggars belief. Human diversity cannot simply be erased in order to make the sporting world fair, and such an endeavor as has targeted Semenya which does not also target athletes who happen to be taller, who happen to retain more oxygen in their blood, or who happen to have a certain shoe-size, reveals itself for what it is—a prejudicial decision that goes against the 2019 United Nations Human Rights Council (UNHRC) resolution on the Elimination of Discrimination Against Women and Girls in Sport. (Iranti and Intersex South Africa 2020)

Like Semenya, activists insist on the recognition that womanhood includes intersex women. In this same statement, Nthabiseng Mokoena argues that "it is unfortunate that the Federal Court Tribunal has chosen to uphold a policy that legitimises discrimination against women with diverse sex characteristics" (quoted in Iranti and Intersex South Africa 2020). Activists also consistently point out that intersex coexists with identifications as woman (or, increasingly, womxn), other genders, or no gender at all.

Several campaigns with a focus on normalizing intersex and increasing visibility have been spearheaded by Intersex South Africa (now abbreviated as ISSA), initially founded by Gross in 1999, and by Iranti, an organization that uses visual mediums to "destabilize numerous modes of discrimination based on gender, sexuality, and sexual orientation."[2] Many of their campaigns and posted videos combine education with personal stories. For example, in a YouTube video titled *Intersex Day of Solidarity with ISSA* (Iranti 2017), four self-identified intersex activists share their views and priorities for social change. Each narrator is identified by home province and provides accessible definitions in their own words. Babalwa Mtshawu explains that intersex goes beyond categorization: "Intersex is a general term that is given to human beings who do not fall into the gendered social categories that is male and female." Crystal Hendricks adds a fun twist: "Sometimes it's not a physical thing that you can see, which most people think that it is, but it's internally itself. So your chromosomes is not just the standard XY . . . *it's a combustion explosion of magical things*" (Iranti 2017).

Such campaigns on social media have significant effects.[3] Less than a month after *Intersex Day of Solidarity with* ISSA was posted on YouTube, a conference hosted by Iranti and ISSA featured South African deputy minister of justice and constitutional development John Jeffery as the keynote speaker. Jeffery specifically commented on the video in his remarks, acknowledging his prior ignorance and its impact on him. As reported by local mainstream media at the time, he went on to express strong support for intersex rights and concluded, "There's no doubt intersex people face appalling stigmatisation and discrimination as children and adults" (quoted in Green 2018).

The important role intersex visibility plays in shifting mindsets is appreciated and honored by contemporary activists. Many recall Gross's pioneering work in South Africa and regularly mention her organizing and its impact as well as their personal relationships with her as a mentor. In a collectively written report titled *National Dialogue on the Protection and Promotion of the Human Rights of Intersex People* (2018), activists celebrate Gross and countless unknown South Africans for "daring to be visible" and speaking out: "Almost four years after Sally's passing, we continue to hear intersex South Africans recount experiences of violations in all spheres of life; within their families, within rural and traditional settings, within medical settings, in schools and in prisons. We honour them as well, for daring to be visible in the face of pervasive ignorance, violence, discrimination and stigma. We honour them for telling and retelling their stories, for refusing to be silenced, for being prepared to stand up for the next generation of intersex children" (Lungile Maquba and Joshua Sehoole, quoted in *National Dialogue* 2018, 1).[4] Activists' respect is paired with multidimensional efforts to grow the movement and embrace visibility of their own design.[5] Following Gross's death, ISSA was initially relaunched under the financial and logistical auspices of Iranti, and intersex delegates "took charge of meetings and laid out clearly their own hopes and goals with optimism" (Botha 2016). As Mokoena stated at the time, "There's only a handful of us, but intersex activism has never been about the numbers. As a handful, or as one person, we are capable of achieving so much" (quoted in Botha 2016). Activists further challenge invisibility in campaigns comparing the commonality of intersex to more visible populations with genetic variations—such as redheads, albinos, and twins.[6] Their visually arresting and educational campaigns effectively raise awareness about intersex in South Africa.

Activists' interventions form the foundation of a theory about visibility in intersex medicine. South African activists identify two strategies that are integral to intersex medicine—visual objectification and concealment—as seemingly paradoxical practices that work together to harm intersex children. *Visual objectification* occurs in medicalized settings, including the demeaning clinical photography analyzed throughout this book, and has lifelong ramifications. Medical curiosity and scrutiny prevents intersex people from seeking medical care as they are "more likely to be subject to abuse due to the scarcity of knowledge, lack of doctors and medical hunger for 'cases'" (Husakouskaya 2013, 18). Intersex activists analyze the psychological, physical, and social distress caused by medical protocols in South Africa, pointing out that they have been recognized by several United Nations committees as "constituting a harmful practice, violence and torture or ill-treatment" (*National Dialogue* 2018, 16). Doctors falsely assert that patients will forget the voyeuristic medical exploitation they experience as children. But former patients unsettle this lie with their painful memories, demanding that intersex people be spared from experiencing this exploitation in the future.

The second element of an emerging theory of intersex visibility/invisibility critiques what activist Crystal Hendricks describes as *concealment*. Doctors conceal the truth that intersex bodies are normal and need no medical intervention, and they require secrecy of patients and their families as well. At a meeting of intersex activists in 2017, participants discussed the way they see this operating:

> Crystal Hendricks noted that [doctors] act from a "concealed-centred method of care." The concealed-care method of care is rooted in the notion that a child can be nurtured into a specific gender and that ambiguous genitalia must be surgically and medically fixed clearly as either male or female.[7] The concealed-care method is supported by various unethical medical behaviours including misrepresentation of the medical impact of atypical genitalia. This misrepresentation allows medical professionals to frame atypical genitalia/intersex characteristics as a medical problem and an abnormality requiring invasive genital mutilation rather than a natural variation/sex characteristic.
>
> The characterising of intersex traits as an "abnormality" and as disorders is problematic as it directly encourages, supports and results in intersex genital mutilation and prevents affirming access to healthcare. There needs to be a conceptual shift in how intersex variations are seen, named, discussed and framed, to more neutral medical terms that are neutral and descriptive rather than negative and implicitly directive. Crystal Hendricks noted that this entire medical approach is based on "normalisation" and isolation of intersex children, rather than a celebration of natural human diversity. Hendricks noted that growing up and having your body framed within a model of "abnormality" induces depression, shame and a sense of being a "liar" (*National Dialogue* 2018, 14).

This passage describes how concealment and pathologization work concurrently in intersex medicine. Hendricks also articulates the effects of the concealed-care model: creating confusion within families and encouraging patients to feel ashamed of their own bodies.

Activists detail severe consequences of this enforced secrecy and the violent practices that accompany intersex medicine: "Children with intersex traits are subjected to repeated genital traumas which are kept secret both within the family and in the culture surrounding it. They are frightened, shamed, misinformed, and injured. These children experience their treatment as a form of sexual abuse. This is not surprising, considering practices like regular vaginal dilation" (*National Dialogue* 2018, 19). Severe psychological effects obviously result from medical practices such as nude photography and genital trauma, and these effects are exacerbated by doctors' instructions that patients keep their experiences concealed. Intersex activists reject the euphemisms of medical jargon and label these practices as sexual abuse and mutilation. Major health consequences, both mental and physical, result from doctors' treatments. But intersex bodies are normal, and this argument is strong and clear as activists assert that their bodies do not need medical "corrections."

Reclaiming Intersex while Black Genderqueer + Feminist in South Africa, a powerful documentary focused on the experiences of Nthabiseng Mokoena and co-directed by Mokoena and Gabrielle Le Roux, confronts doctors' practices directly (Le Roux and Mokoena 2016). Mokoena, who identifies as a "black, intersex, genderqueer, feminist person," reverses objectifying medical gazes by putting doctors under scrutiny. Mokoena details their difficulty finding medical care and why their initial excitement about finding a doctor was quickly replaced with sadness:

> I get there, and the doctor, after I talked with him, he was like, "Oh, I'm so excited to meet a case like yours; I'm going to include this in my paper at the end of the year." And then bells rung at that point. At that point I just heard bells that this person is excited so that I can be part of his paper. Suddenly, I'm becoming his subject; I'm becoming a guinea pig.
>
> And so I was there in the consultation room, and he said, "Take off your clothes, be free," and I did as I was told. Then he left, and then after a while a doctor came and said, "Oh, I left my pen in here," then left; another one came and said, "Oh, I left my jacket in here," looked at me, and left; another one came, and it went on. And I realized what was happening at that moment: none of them had left anything in that office; that doctor went and told more doctors and they were coming in here to see the

"hermaphrodite," as it was written in my paper. After that, he came back with medical students, about five to seven medical students, and he was literally giving a lecture about intersex, about disorders of sexual development, that's what he said, actually. Right there, naked sitting on the bed. After that, I went home and I cried and I cried, going home to the North West.

He gave me an appointment, [but my home in] the North West . . . is far from Johannesburg. There are no taxis where I used to live. There was no way I could get to Johannesburg easily. But every Friday I would be sitting hitchhiking all the way to Johannesburg, come back, just so I could be treated as a guinea pig. Eventually, I just thought, "No, I can't do this." And I only did that when I met other intersex people. . . . You know, people had horrible stories.

At that point I realized that having escaped from the doctors' eyes, having escaped surgery as a child was by far the best thing that could have happened to me as an intersex person. . . . [Their stories] opened my eyes to see, number one, that I'm not the only one, there are thousands of us out there. And, number two, that the experiences are so similar, that the violations, the violence, the prejudice, the stigma, the stereotyping, is so similar it's scary. You realize how much of a system and a structure is actually formed against intersex bodies. (Le Roux and Mokoena 2016)

In this recollection, Mokoena rejects doctors' and students' scrutiny and poignantly describes their "escape from the doctors' eyes." They only consent to examination under great duress, as obligatory gatekeeping in exchange for their medical care, hitchhiking over one hundred miles between their home and Johannesburg/Soweto to be treated as a "case" and "guinea pig" for research.[8] Mokoena realizes the threat the doctor poses to their life and puts an end to these traumatic experiences following conversations with other intersex activists such as Gross (who was a close friend), theorizing their experiences as systemic and institutionalized violence.

Crystal Hendricks has also publicly shared her experiences of medical scrutiny and how they inform her thinking on intersex medicine. While going through puberty, she started seeing a doctor to determine the cause for her lack of menstrual periods. She recounts the procedures she endured; "At one stage I was lying in the hospital robe, naked and had a professor and student look over my body. That was pretty terrifying for a 15-year-old" (quoted in Akoob 2018). Echoing comments by so many other intersex South Africans, Hendricks explains that during this experience, she felt that "clearly I was a science project or an experiment for them" (quoted in Akoob 2008). Doctors then told her that she had underdeveloped ovaries that would need to be immediately removed. As she was prepared for surgery, she recalls, "I remember going in for surgery, doctor asked me, 'Can you please put your robe over your face?' I am 16, I was in grade 12 that year, so the doctor says, 'Put your robe over your face,' and that's what I did. After that few seconds, I heard camera sounds going off. I mean at 16, for me it's like there's really something wrong with you. They're calling 10 people into the room, now they're taking pictures of your body, you should never speak about this" (quoted in Iranti 2018). Hendricks's experiences of photography and surgery were not only harrowing but medically unnecessary. Several years later she learned that her family had been falsely told that she might have cancer and that her "emergency" surgery had actually removed her testes, not her ovaries. Journalist Amy Green explains, "But it was only at the age of 22, after she started working and had access to a medical aid[e]—and private doctors—that Hendricks was told the truth about her operation; and body" (2018).[9] The scrutiny and injustice she faced motivated her activism. As she explains, "There's people that will never come out because of the shame, and fortunately there are people like myself, activists, people in ISSA, Iranti, that are bringing light to this" (quoted in 2018).

Even self-directed visibility has its costs, and many intersex activists in the public eye have faced severe backlash. Mokoena publicly shared their experiences as a form of intersex advocacy and reflects on what followed:

The first time I appeared in a national magazine, I had to spend an entire month avoiding calls or being alone in public. The hate mail was tremendous and people were more curious about my genitals than the issues I was trying to raise. In time I became used to the public sneers and the curiosity over my gender. I soon realised the social stigma that surrounded being intersex, I knew the secrecy we were all raised under, but I did not expect that speaking out would involve isolation and literal threat to my life at times. Stories of intersex primary school children being undressed in front of their classmates by their teachers suddenly did not become shocking, they became a reality of being intersex and living in the townships.[10] For these reasons I decided to stay as an activist and know other activists such as Sally, if not for mentoring at least for support. (quoted in *National Dialogue* 2018, 15)

Mokoena vividly explains the costs of public disclosure, comparing the consequences of media visibility to the medical examinations they endured. For many activists, including Mokoena, the difficult choice of whether to be visible entails significant risk and sacrifice. But it is made easier through solidarity with other intersex activists and mentors.

Self-Directed Priorities: Challenging Medical Protocols and Racist Histories

TOWARD A NEW "REFERENCE OF INTELLIGENCE"

While much of this book focuses on South Africa, coalitional work among African intersex activists is strong and decolonizing in its approach and strategies. Ugandan feminist scholar and activist Sylvia Tamale reminds us that despite vast differences on the African continent, oppressive colonial strategies had similarities: "When the empire strikes the African 'Other,' it completely disregards the nuanced diversities" (2020, 11). Tamale continues by recommending activist strength in African unity, suggesting, "Africa's decolonial and decolonization struggles must also be solidified to act as one ecosystem" (11).[11] With similar objectives of African collectivity, beginning in 2017 and continuing to the present, activists representing organizations from seven African countries have worked under the auspices of the African Intersex Movement (AIM) to issue public statements with unified demands. They envision African intersex futures that include ending nonconsensual surgeries, providing training for health-care providers, and halting the significant traumatic events facing intersex people (Iranti 2018). These collaborations position activists as the critical authority—the "reference of intelligence"—for intersex liberation.

Taken together, statements collectively authored by AIM engage in dialogue with doctors and government officials and call out violence against and killings of intersex people. Activists' work is elaborated in contexts as varied as YouTube videos, feature films, Instagram posts, and television interviews, forming new activist strategies with global resonance. Perhaps the strongest push of these initiatives focuses on bodily violence, including the following aims:

- *To put an end to mutilating and 'normalising' practices* such as genital surgeries, psychological and other medical treatments through legislative and other means (such as education, policy, and treatment protocol change). Intersex people must be empowered to make their own decisions affecting their own bodily integrity, physical autonomy, and self-determination.
- *To put an end to non-consensual sterilisation of intersex people.*

- *To depathologise variations in sex characteristics* in medical practices, guidelines, protocols and classifications, such as the World Health Organization's International Classification of Diseases.
- *To ensure that intersex people have the right to full information* and access to their own medical records and history.
- In view of ensuring the bodily integrity and well-being of intersex people, *autonomous non-pathologising psycho-social and peer support be available to intersex people* throughout their life (as self-required), as well as to parents and/or care providers. (Iranti 2020a, emphasis added)

Activists' priorities challenge medical norms and protocols. Their policy recommendations are personalized through intersex activists' self-representations, especially on social media.

South African influencer and vlogger Babalwa Mtshawu has a strong presence on YouTube, where more than 150 video logs posted since 2016 document her views, travels, and relationships, including what she terms her "intersexperiences."[12] One of Mtshawu's (2017a) vlogs that received significant attention—titled "Intersex Struggles: I Do Not Love Doctors"—explores her experiences with South African physicians. Using a characteristic charm and disarming humor, Mtshawu shares her knowledge and critiques. This vlog intersperses Mtshawu's narrative with music and video clips, and even includes a skit of her acting out the part of her doctors in ways that are both revealing and compelling.

The video begins with Mtshawu speaking directly to the camera from what appears to be her dorm room.[13]

Guys, the first experience I ever had with a doctor—like, I wasn't a sick baby; I've never been a sick baby—but the first time I remember going to the doctor was when I was twelve years old. And I was going to have my gonadectomy, is that what they call it? Gonadectomy? I don't know; I'll write the name in English, not my mother tongue. But that was like the first time they were going to remove my testes. I was, like, around twelve years old. And I went to, like, this really fancy hospital, but it was an academic hospital. The doctor was creepy as hell, and he said:

[*Cut to Mtshawu dressed as her own doctor in scrubs with an official-looking nametag reading "Dr Babalwa." She puts on gloves and applies lubrication to them while preparing to conduct an internal exam and speaks directly to the camera*] "Can you please take off all your clothes? Lie on the bed, open up!"

[*Return to narrative*] Guys, ew! Like that was not enough, the following day I was busy sleeping because I'm not sick! Right? They are going to remove something in my body that is not bothering me at any point, so I'm not sick; I'm just wondering why are they doing this? Why am I here? Because my parents never really, like, communicated with me what the hell was going on. So the following day, because this is an academic hospital, the doctor walks in and he's with a bunch of students, and they start like taking the blankets off and they're talking amongst each other, and I don't know what's happening. It was the most frightening time of my life. I went to the operating room, they operated me, I got out, and now I was sick, I was in pain. So I never understood, what the hell? I went to the hospital not even sick; the next thing I came out and I'm sick now, and they're letting me go home? What kind of bullshit is that? Like what is that? So that was my first encounter with a doctor that made me, like, not like doctors to begin with. . . .

So my endocrinologist sends me to a gynecologist to actually do an ultrasound so that they can confirm that I really do not have the uteruses and those kind of stuff. So I go to this doctor—private hospital, my dear. I'm in the waiting room. I give the doctor the letter, because it is a referral, I give the doctor the letter; the doctor looks at the letter.

[*Cut to repeat scene of Mtshawu acting the part of her doctor*] "Can you please take off all your clothes? Lie on the bed, open up!"

[*Return to narrative*] I just met you! But still take off your clothes? [*laughing*] And I lied on the bed, and she did her thing. She reads the letter again. She does her thing. She looks on the screen. She reads the letter again. And then she's like, "Wait a minute." Goes out, comes back with another doctor, and they're saying something in Afrikaans. Goes out, comes back with two nurses; they're busy saying something in Afrikaans. And everyone is like, "Ah! Oh my god!" And they're looking at me, and they're like, "Oh my god!" They walk out; they come with two cleaners! Now this small little consultation room is becoming crowded. The next thing, there's like even a gardener, like, there with a lawnmower! [*Mimes mowing grass*] Like everyone is, like, so shocked this girl doesn't have a womb! Okay, I'm pushing it, but you get what I mean! This doctor went to call other people to come show them this miracle; it's not supposed to happen: girl without a uterus. And then she turns around, and she's like, "So how does it make you feel to be born without a womb? How do you feel?"

[*Cut to a music video clip with lyrics featuring US rappers Playboi Carti and UnoTheActivist. In the video, they crash a party of rich white guests, disrupting the party while rapping and sipping champagne. Music and lyrics:*] "What? What? You're not my ho! What? What? Get it through your head!"[14]

[*Return to Mtshawu's narrative, speaking briefly in Xhosa*] I hate psychologists, so I don't know, maybe she was just trying to practice her psychology 101 on me. I don't know. Doctors have to go through psychology. I don't know what they teach you in med school, but seriously that doctor was creepy. . . .

So, like, those are my experiences with doctors; like, I just don't like doctors for that reason. I really do not like doctors. And for the fact that I have to disclose, even if I have flu, then they ask, "So are you taking anything extra?" I'm like, "Oh yeah, I'm taking premarin." And they're like, "Oh you're so young!" Fuck! Anyway, I'm going to end this video. I just shared all my feeling about doctors. Thank you for tuning in. Subscribe. Like. Share this vlog. I love you! Come here, let's hug! [*moves to hug camera as the vlog ends*] (Mtshawu 2017a)

This vlog presents a brilliant critique of medical hegemony. It confronts discourse that is usually one sided and rests on patients' silent complicity by voicing Mtshawu's thoughts as a patient. Her use of video clips featuring artists like Playboi Carti and UnoTheActivist also implicitly critiques white doctors' racist assumptions and speaks to younger generations. Language throughout this vlog offers an embedded critique. Mtshawu discusses medical jargon while subtly critiquing it, speaking about her "gonadectomy" while noting her distance from the word, procedure, and the English language—"not my mother tongue." She describes how Afrikaans is spoken among doctors and staff in front of her to exclude her from conversations about her own body. When Mtshawu responds to these exclusions with Playboi Carti and UnoTheActivist's lyrics, she follows this with her own comment to the camera in Xhosa, which she describes in another vlog as her native tongue. Code switching is common in multilingual South Africa, and here she communicates directly to those who understand the exclusions of racist medicine.[15]

Mtshawu was featured as a social media influencer on *OkayAfrica*, a digital media platform with a large African and African diasporic following, and she explained the thinking behind this and other vlogs. She begins by reflecting, "I grew up thinking that my story was insignificant and that no one wanted to hear it" (quoted in Samanga 2019). But this feeling was displaced as the popularity of her YouTube channel content "landed her many gigs she never imagined she'd even be offered," including panel presentations and a viral BBC interview, earning her a "seat at the proverbial 'table' that Mtshawu has always wanted" but did not feel she deserved (Samanga 2019; Mtshawu and Hlope 2019).

Discussing how she began posting videos on YouTube, Mtshawu explains that when she was diagnosed as intersex at age twenty-five and began medical treatment, she initially lied to her friends and told them she had cancer. When she decided to come out to them, instead of approaching them individually, she took to YouTube out of convenience: "So I decided to shoot a video and put it online. Initially, I thought this video was just going to be for my friends because I just gave them the link. I was shocked when the initial video hit 20k views. That led to me releasing similar content, but because I didn't want it to be a very morbid channel, I tried to diversify the content and include new things like travelling, my career and that kind of stuff" (quoted in Samanga 2019). Mtshawu discusses the resulting visibility and challenges of these personal disclosures, including backlash and pressure from viewers to share about topics that were uncomfortable for her.[16] But when asked about fun moments she had in creating her content, Mtshawu reflects, "There's a video I did entitled 'The reason why I hate doctors.' I mean, that whole story-line is very sad, if you're presenting it in a sad way but for me it has always been funny. So, there are some videos that when you're thinking about them, they bring tears to your eyes, but the more you shoot the content, the funnier it can sometimes take" (quoted in Samanga 2019). This humor and her candid charm earned Mtshawu a large online following, with an important educational influence.

Activists confront the scrutiny and violence of intersex medicine with a wide range of strategies. A report titled *Intersex Genital Mutilations: Human Rights Violations of Children with Variations of Sex Anatomy* (Bauer and Truffer 2016) similarly analyzes objectifying intersex medicine but with a much more confrontational and litigious approach. Authors Markus Bauer and Daniela Truffer hold South African doctors and government officials accountable for practices they criticize as harmful, abusive, and torturous.[17] They expose sterilizing procedures, "feminizing" and "masculinizing" cosmetic genital surgeries, and forced examinations and photography. This report directly challenges medical protocols and even engages the citational chain of racist medical literature I have traced throughout this book by highlighting two prominent South African authors of medical literature.

First, the work of physician Rinus Wiersma (2001, 2011) is interrogated for promoting surgical and hormonal sterilization and genital "normalization." Wiersma figured prominently in the citational chain of published references I detail in chapter 2. Like so many others, he repeatedly makes the unsubstantiated claim that "a disproportionately high incidence of true hermaphroditism has been reported among the South African black people, the cause of which has not yet been elucidated" (2001, 397).[18] Activists point out that Wiersma recommends medically unnecessary "feminizing" and "masculinizing" cosmetic surgeries, including clitoridectomy and other forms of genitoplasty to "normalize" genitals.

The master's thesis by H. J. Grace (1970) that I interrogate in chapter 2—"Intersex in Four South African Racial Groups in Durban"—is also problematized in this report. Bauer and Truffer point out that "Repeated Forced Genital Exams and Photography are also common place in South Africa" (2016, 9), and their report includes six images (both medical photographs and test imaging) and captions from three of Grace's case studies. For these activists, such images exemplify the visual exploitation of South African intersex patients that must be challenged. They describe the images in Grace's work as "typical pictorial examples of forced medical display and genital photography of intersex humans from a 1970 Durban (Natal) zoology thesis" (2016, 9).[19] In this activist context, the images are framed to give readers a sense of the extreme violence of their capture. Rather than being gratuitous, the use of the photographs in this report pushes back against the euphemisms and glossing over of violence so common in medical journals.

MEDICAL TRADITIONS AND TRADITIONAL MEDICINE

African intersex activists are concerned with a range of harmful practices, arguing, "It is essential to urgently address intersex infanticide, child abandonment, familial stigma and other concerns in rural and traditional settings across the country" (*National Dialogue* 2018, 13). While they are working "to put an end to infanticide and killings of intersex people led by traditional and religious beliefs" (AIM 2019), research on how and why intersex infants are targeted is scant and largely informal.[20] Intersex infanticide is widely known anecdotally, but shame and fear of retribution make those who know about such practices reluctant to speak publicly.[21] South African activists demand that national studies of infants and children address infanticide, as "the absence of [research-based] figures at a state level perpetuates the silence around intersex existence" (*National Dialogue* 2018, 29).

The simultaneous visual objectification and concealment theorized by Hendricks and other activists again provides a framework for understanding the harm that intersex children face. Infants may be scrutinized as physically ambiguous, concealed from community view, or secretly killed as a result of judging gazes. Within communities, infanticide is sometimes committed by midwives and is framed as an "act of love," described as "saving the mother from too many questions from the community" (*National Dialogue* 2018, 13). Research by the organization LEGBO Northern Cape is cited by activists as the earliest and most extensive study of intersex infanticide to date.[22] Journalist Carl Collison (2018) shares part of an interview with activist Shane Griqua on this work:

> From 2008 to 2010, the organisation [LEGBO] conducted interviews with midwives and traditional birth attendants across the province: "We undertook the research after a resident in one of the villages told us that her mother, who was a midwife, had said that when she 'sees funny things' on a child, she would—and this sounds really cruel to say—but she would 'get rid of the child.' She felt it was her responsibility to do this because [these children] were a punishment from God." Of the 90 traditional birth attendants and midwives interviewed, 88 admitted to having done this. Griqua adds that, since this research was conducted, a lot has changed as a result of educational drives by nongovernmental organisations working at securing greater rights for intersex people. "But," he concedes, "the pace of this change is very slow."

These interviews suggest that midwives and traditional birth attendants are the eyes of the community who evaluate ambiguous genitals as "funny things" and believe they act as servants of God.[23] Research by LEGBO is consistent with other work that shows many condemn intersex infant births using spiritual judgments—in this case, a "punishment from God." Activist-based research by Tunchi Theriso (a self-chosen pseudonym) that began in 2015 found a similar spiritual focus. Theriso documents connections between intersex and witchcraft beliefs, shared anecdotally and in media accounts, in which infants are seen as curses or "bad omens" for families and communities. Theriso's research suggests that in some contexts, midwives may commit infanticide, telling mothers that their infants were stillborn and then using the infants' bodies for witchcraft and financial gain (Collison 2018).

Intersex infanticide can be connected to historical representations of intersex people as "monstrous." Poppy Ngubeni is a traditional healer and independent researcher who conducted research into infanticide in KwaZulu-Natal, Lesotho, Gauteng, Limpopo, and the Eastern Cape (Collison 2018) and who travels around South Africa to speak with Christian leaders and "abelaphi (diviners, healers and initiates) in an attempt to change their perceptions of intersex people, and intersex newborns in particular" (Collison 2022). Ngubeni explains, "When an intersex baby is born, it is viewed as a sign that the ancestors are angry about something" (quoted in Collison 2018). She recounts that in her interviews, traditional birth attendants claimed that "when the ancestors have spoken it would be suicide for the family not to heed that order. 'Who wants to keep a monster?' they would say" (quoted in Collison 2018). Ngubeni's specific terminology—recounting references to intersex infants as "monsters"—recalls the centuries-old colonial science of teratology addressed in prior chapters.[24]

Gross's final unpublished writings directly connected scientific theories of monstrosity and intersex to infanticide in South Africa. Hearing growing numbers of informal accounts of infanticide through her work with ISSA, Gross attempted to gain support from South African governmental and Catholic leaders on behalf of infants to no avail. Gross lamented, "The silence is telling. It has been abundantly clear that the general sense is that this is not a matter which [concerns] anyone" (2013).[25] She felt strongly that connections between religion and rigid gender binaries enable intersex infanticide to continue as an ignored and genocidal practice.

Intersex activists in South Africa seek to understand and prevent infanticide rather than simply to condemn those involved with it. They collectively suggest that analyzing secrecy, stigma, and heterosexism will prove integral to curbing the practice: "What these behaviours indicate is a profound degree of stigma and fear regarding the birth and meaning of intersex children for communities. For children that do survive, parents often experience deep shame, and it is common for them to not talk to their children about their intersex status. Parents also often question their child's sexuality and identity and, indeed, their own. This stigma and secrecy are self-perpetuating in that it is difficult for intersex individuals to come out and speak on their own behalf. this [is] particularly true for Black intersex people from rural communities" (*National Dialogue* 2018, 13). Violence targeting those deemed intersex and their families goes hand-in-hand with the degradation facilitated by allopathic medicine. Activists explain that in formal medical settings, parents experience almost no support or understandable medical information and are humiliated by demeaning medical attitudes. Unpacking these contexts of shame and judgment are integral to understanding and preventing infanticide.

In *Reclaiming Intersex while Black Genderqueer + Feminist in South Africa*, Mokoena explains that they see the invisibility of intersex as tied to an intentional erasure of those outside gender norms. As part of their activist work with Transgender and Intersex South Africa (TIA), Mokoena and other organizers regularly spoke to those in rural villages to debunk their views of intersex as a fearful curse. They found connections linking negative ideas about intersex with missionary histories and Christian enforcement of rigid gender binaries.[26] Mokoena grounds contemporary intersex rejection in colonial legacies: "The history of intersex people in South Africa [is] that we have been part of our communities, but at some point in our history there was a direct effort to erase us, there was a direct effort to normalize us, there was a direct effort to ensure that we fit typical definitions of what a man is, what a woman is, what a male is, what a female is" (Le Roux and Mokoena 2016). Because access to physicians is limited, and their authority is valued in rural areas, Mokoena suggests that doctors' pathologizing views of intersex are more readily accepted. Further, medical professionals in the public health system usually have limited knowledge of and experience working with intersex people. All these factors work together to facilitate stigma and harm and to exacerbate the medical exploitation of children and their families.[27]

While infanticide is often portrayed as happening only in rural communities, risky and often fatal allopathic medical procedures performed on intersex patients can constitute another kind of institutionally sanctioned infanticide. Born in 1987 in a small town in the North West province, Mokoena avoided life-threatening interventions as a child thanks to the amazing care of their mother, Kedibogetsi Mokoena.

> The story that I inherit from my mother is that when she gave birth to me, on that day, I was born at home. Lucky me, I was not born in the clinic; otherwise the story might have changed. So I was born at home, and when she gave birth, the midwives were a bit confused because I was very atypical. And the midwife said, "Okay, first thing you need to do is take the child to the clinic" after the home birth. So she waited a few days, went to the clinic, and the doctors said, "Intersex child." Of course they didn't use "intersex child"; I'm pretty sure they used some "disorder" language or condition language, and they said, "intersex child—you need to have surgery." And of course living in that poor environment and in this community where we didn't have access to good healthcare, the perception of the community is that if you go to hospital, you are basically going to die because healthcare was that bad. The people who went for surgeries probably never came back sometimes.
>
> So my mother was like, "No! You want my child to go for surgery? I've just had this child for a couple of days and already you want to kill this child!" And she said, "No!" Packed her bags, ran away with me, and we ran away to a very small little village . . . in the North West, and there are basically just five houses in that whole village. Five houses! And the road is far! So you can't escape; once you're there, you're there. It's a camp away from the world. And so I was raised, and I love that little place, because it's my getaway from the rest of the world. (Le Roux and Mokoena 2016)

Mokoena's story is unique, yet it also parallels narratives shared by other intersex South Africans who were able to refuse treatment. Both allopathic and traditional medical contexts are often places of harm and death for those who are intersex. Activists confront the silence and secrecy that have surrounded all forms of bodily harm and unsettle dualistic gender systems—with strong links to colonial histories—to challenge their violent proliferation.

CENTERING ACCOUNTABILITY AND RETRIBUTION

The priorities described here work in concert with a final demand from activists that I want to highlight: accountability for continuing practices that are discredited, harmful, and medically unnecessary. African activists are leading calls for acknowledgment of "suffering and injustice caused to intersex people" and recognition that "medicalization and stigmatisation of intersex people result in significant trauma and mental health concerns" (AIM 2019). South Africa has long been a forerunner in intersex rights and was also the first nation to highlight and recognize harm done to intersex people at the United Nations in 2016. Building on these milestones and their growing collective power, African intersex activists have organized against medical interventions they increasingly deem intersex genital mutilation (IGM).

In contemporary African contexts, IGM is used by activists as a way to describe "cosmetic surgeries performed on intersex infants/babies": "These surgeries are often coerced, uninformed and unnecessary aimed at altering the sexual and reproductive anatomy to suit social classifications of male and female. The surgeries are performed without the informed consent of the minor (and in some cases, without that of their parents). IGM surgeries are irreversible causing permanent infertility, permanent pain, incontinence, loss of sexual sensation, and lifelong mental suffering, including depression. IGM may include other harmful medical interventions/treatments which may not be considered necessary for 'normal' children without evidence of benefit for the child concern[ed] but justified by societal and/or religious standards" (*National Dialogue* 2018, 8). This language of IGM is possibly controversial but certainly deliberate in its connection to African practices referred to as female genital mutilation (FGM).[28] Comparisons between FGM and IGM have been forwarded by intersex activists since the 1990s, including through the highly influential (and now-defunct) Intersex Society of North America (ISNA).[29] Reflecting on efforts in the 1990s, ISNA founder Cheryl Chase explains that while African activists who opposed the practice labeled FGM were receptive to the comparison to intersex, feminists from the Global North routinely expressed that they were only interested in practices affecting "African girls." Their opposition also had a temporal component, as Chase puts it: "First-world feminist discourse locates clitoridectomy not only elsewhere but also 'elsewhen'" (2002, 143). Chase describes how these debates falsely situated all genital surgeries in the distant Global South (elsewhere) and the primordial past (elsewhen).[30]

South African intersex activists today are taking these conversations in new directions, merging their experiences of the damage of intersex medicine with deep analyses of African histories. They collectively argue, "In the Global North FGM is mostly frowned upon and considered a barbarous crime. It is often used as a marker of the progressive nature of Western nations versus their African, Asian and Arab counterparts" (*National Dialogue* 2018, 10). These organizers point out that "corrective" genital surgeries on infants diagnosed as intersex are treated as medical emergencies and sanctioned because they are undertaken by doctors in hospitals, while "traditional" procedures deemed FGM are largely banned.[31] Activists also extend comparisons to "male circumcision," generally viewed favorably and as completely different despite "significant overlap in practice, purpose and cultural meaning" (*National Dialogue* 2018, 10). These hypocrisies guide global practices and discussions of genitals.

While medicalized IGM is accepted and even celebrated, FGM continues to be judged and legislated as a regressive "primitive" practice. Mokoena critiques the racism of perceptions of FGM and simultaneous acceptance of IGM, pointing out, "There is a racial division on how we view them. . . . Female genital mutilation, we're like, this does not affect the white community, this happens in some village in Africa, so it must be wrong. [IGM] is close to home, it happens in every hospital, and because it happens in every hospital, it must be right. And that is the problem with the racial view of these two" (Le Roux and Mokoena 2016). Activists strategically compare FGM and IGM as similarly damaging and medically unnecessary, while retaining a strong critique of the politics of FGM in the Global North. They are demanding action in various fora and explicitly use the hashtags #EndIGM and #StopIGM as part of their actions.

In the quest for accountability, activists seek to hold the South African government responsible for its official knowledge of intersex harm, pointing to two decades of ongoing conversations between officials and activists. For instance, in 2004, the South African Human Rights Commission considered banning IGM but chose not to do so. As a result, surgeries have continued, and "most disturbing is that much of these practices take place at University clinics and state hospitals. In light of this, there is an argument to be made that not only does the South African state do nothing about IGM but directly funds its continuation" (*National Dialogue* 2018, 21).[32]

On Human Rights Day in March 2021, a day historically linked to the 1960 Sharpeville massacre and widely commemorated since the end of apartheid,

Iranti issued a press release with the title, "Human Rights Day Should Also Be for Intersex Children." It condemned the inaction by the government on behalf of intersex children, arguing that IGM "has continued as an acceptable practice unabated, violating intersex people's rights and inflicting lifelong damage," and enabled by state funding (Iranti 2021a). The press release strongly asserts that the South African Department of Health has a responsibility to ensure the health of all children, including intersex children. Iranti calls on the Department of Health: (1) to enact a moratorium on IGM, (2) to depathologize intersex in medicine by removing disorders of sex development from the international classification of diseases code, and (3) "to ensure access to health based on ethical medical standards and to ensure that intersex persons have full access to their medical history" (Iranti 2021a).

Taken together, these health-based demands draw on South African and international law as they call for historical correctives. Activists are concerned with both prevention of future harms and reparations for the violence they have endured. Some even call for "fair and adequate compensation" and "the means for full rehabilitation" from medical harms (Bauer and Truffer 2016, 18). The potential for legal action is under consideration by strategists who demand the end to what they refer to as archaic colonial medical protocols (AIM 2020). The deception and abuse publicly shared by intersex activists discussed throughout this chapter—ranging from withholding medical information to nonconsensual and experimental surgeries, exams, and photography—all demonstrate the ongoing violence of intersex medical treatment and mandate immediate action.

"We Are Just Waiting for South Africa to Come to the Party": African Intersex Futures

We have accepted ourselves and we are just waiting for South Africa to come to the party. —CRYSTAL HENDRICKS, in *National Dialogue on the Protection and Promotion of the Human Rights of Intersex People*

This is a new era for intersex activism in South Africa. Rather than relying on medical institutions as intermediaries to reach intersex patients and on mainstream media outlets to convey their messages, now intersex activists and influencers reach out directly. They come out publicly via social media, and wide online access through mobile phones allows instant connections. They continue to navigate the challenges of invisibility and hypervisibility while defining innovative agendas and strong demands. At an important conference held in Pretoria and online in November 2021—titled "SA-EU Dialogue on Policy Improvements for Transgender and Intersex Persons"—delegates repeatedly articulated their frustration with pity and empty words from the government. Intersex activists attending called for policy implementation, curricular development, and substantive changes to protect intersex children from harm. In 2000, Sally Gross told me that she was battening down for a long haul, as "seeds" that she had sown in founding Intersex South Africa needed to "germinate and grow" (2000). Growing seeds have been nurtured over the past two decades, and now activists are understandably growing impatient.

Activism is rife with challenges. Intersex organizers face tokenization and the marginalization of their priorities, and intersex organizing still receives scant funding. Activists call international human rights organizations and funders based in the Global North to action, warning that structural support is needed for substantial engagement. They mandate that "this should be done in a spirit of collaboration and no-one should instrumentalise intersex issues as a means for other ends" (AIM 2019). Funders need to deepen their commitment to and involvement in intersex organizations and "support them in the struggle for visibility, increase their capacity, the building of knowledge and the affirmation of their human rights" (AIM 2019).[33] Remedying neglect is a priority of South African intersex activists seeking to promote educational initiatives, confront abuses, and foster solidarity. Further, even in contexts that include intersex activists, "LGBTI or trans NGOs often perpetuate offensive behaviour such as expecting intersex people to prove they are intersex" (*National Dialogue* 2018, 29). Mokoena contends that intersex people can be particularly vulnerable to exploitation, and demanding bodily "proof" reinscribes intersex stigma and trauma (29).

South African activism has never been about single-issue politics, and Crystal Hendricks articulates this clearly, asserting that "intersex persons do not only lack access to appropriate and affirming health care, but also lack access to justice, education, social and employment services, and opportunities" (Iranti 2021a). The start of the COVID-19 pandemic in 2020 temporarily brought in-person activism to a halt as basic needs intensified.[34] An online community-led conversation in October 2020 focused on the impact of COVID-19 on intersex organizing in southern Africa. This conversation brought together activists from Namibia, Malawi, Zimbabwe, and South Africa, and it had even broader online reach as it was tweeted, live streamed, and recorded. Critical considerations in the discussion included how unemployment forced some intersex Africans to choose between gender-affirming healthcare and food, while financial losses obligated others to sell cell phones and lose touch with essential support systems. Early reporting also revealed that vaccines have been difficult to access. For instance, Ronnie Zuze of the Intersex Community of Zimbabwe (ICoZ) described how COVID-19 vaccination programs in Zimbabwe have discriminated against intersex people, as they faced rejections and accusations of using identity documents that did not belong to them (Matimaire 2021).[35] The effects of the pandemic on intersex Africans have already been notably dire.

Holistic efforts to ameliorate challenges faced by intersex Africans are supplemented by activists' efforts to change the way gender is understood. Despite the constraints the pandemic placed on organizing, South African activists' collaborative work with the Department of Home Affairs (DHA) has led to recent shifts with national and transnational significance. In December 2020, the DHA sought comment for a proposed policy change that would let identification applicants chose gender markers—male, female, or x—and would randomize South Africans' identity numbers (the seventh digit had long been gendered male/female). Early governmental documents described the x designator as a "third gender" option, but activists insisted on a more complex articulation of how gender works.[36] As discussed in the introduction, from the 1970s onward, anthropologists often referred to those outside the male/female binary in the Global South using the troubling language of "third gender." This usage reiterated the gender binary and homogenized anyone identifying outside it. Speaking on the proposed legislation, Sibusiso Kheswa asserts, "The notion of third gender should be discarded . . . we do not want a third gender—it implies those people are abnormal and different" (Nortier 2021). Jabulani Pereira discusses the important "huge shift" this represents for the government and further explicates concerns about "third gender" labeling for intersex South Africans:

> We believe there should be male, female, and "undetermined." Intersex is not a gender identity. And the government does not fully understand this in the policy document. So in relation to intersex persons . . . we believe that a third gender category is going to stigmatise and *add* stigma to people, which is highly problematic. We want parents to have the option of the category 'undetermined' because with intersex-born children, medical practitioners are the biggest violators [of their rights], often compelling parents to decide what gender they want an intersex-born child to be at the time of birth. (quoted in Collison 2021)

Coalitional activist goals are clear in Kheswa and Pereira's statements: "third gender" does not represent an accurate view of gender and could increase discrimination.[37]

What does it mean to broaden societal ideas about gender, allowing anyone to choose ungendered identity documents for any reason? The x designation was at first intended by the South African government as a way to accommodate nonbinary, transgender, and intersex people (Igual 2021), but a coalition of activists called for this option to be open to anyone without stigma or restriction. They wanted to avoid deferral to medical authority and to prevent violence against those who choose it, for any reason. Kellyn Botha (2021) pointed out that cisgender (or endosex) South Africans could choose the undetermined x designation as a way to limit gendered information stored online. Tebogo Makwati also enthusiastically welcomed the change as sending a strong message about the problems of gender binaries and the importance of alleviating pain inflicted on intersex South Africans. He explains, "These binaries have perpetuated violence in that it has classified how people must live. So I think this would give an opportunity to people to decide how they want to live. It will show people that you can be whoever you want to be" (quoted in Collison 2021).[38]

Intersex activists model new ways of understanding gender through their self-representation and statements. These are not abstract conversations but are deeply personal. In an article in the *Daily Maverick*, Dimakatso Sebidi emotionally reflects on the impact of doctors' ideologies and years of surgery on her life and body: "'I am angry at the doctors, I am angry at my parents for agreeing to take my penis,' [Sebidi] cries, tears streaming down her face. 'Let your child grow until they can make the decision. Until they say they want to keep them both or remove a penis or vagina. They have a right—don't take that right away from them.' Today she sees herself as neither male nor female. 'I am something completely different. I am me'" (Maguire 2019). The violent and lasting impact of medical interventions is undeniable. Sebedi demands her categorical recognition as "something completely different" and outside male/female binaries, challenging simplistic ideas of dualistic gender.

Mokoena similarly argues for rethinking gender, stating, "Intersex means being born with sex traits that do not fit the neat little boxes that doctors have created, that society has created. [It means] saying only people like this fall in this box, and only people like that fall in this box, and there are no overlaps, no grey areas, and there is nothing. There are just two separate neat little boxes. Which is a lie" (Le Roux and Mokoena 2016). The lies of gendered science that Mokoena exposes are falsehoods that violently force bodies into gender binaries. Norms of gender and genitals demand that "because you are disturbing these two neat boxes, something needs to be done to you. You need to be 'normalized.' And I don't know who gets to determine what normal is. In our cases, most of the time, doctors get to determine what normal is" (2016). By pointing toward the violence of "normalization," activists including Sebidi and Mokoena theorize a new reality outside gender.

Today's South African intersex activists refuse to accept dominant gender theories and lies and directly confront invisibility and exploitation. South Africans have long been leaders in both gender theorizing and intersex organizing, and contemporary strategists continue to envision and decolonize intersex. At the end of *Reclaiming Intersex while Black Genderqueer + Feminist in South Africa*, Mokoena leaves us with this final message, stated directly into the camera:

> To the doctor that told my mother that surgery is necessary when I was an infant, to the doctor that told my parents that I was a mistake at thirteen, to the doctor that told me I'm a hermaphrodite and he's excited that I'm part of his little "project" when I was in university—I really want to say that here I am right now, still no surgery, still not sick, still healthy, still bouncy, still happy, still awesome. That I am full, free; I'm happy and I am normal. That I did not need anyone to tell me that this is what normal is. I am who I am, and who I am is what is best for me. (Le Roux and Mokoena 2016)

The priorities and leadership of contemporary activists and an "African intersex reference of intelligence" should make the rest of the world take note.

Epilogue. Reframing Visions of South African Intersex

One of the most poignant recollections shared in this book is Keguro Macharia's encounter with a photo of a South African described as a "hermaphrodite" on the pages of G. P. Charlewood's *Bantu Gynaecology* (1956), a fundamental medical text that claimed African women's bodies as innately inferior and hermaphroditic. Texts like Charlewood's justified colonialism and apartheid, and the readership of such books went far beyond scientists and doctors. Macharia describes his disquieting experience: "The picture made me uncomfortable, made me wonder if it told a truth about sex, a truth about me, about my own gender non-normativity. It made me wonder about the truth of bantu sex, a truth that was medically certified" (2009). He felt strongly that "something traumatic happened to those who, like me, dared to look at it." This photographic attempt to enforce a medicalized and African "truth" of the body exemplifies how disproportionate intersex among black South Africans has been illustrated. False assertions gain authority through citational practices, and a primary objective of *Envisioning African Intersex* is to expose these visual and recitative strategies. Images like the one viewed by Macharia, the same photo torn from the pages of my borrowed copy of *Bantu Gynaecology*, circulate and build on each other to produce a fictitious reality of African intersex that is reconstituted over centuries in books, articles, films, and social media.

Exploitative photographs and their widespread replication have been traced throughout *Envisioning African Intersex*. They form essential parts of citational chains linking colonists' observations, popular representations, and medical literature from the 1600s to the present. Images are critical to this scientific scholarship; they are explicitly displayed and manipulated to create a skewed sense of reality and support for unsubstantiated data. In the citational chain analyzed in this book, photographs, X-rays, drawings, charts, and slides graphically depict intersex people from South Africa as abnormal and in need of "correction." But these images have not remained confined to the pages of medical journals, moving instead in and out of popular culture. They enter public consciousness through their use in films and television programs. They are ripped from books for individual consumption. They are manipulated and sent as postcards or published in textbooks. They circulate for decades in reference books. They continue to be reproduced in the media and online.

In this epilogue, I want to revisit the most prominent visual citational chain threaded throughout this book. Photographs first published in H. J. Grace's 1970 master's thesis include eighteen identifiable patients, all pictured nude. While I choose not to include these images here, they are what motivated me to complete this book. I was haunted by images of the faces of anonymous people in torment, photographs of body parts dissected and starkly displayed. People, labeled only with case numbers and in obvious pain, look at the camera with facial expressions that seem to indicate shame, sadness, and defiance. Close-up images show black patients' genitals manipulated by white hands. Dead infants' tiny bodies, which withstood invasive procedures to "discover" gender, are displayed as examples of intersex abnormality. To imagine the circumstances in which these photographs were taken is horrific, and to find them circulating in so many contexts today is unconscionable. But those seeking to reinforce unsubstantiated scientific truths have reprinted these images in countless academic and popular contexts.

In the decades since their first publication, activists' replication of these same photographs expose the images to a different kind of scrutiny and let them do a different kind of work. Whereas scholars and journalists capitalize on these photographs, activists reverse the camera's gaze to uncover the motives and practices of scientists and doctors who compelled their initial capture. Consider *The 3rd Sex* (van Huyssteen 2003) documentary discussed in chapter 3, for which activist Sally Gross was an active consultant. In the film footage, Grace's 1970 photographs and other images from medical journals of this era form a startling backdrop to narration that strongly critiques medical violence. These same images punctuate interviews with Gross and Nombulelo Soldaat about their exploitative experiences of intersex medicine.

Photographs of patients' full bodies standing against white backgrounds, and other similar images from South African medical literature, flash across the screen in succession. They constitute a macabre lineup, images of black intersex patients, positioned against stark walls with their eyes obscured as if awaiting execution. At first, the camera pans quickly over their bodies as multiple photographs are screened, but unlike in the pages of medical journals, the images are intentionally blurred by the camera's movement. The camera zooms in and begins to focus only on the faces of the patients, and the viewer is prevented from scrutinizing their bodies. Patients' faces are shown for a few long seconds each. They seem to stare back at the camera despite white boxes of feigned anonymity imposed over each eye, forcing the viewer to humanize those pictured as whole people instead of dismembered body parts. These remade images from the 1970s establish a parallel visual commentary to the film's intersex narrators' personal stories and theories. This link in the citational chain creates new South African intersex histories that expose the barbarism of medical protocols reflected in images broadcast on South African public television.

Grace's thesis photographs are also reprinted in a 2016 activist report, *Intersex Genital Mutilations: Human Rights Violations of Children with Variations of Sex Anatomy* (Bauer and Truffer 2016). As in *The 3rd Sex*, in the context of this report, photographs are not sensationalized. Instead, they are framed as evidence of the harms of medicine to support the report's demands for change and reparations. The activist authors describe Grace's use of photographs in his master's thesis as "typical pictorial examples of forced medical display and genital photography of intersex humans" (2016, 9). In chapter 5, I describe how the context of this policy-based initiative is not intended to be objectifying but instead serves as a link in the citational chain that exemplifies intersex decolonization. In this report, intersex activists challenge, in decisive and condemnatory terms, medical protocols and the traumatic damage physicians cause. They describe imaging and treatment of intersex patients as nonconsensual "mutilation" with physical and emotional effects, thus pushing back against euphemisms. These activists recast photographs from Grace's thesis to demand accountability and legal retribution.

When I first saw the images in Grace's work in 1997, I was most struck by their brutality. The lives of the patients in the photographs have occupied my mind for more than twenty years. I kept thinking about the conditions before and after the photos were captured as well as about the violence of their repeated use to reinforce racist notions of gender and genital "abnormality." Because I found the images unforgettably disturbing and was compelled by intersex activists' struggles against medical violence, I wanted to put doctors under the same kind of scrutiny as they had focused on patients in the photos. I also wanted to challenge the ways in which many in the Global North respond to discussions and representations of intersex in Africa with voyeuristic fascination. For these reasons, *Envisioning African Intersex* is a book centrally about images, especially medical photography; but I refuse to include the photographic images under consideration. We have all picked up a book and flipped to the pictures, not reading the text but scanning the images and stripping them of their meaning. Sharing these photos felt like it would constitute another act of violence, and I decided that it would be better for the reader to have to rely on my descriptions than to risk reinscription of centuries of objectifying pathologization.

I continue to be haunted by these images. Queer and feminist theorists, following Derrida (1994), describe "haunting" as a way that history registers as emotion in the present. Avery Gordon (2008, 8) explains it this way: "Being haunted draws us affectively, sometimes against our will and always a bit magically, into the structure of feeling of a reality we come to experience, not as cold knowledge, but as a transformative recognition." These images of intersex patients are haunting in this sense, affectively recalling living people and ghosts captured by doctors' cameras. Images intended to represent intersex in medical journals are framed in ways that are cold and impersonal. They are meant to be evidentiary and atemporal, timeless. My refusal to display these images creates another haunting absence but one that is intentional. These images are hauntings of the past that are also brought to the present. Activists' repurposing of these same photos to advocate for change connects medical histories and activist futures as the images take on new memorial and decolonial life.

The ways images with colonial and apartheid roots are reframed and replaced by new images proves integral to intersex decoloniality. Louis François Charon's 1814 cartoon of the scrutiny of Sara Baartman is an iconic image brought to the present by activists, as analyzed in chapter 4. In the 2016 meme by the anonymous radical collaborative group Xcollektiv—*The Unrelenting Gaze, 1789–2016*—Baartman is replaced with Caster Semenya, staring back at onlookers in annoyance and implicit critique. Colonial castings in museums and travel postcards that posit black bodies as innately abnormal are similarly displaced in public discourse by memes and videos from Intersex South Africa and Iranti that picture self-described intersex activists with their demands for equity. In these ways and more, self-determined images compel decolonial reconceptualizations of intersex.

On January 10, 2021, an article in the South African *Weekend Argus* newspaper about activists' efforts to add the x gender designator to government identification was accompanied by a color photograph of two parents and a small alert baby. The caption read, "Abongile Qwenye, father, and Ntabeleng Tsoanyane, mother, and their baby, Thateho, who was born intersex back in 2019. The Delft mother welcomes government's move to propose legislation that would recognise the registration of intersex children to spare future mothers the burden of assigning gender" (Lepule 2021). This was not an exceptional photograph, but its publication indicates an important recent shift in thinking about intersex and imaging in South Africa. It replaces secrecy and shame about intersex babies with Thateho's parents' pride and openness. The baby's mother explains her support of legislation to add an x option to government identification: "It was a confusing time for us when faced with decisions about how to raise her, things that would determine how she viewed herself later in life. But right now we are sort of in the middle, while I raise her as a female I try to buy her gender neutral clothes for her, her name is also neither a male or female name. How she identifies should be something she decides once old enough to do so" (quoted in Lepule 2021).

South Africa is not a panacea, and intersex people face violence daily, but images and stories like this indicate a new vision of intersex. African intersex activists are working to foreground their self-representations and reconceptualizing theories of gender to influence medical protocols and public policy. They will continue to demand new visualizations of intersex and unsettle the violence of gender binaries as they lead conversations for the future.

This project has spanned more than twenty years, and during that time I incurred more debts of gratitude than I can ever repay. Early ideas about the necessity of this book began in 1997, when I came across publications that claimed intersex was disproportionately common among black South Africans. The overt racism of this medical literature constantly nagged at me. A few years later, I met Sally Gross as she was starting Intersex South Africa, and a lifelong friendship began. It was too soon to write this book then, but when Sally passed away in 2014, I resolved to write about what I knew in her honor.

So I start with deep gratitude to Sally for her friendship and tireless commitment to intersex equity. I am grateful to Midi Achmat, Theresa Raizenberg, Conny Mchunu, Phumla Masuku, Barbara Rass, Dawie Nel, Juan Nel, and Flo Belvedere, who opened their homes and hearts to me for months and years on end (more times than I can count). I am thankful for my sweet connections with and learning from Prudence Mabele, Bass John Khumalo, Elaine Salo, Dereck Dryer, and Charl Marais, all of whom are no longer with us. I'm also grateful for lasting friendships with and lessons from Zanele Muholi, Zackie Achmat, Jack Lewis, Liesl Theron, Gabrielle Le Roux, Yvonne Shapiro, Deena Bosch, Funeka Soldaat, Simone Heradien, Nazmah Achmat, Phumi Mtetwa, Nazz Booysen, Tshidi Telekoa, Sophie Oldfield, Koni Benson, and Premesh Lalu.

I have had the opportunity to learn about intersex, trans, queer, and gender activism over many years and through many organizations; some are still operational and others, historical memories. I want to thank a few of them here: the AIDS Law Project; Association of Bisexuals, Gays, and Lesbians (ABIGALE); Behind the Mask; Forum for the Empowerment of Women; Free Gender; Out in Africa/Gay and Lesbian Film Festival–Cape Town; Gay and Lesbian Legal Advice Center (GLLAC); Gays and Lesbians of the Witwatersrand (GLOW); Gay and Lesbian Organization of Pretoria (GLOP)/OUT; Gender DynamiX; Hope and Unity Metropolitan Community Church (HUMCC); Idol Pictures; International Gay and Lesbian Association (ILGA)–Africa; National Coalition for Gay and Lesbian Equality/Equality Project; Sex Workers Education and Advocacy Taskforce (SWEAT); Sistahs Kopinang; Treatment Action Campaign (TAC); Triangle Project; Umanyano; and Uthingo.

Financial support for preliminary stages of this research came from the University of Minnesota Graduate School, the Center for Advanced Feminist Studies, the Anthropology Department, and the Schochet Center. The MacArthur Interdisciplinary Program on

Social Change, Sustainability, and Justice/Interdisciplinary Center for the Study of Global Change also supported this early work, and thanks go especially to Allen Isaacman, Bud Duvall, Karen Brown, and the late Jim Johnson for creating an incredible sense of home and intellectual community. I benefited from the mentorship of brilliant feminist thinkers at the University of Minnesota in the Department of Gender, Women and Sexuality Studies, and I especially want to thank Richa Nagar, Amy Kaminsky, Naomi Scheman, Helen Longino, Lisa Disch, and Jigna Desai. An invitation to present on this project at a symposium titled Reframing Mass Violence in Africa at the University of Minnesota, sponsored by the Interdisciplinary Center for the Study of Social Change, came at an opportune moment in 2018, and generous feedback from Richa Nagar and Sima Shakhsari, in particular, importantly advanced my thinking.

A Mellon Postdoctoral Fellowship from Barnard College also supported my early research and writing and provided a welcoming place to think and learn. I am especially appreciative of encouragement in these formative stages of work from Chi-ming Yang, Chris Cynn, Janet Jakobsen, Rebecca Jordan-Young, Elizabeth Bernstein, and Lila Abu-Lughod.

More recent support for my work on this book came from the University of Washington through a Royalty Research Fellowship as well as through a Society of Scholars Fellowship and a Second Book Fellowship from the Walter Chapin Simpson Center for the Humanities and the College of Arts and Sciences. I am grateful to Kathleen Woodward, Miriam Bartha, Annie Dwyer, Kalia Walker, and Rachel Arteaga with the Simpson Center. I am also grateful to Barbara Thompson, Katherine Stovel, Karen Luetjen, and Peter Wilsnack with the Royalty Research Fellowship.

Facilitating open access to this text online and purchasing hundreds of hard copies to distribute was essential to ensure its wide availability to African audiences, including intersex activists. This was made possible by the Royalty Research Fellowship; the Department of Gender, Women, and Sexuality Studies; the College of Arts and Sciences; and the Robert M. Eichler Gay and Lesbian Studies Endowed Library Fund, all at the University of Washington.

Gisela Fosado was an amazing editor, providing brilliant and kind encouragement throughout our work together. Her unwavering support was, frankly, the perfect catalyst for the completion of this book. Alejandra Mejía assisted with the logistics of completion, and I thank her for this help. Anonymous reviewers at Duke University Press were incredibly generous and helpful with their comments, and I am grateful for their assistance in developing my manuscript in such productive directions. Andrew Ascherl provided careful indexing, and Courtney Leigh Richardson, Lisl Hampton, Lisa Lawley, Emily Lawrence, James Moore, Christopher Robinson, and Chad Royal from Duke all kindly helped with various stages of the production process.

Smart specialists have always guided me in my scholarship and inquiries. University of Washington librarians Nicole Dettmar, Cass Hartnett, Theresa Mudrock, Sally Pine, and Elliott Stevens were helpful with integral pieces of this project. I am also grateful for archival assistance from the GALA Queer Archive at the University of the Witwatersrand in Johannesburg over many years, especially Linda Chernis, Anthony Manion, Sibusiso Kheswa, and Ruth Morgan, as well as from the Wellcome Collection in London and the Glasgow University Archive Services at the University of Glasgow in Scotland.

My home Department of Gender, Women and Sexuality Studies at the University of Washington has been a supportive refuge for seventeen years. I am one of the rare, lucky people with colleagues who are all brilliant, kind, and generous. Huge gratitude goes to Kemi Adeyemi, Angela Ginorio, Michelle Habell-Pallán, Judy Howard, Bettina Judd, Nancy Kenney, Cricket Keating, Priti Ramamurthy, Chandan Reddy, Luana Ross, and Shirley Yee for creating a sustaining space in Padelford. My thanks also go to Young Kim, Laura Marquez, Whitney Miller, and Catherine Richardson for their support of the department and to Sean Jarvis, Logan O'Laughlin, and Jey Saung for their research assistance. I appreciate my colleagues in African studies at the University of Washington for keeping me anchored, especially Catherine Cole, Ben Gardner, Danny Hoffman, Ron Krabill, Stephanie Smallwood, Maya Smith, Lynn Thomas, and Sarah Zimmerman.

The African Feminist Initiative was an invaluable source of community and inspiration, and I am especially grateful for Gabeba Baderoon and Alicia Decker's leadership. Much of this book was written during many visits to the Helen Riaboff Whiteley Center. I am appreciative of Arthur H. Whiteley and Helen Riaboff Whiteley for this incredible space and the staff at Friday Harbor Laboratories at the University of Washington who made my visits possible, especially Kathy Cowell and Stephanie Zamora. Meshell Sturgis's daily writing group through the UW Center for Communication, Difference, and Equity and graduate students in GWSS 593—Amalie Goul Dueholm, Erin Gilbert, Leah Rubinsky, Maxine Savage, Jingsi Shen, Ananya Sikand, Meshell Sturgis, Kelia Taylor, and Paulette Thompson—were thoughtfully brilliant as I was pushing to finish this book. My thanks also go to Hil Malatino, Shireen Hassim, Premesh Lalu, Sylvia Tamale, Rebecca Jordan-Young, David Rubin, Michelle Wolff, Ariana Ochoa Camacho, Adair Rounthwaite, Lauren Mark, Catherine Burns, Pamela Scully, and Sean Saifa Wall for their wisdom.

This book would not exist without the support of Sasha Su-Ling Welland, who was a thoughtful and always smart interlocutor over many years of weekly meetings. I have immense gratitude for our endless cups of coffee and then Zoom connections, which kept me moving forward through the most difficult times. I am indebted to Sam Bullington, who supported me as this book began in 1997 and is still doing the same at its completion. His lifelong comradery, memory, and calm presence were a touchstone during our times living in South Africa and far beyond. He has had immeasurable impact on me and on this project. There are a few other people who are also, as Toni Morrison put it, friends of my mind and who make the world and work more bearable. I'm grateful to Joel Wainwright, Chi-ming Yang, Lynn Thomas, and Katrina Karkazis for their help and encouragement on this project.

My family has always supported me. Barbara Harvey inquired about my progress every day and listened patiently to my detailed chattering. Dan Harvey taught me how to write and, along with my beloved Jessica Ellinger, endured endless grammatical questions and nerdy jokes. I thank my Swarr family—Fred, Val, Gabe, Karla, Zach, and Laura— for keeping me grounded, and Jennifer Muchow for kind encouragement. Tori Stevens played the Rocky theme when I was faltering, left encouraging notes and cute photos on my desk, and always said the right thing when I doubted everything. Her unwavering love and belief in me made this book a reality.

The completion of this book was heavily affected by the pandemic. In 2019, I received a Royalty Research Fellowship to spend six months in South Africa connecting with intersex activists. Lockdowns meant that this trip was repeatedly postponed and eventually cancelled. I was able to connect with some folks over social media and email and to participate in an important conference via Zoom, but this was a far cry from being back in South Africa in person. Nevertheless, I am grateful to those activists who corresponded with me about this project over the past few years, including Babalwa Mtshawu, Crystal Hendricks, Jabulani Chen Pereira, Zanele Muholi, Liesl Theron, and Gabrielle Le Roux. Writing this book was a lesson in humility and patience. The manuscript is limited by both my own faults and those of circumstance, and all errors are my own.

All author royalties from *Envisioning African Intersex* will be donated to Intersex South Africa in honor of Sally Gross and in anticipation of work by activists that will shape our collective future. The entire book is also available in a free electronic edition to allow for the fullest access possible. At the end of her life, Sally wrote about the importance of a support system for intersex activists. Envisioning such a project, she said, "This longer-term project would be unlikely to benefit me personally: it would be a matter of legacy and a project and resource for all of us." I hope that this book can contribute to Sally's activist visions and her legacy in some small way.

APPENDIX 1

Compilation of Works by and Featuring Sally Gross

WORKS AUTHORED BY GROSS

Gross, Sally. 1997. Personal communications and notes, beginning in 1997. Sally Gross Collection, GALA Queer Archive at the University of the Witwatersrand, Johannesburg, South Africa. https://gala.co.za/.

Gross, Sally. 1999. "Intersexuality and Scripture." *Theology and Sexuality: The Journal of the Institute for the Study of Christianity and Sexuality* 6 (11): 65–74.

Gross, Sally. 2009a. "Intersex and the Law." *Mail and Guardian* (Johannesburg), September 19. https://mg.co.za/article/2009-09-19-intersex-and-the-law.

Gross, Sally. 2009b. "Life in the Shadow of Gender." *Witness* (Pietermaritzburg), August 29.

Gross, Sally. 2009c. "Response on the Mistreatment of Caster Semenya." *Intersex Initiative*. Accessed June 26, 2018. http://www.intersexinitiative.org/media/castersemenya.html.

Gross, Sally. 2009d. "Sex Typing Is Fuzzy Science." *Times* (Johannesburg), August 26.

Gross, Sally. 2009e. "Updated Feature Article" [Re: Stephen Coan's "The Journey from Selwyn to Sally," published in 2000]. *Witness* (Pietermaritzburg). Sally Gross Collection, GALA at the University of the Witwatersrand, Johannesburg.

Gross, Sally. 2011. "The Chronicle of an Intersexed Activist's Journey." In *African Sexualities: A Reader*, edited by Sylvia Tamale, 235–37. Cape Town: Pambazuka Press.

Gross, Sally. 2013. "Not in God's Image: Intersex, Social Death, and Infanticide." Paper presented via Skype at the Intersex, Theology and the Bible conference, University of Manchester, March 12.

Swarr, Amanda Lock, with Sally Gross and Liesl Theron. 2009. "South African Intersex Activism: Caster Semenya's Impact and Import." *Feminist Studies* 35 (3): 657–62.

INTERVIEWS WITH AND FILMS FEATURING GROSS

Beaver, Trish. 2012. "The In-Betweeners." *Witness* (Pietermaritzburg), February 11. https://www.news24.com/witness/archive/the-in-betweeners-20150430.

Brömdal, Annette. 2008. *Intersex: A Challenge for Human Rights and Citizenship Rights*. Saarbrücken, Germany: VDM Verlag Dr. Müller.

Coan, Stephen. 2000. "The Journey from Selwyn to Sally." *Natal Witness*, February 21.

Gross, Sally. 2013. *Sally Gross, Founder and Director of Intersex South Africa*. It Gets Better South Africa, video, 3:03, April 3. https://www.youtube.com/watch?v =Xe8ngRLiUH0.

[Gross, Sally, and Aaron Nicodemus]. 1999. "Lifting the Veil on Intersexuality." *Mail and Guardian* (Johannesburg), August 13. https://mg.co.za/article/1999–08–13-lifting-the -veil-on-intersexuality.

Lahood, Grant, dir. 2012. *Intersexion*. San Francisco: Frameline.

van Huyssteen, Wessel, dir. 2003. *The 3rd Sex*. Johannesburg: Tin Rage Productions for the South African Broadcasting Company (SABC3).

Afrika, Azania (@SAYoungLion). April 26, 2018, 3:57 a.m. https://twitter.com
/SAYoungLion/status/989458454589352000.

Awu, Mel (@MelAwu). April 26, 2018, 10:03 p.m. https://twitter.com/MelAwu/status
/989731704427266049.

Beningfield, Perry (@beningfield). April 28, 2018, 10:43 p.m. https://twitter.com
/beningfield/status/990466637072609280.

Chuene, Rami (@ramichuene). May 2, 2019, 3:54 a.m. https://twitter.com/ramichuene
/status/1123903602324647936.

DASH, Daniellé (@DanielleDASH). May 3, 2019, 2:08 a.m. https://twitter.com
/DanielleDASH/status/1124239274998685698.

Du Plessis, Anzet (@Zetsaid). April 26, 2018, 8:40 p.m. https://twitter.com/Zetsaid
/status/989710900771938305.

Eunice (@Eunice_Kuhle). April 29, 2018, 11:55 a.m. https://twitter.com/_Eunice_Kuhle
/status/990665841577472005.

Gudani, Masbe (@MasbeGudani). April 26, 2018, 10:27 a.m. https://twitter.com
/MasbeGudani/status/989556628881072128.

King Sbu (@SbuIsKing). April 25, 2018, 11:38 p.m. https://twitter.com/SbuIsKing/status
/989393238741176320.

Mafu, Sibongile (@sboshmafu). August 13, 2018, 1:37 a.m. https://twitter.com/sboshmafu
/status/764380224138141696.

Malume (@bozzie_t). April 27, 2018, 2:31 p.m. https://twitter.com/motaut/status
/989980328638009344.

Miss_Barbara-B (@Eng_Precious). May 3, 2019, 1:59 p.m. https://twitter.com/Eng
_Precious/status/1124418147157594112.

Mokgobedi, Onicca (@tp1_moloi). April 27, 2018, 7:44 a.m. https://twitter.com/tp1
_moloi/status/989877979844173825.

Mologadi, Ramaesela (@Lebza_leo08). May 2, 2019, 1:43 a.m. https://twitter.com/Lebza
_leo08/status/1123870519969894400.

Motsepe, Andi (@AndiMotsepe). September 9, 2020, 1:49 a.m. https://twitter.com
/AndiswaMadikazi/status/1303616474322526209.

Ntuli, Lynette (@MsNtuli). April 26, 2018, 3:07 p.m. https://twitter.com/MsNtuli/status
/989627153900822528.

Ona (@kagisolatane). April 26, 2018, 6:57 p.m. https://twitter.com/kagisolatane/status/989685007076782080.

Phelani, Mfana Koko ZA (@PerkinPangolin). April 26, 2018, 1:21 a.m. https://twitter.com/PerkinPangolin/status/989419088295456768.

Semenya, Caster (@caster800m). April 26, 2018, 2:35 a.m. https://twitter.com/caster800m/status/989407535856832512.

Semenya, Caster (@caster800m). September 8, 2020, 1:21 p.m. https://twitter.com/caster800m/status/1303428263663079424.

Shangase, Nokuphila (@NokuPh). May 2, 2019, 12:37 a.m. https://twitter.com/NokuPhila_Live/status/1123854045133856768.

Sigidi, Mbali (@MBali_N). May 4, 2019, 1:19 a.m. https://twitter.com/Mbali_N/status/1124589409742016512.

StreamCaution (@joelkings80). May 4, 2019, 3:27 a.m. https://twitter.com/joelkings80/status/1124621624471429120.

TaMphanyaTeam (@Tamphanyos3). April 26, 2018, 10:51 p.m. https://twitter.com/Tamphanyos3/status/989743776200511490.

African Intersex Movement Priorities (2017, 2019, 2020)

Aims of the African Intersex Movement, the critical "reference of intelligence" for stake-holders and allies:

- To put an end to infanticide and killings of intersex people led by traditional and religious beliefs.
- To put an end to mutilating and 'normalising' practices such as genital surgeries, psychological and other medical treatments through legislative and other means (such as education, policy and treatment protocol change). Intersex people must be empowered to make their own decisions affecting their own bodily integrity, physical autonomy and self-determination.
- To include intersex education in antenatal counselling and support.
- To put an end to non-consensual sterilisation of intersex people.
- To depathologise variations in sex characteristics in medical practices, guide-lines, protocols and classifications, such as the World Health Organization's International Classification of Diseases.
- To ensure that sex or gender classifications are amendable through a simple ad-ministrative procedure at the request of the individuals concerned. All adults and capable minors should be able to choose between female (F), male (M), intersex or multiple options. In the future, sex or gender should not be a category on birth certificates or identification documents for anybody.
- To raise awareness around intersex issues and the rights of intersex people in communities and society at large.
- To create and facilitate supportive, safe and celebratory environments for intersex people, their families and surroundings.
- To ensure that intersex people have the right to full information and access to their own medical records and history.
- To ensure that all professionals and healthcare providers that have a specific role to play in intersex people's well-being are adequately trained to provide quality services.
- To acknowledge the suffering and injustice caused to intersex people.
- To build intersex anti-discrimination legislation in addition to other grounds, and to ensure protection against intersectional discrimination.

- To ensure the provision of all human rights and citizenship rights to intersex people, including the right to marry and form a family.
- To ensure that intersex people are able to participate in competitive sport, at all levels, in accordance with their legal sex. Intersex athletes who have been humiliated or stripped of their titles should receive reparation and reinstatement.
- To recognise that medicalization and stigmatisation of intersex people result in significant trauma and mental health concerns.
- In view of ensuring the bodily integrity and well-being of intersex people, autonomous non-pathologising psycho-social and peer support be available to intersex people throughout their life (as self-required), as well as to parents and/ or care providers.

INTRODUCTION

1   Most contemporary published sources cite Richard Goldschmidt (1917) as the earliest author to deploy the term *intersexual*, but dozens of citations throughout the
nineteenth century use this language as a way to describe bodies, sexual attraction,
communication styles, and even marriage arrangements. In 1866, the *Oxford English
Dictionary* first defined *intersexual* as "existing between sexes, pertaining to both
sexes." German geneticist and biologist Goldschmidt then used the word *intersex* to
refer to sex determination and a continuum of gender in moths in a precursor to its
accepted uses today (Stern 1967). Even when the word gained widespread acceptance in the 1950s, its meanings continued to differ over geographic and temporal
contexts.

2   I rely on Judith Butler's conception of "citationality" (via Derrida and Lacan) in
this formulation. In her discussion of gender and performativity, she explains cited
reiterated norms as those that "precede, constrain, and exceed the performer" (1993,
234). I expand on the meaning and power of citationality in the chapters to come,
especially in chapter 2.

3   I use the phrase "always already," following conventions in critical theory and
coined by Martin Heidegger, to refer to assumed actions without definable begin-
nings. It describes what is "always" present and "already" preexisting in common
thought. This concept works in concert with the quotidian to explain black intersex
frequency, especially in the Global South, as seemingly unremarkable because it
forms part of daily life.

4   I appreciate Iain Morland's explanation of these diagnostic processes: "Intersex is
often popularly conflated with ambiguous genitalia—external sexual anatomy that
cannot be easily described as entirely female or male, such as a larger-than-typical
clitoris. However, for clinicians, an intersex diagnosis can refer also to attributes that
are not apparent on the body's surface, including xxy sex chromosome or indifference to the hormones that produce effects connotative of masculinity" (2014, 111).

5   Amadiume's influence is immense and recently inspired a thirty-year retrospec-
tive in the *Journal of Contemporary African Studies* (Magadla, Magoqwana, and
Motsemme 2021). In this special issue, Zethu Matebeni (2021) smartly articulates

the dominance of colonial understandings of gender and their implications for present-day considerations.

6 Oyěwùmí's work has been critiqued as imagining an ungendered precolonial community without adequate empirical data (Mama 2001) or as giving too much agency to Euro-American colonizers (Thomas 2007). Nevertheless, the bones of her intervention have inspired related research for decades.

7 I agree with Desiree Lewis and Gabeba Baderoon's arguments about the importance of foregrounding African feminisms and "feminist knowledge produced on the continent *in conversation with, in response to, and as part of* a broader conceptuali-sation of black feminism than what is commonly known" and follow their directive here (2021, 4).

8 Decolonial, postcolonial, and anticolonial feminisms emerge from multiple loca-tions and periods but commonly critique the ubiquity of raced and colonial histo-ries and amplify the political importance of challenging their legacies (Asher and Ramamurthy 2020).

9 Desiree Lewis and Gabeba Baderoon point out that the recent revival of interest in African feminism in South Africa today has been a response to widespread calls for decolonization and the importance of feminisms to these efforts (2021, 6).

10 I am drawing on Olajumoke Yacob-Haliso's presentation, "Decolonisation and Disputations in African Women's Studies," for the Centre for Social Change at the University of Johannesburg, where she shared ideas from her then-forthcoming vol-ume, edited with Toyin Falola, *The Palgrave Handbook of African Women's Studies* (Yacob-Haliso and Falola 2021).

11 Eve Tuck and K. Wayne Yang's discussion of the appropriation of decolonialization —and their pointed assertion of what it is not—is relevant here; "It is not convert-ing Indigenous politics to a Western doctrine of liberation; is it not a philanthropic process of 'helping' the at-risk and alleviating suffering; it is not a generic term for struggle against oppressive conditions and outcomes" (2012, 21).

12 I especially appreciate P. J. DiPietro and colleagues' detailed analysis of this ele-ment of Lugones's thinking, borne of the authors' close collaborations with her: "For Lugones, gender does not signify the binary categories of either male or female, or even a spectrum of genders between these poles, but a system of relations with light and dark sides. The light side of the colonial/modern gender system . . . is based on the ideas of biological dimorphism and heterosexuality between men and women, opposing an ideal of the weak, passive, domestically bound, and sexually pure woman to that of a strong, active, self- governing, and sexually aggressive man. The light side is hegemonic in that it establishes the modern meanings of 'woman' and 'man,' and thus of 'human'—those who are civilized and evolved enough to warrant the labels 'woman' and 'man.' By contrast, the dark side of the colonial/modern gender system does not organize gender in these terms; colonized/nonwhite females were 'under-stood as animals in the deep sense of "without gender," sexually marked as female, but without the characteristics of femininity' [Lugones 2007, 202–3]. . . . Most important, the light side of the colonial/modern gender system is maintained by perpetuating the dark side: the more people of color are dehumanized, the more womanly and manly white bourgeois people become" (DiPietro, McWeeny, and Roshanrava 2019, 15).

13 At the end of this chapter I discuss my reasoning for capitalizing *Black* when referring to those in the United States out of respect for politics in this context while also
following many South African scholars' decisions not to capitalize *black* as a refusal
of lexicons imposed by those in the Global North.

14 The seven countries represented are Burundi, Kenya, Lesotho, Namibia, Tanzania,
Uganda, and Zimbabwe.

15 National and regional distinctions have been artificially imposed, and feminists including Yacob-Haliso (2021) argue that collective African protest is itself
decolonization.

16 Important discussions on this subject include Aizura (2018), Gill-Peterson (2018a),
and Driskill (2016), just to mention a few; see also Wolff, Rubin, and Swarr (2022).

17 Joseli Maria Silva and Marcio Jose Ornat articulate a trans decolonialist approach as
a "strategy with which to overcome the notion of the primacy of scientific knowledge over those who suffer the effects of epistemic violence" (2016, 220).

18 The other pioneering intersex activist of whom I am aware is Julius Kaggwa from
Uganda, who wrote an amazing autobiography presciently published in 1997.

19 Cary Gabriel Costello points out the eugenic components of preventing gender "abnormalities," including the warning on the label of Propecia that cautions, "Women
who are pregnant must not use PROPECIA and should not handle crushed or
broken PROPECIA tablets because the active ingredient may cause abnormalities of
a male baby's sex organs." As Costello goes on to articulate, "intermediate genitalia
are framed as abnormal and as triggering a medical emergency" (2016, 86). I was
recently prescribed a medication with finasteride in it, and a pharmacist personally
called me to issue a required extra warning about possible "abnormalities to male
genitals" that could occur during my pregnancy (though I am physically unable to
become pregnant). Controversies about this drug continue to the present. Merck is
currently being sued in a class action suit brought by men in the Global North who
took finasteride and faced side effects of post-finasteride syndrome, ranging from
impotence to suicide. Further, illegal use of finasteride to mask steroid abuse has led
to athletes being banned from global athletic competitions.

20 For more on the Lamprey grid and its development and use as a tool of scientific
racism, see Landau (2002) and Pinney (2011).

21 Science Channel (@ScienceChannel), Twitter, September 13, 2016, 10:00 p.m.,
https://twitter.com/ScienceChannel/status/775891976768086018.

22 I explore this film's comparative medical claims and discussions of black intersex in
South Africa at length in chapter 2.

23 Sambia is Herdt's pseudonym for the region under his consideration.

24 Interestingly, years after Herdt and Davidson's research began, they suggested that
Imperato-McGinley conduct research in Papua New Guinea herself (e.g., Imperato-
McGinley et al. 1991), and Herdt and Stoller also reference her work collectively
(e.g., 1985), further indicating interdisciplinary and transnational collusions.

25 Herdt and Stoller published their own transcription of their conversation and
inserted their later thoughts in brackets.

26 In the late 1990s and early 2000s, the questionable ethics of Herdt's work more
broadly came to the fore when representatives of the Sambia took court action

and forced him to face public scrutiny, as reported in US-based publications such as *Anthropology Today* and *Anthropology News*. They contested the ethics of his work, lack of compensation, and failure to share his publications in public library repositories in Papua New Guinea. For discussion of this court action and public statements by Herdt and his accusers, see "Media" (1998); Dariawo et al. (1999); Herdt (1999); *Anthropology Today* (2000); see also Eckert (2017).

27 Gronemann's publication apparently includes an unclothed picture of Sakulambei with his eyes blacked out, purportedly for anonymity (Eckert 2017, 129–30); I analyze similar photographs and conventions of photographic dehumanization in chapter 2.

28 For instance, Foucault's ([1963] 1994) analysis of the dominance of the clinical gaze troubles gendered categorical violence and surveillance, disrupting ideas considered diagnostic and definitive.

29 Authors including Donna Haraway (1989) and Paul Landau (2002) juxtapose cameras and guns, discussing how colonial hunting with a camera allows photographers to ultimately control time, nature, consumption, and possession.

30 Rahul Rao's (2020) analysis of the neoliberal spaces of Uganda, India, and Britain is another text that navigates these tensions of exploring the queer archival past, asking if there are ethical ways to explore the "past-in-present" and "future-in-present."

31 The GALA Queer Archive (https://gala.co.za/) was founded in 1997.

32 There are also a range of new, similar terms in use; for instance, the Organisation Intersex International (OII) prefers *intersexuation* as a term "to approach sexuation—known as a set of biological and symbolical phenomena leading a person to recognize him/herself as belonging to one sex or the other—and not sexuality" (Montañola and Olivési 2016, 2). Eckert (2017) suggests *intersexualization* as a way to describe the process through which intersex diagnoses and labels are imposed.

33 DSD is an inconsistent acronym that can include the words disorders/differences, sex/sexual, development/differentiation, and so on, depending on authors' preferences.

34 Dissatisfaction about DSD is not uniform but extends globally; as David Rubin notes, "The proponents of the shift from intersex to DSD adopt medicalized language in an effort to generate improved treatment outcomes, but the DSD nomenclature has generated significant opposition from some intersex activist groups, such as Organisation Intersex International, whose members argue that the DSD nomenclature has discriminatory social and political implications" (2017, 131; see also Curtis 2007).

35 My thinking on this benefits from discussions on social media initiated by Shireen Hassim, who alerted me to Asanda Ngoasheng's publication. I capitalize Black only when referring to the United States, in deference to Black scholars and activists who explain this decision as a claim to power in the face of histories of enslavement (Appiah 2020).

36 Ngoasheng writes the following about her use of lowercase letters: "It is about rejecting linguistic disciplining, because languages are one of the tools used to oppress, erase and challenge black people. The use of small letters is jarring and should be jarring linguistically, because it is done to force the reader to pause and

think—why is 'black' or 'white' not capitalized, and what is the author trying to tell me by not capitalising it?" (2021, 147–48n2).

1. COLONIAL OBSERVATIONS AND FALLACIES

1   *Bantu Gynaecology* defines Bantu to include "Negroid peoples" of southern Africa who speak one or more of two thousand dialects of the Bantu language and who share a set of similar phenotypic characteristics deemed inferior (Heyns 1956, 1–2). Beginning in the mid-nineteenth century, Bantu, a word for "people," was used to refer to speakers of a group of languages in Africa. It was deployed under apartheid to describe Africans as physically inferior and to politically justify violent genocidal policies. The word was later largely replaced with African or black in demographic descriptions by those in power.

I elaborate on the 1950s origins and development of the field of Bantu Gynaecology later in this chapter. *Bantu Gynaecology* is the most influential publication of Godfrey Phillips Charlewood (1905–2003), a South African–born obstetric/gynecological surgeon who was trained at the University of Cape Town and in England. Charlewood served in Britain's Indian Medical Service for over a decade. He returned to South Africa in 1947 and worked first at Baragwanath Hospital in Soweto and then in private practice in Johannesburg. Charlewood was very influential in training physicians and founded the College of Medicine of South Africa in 1954; he also served as president of the Southern Transvaal branch of the South African Medical Association (Van Dongen 2003).

2   I later found that these pages pictured a nude person with the caption "A 'true' hermaphrodite with female breasts, rudimentary vagina, uterus, penis and ovotestis" (Charlewood 1956, 13–14).

3   Library censorship and theft of medical and sexology texts like Havelock Ellis's *On the Psychology of Sex* for pornographic purposes provide important points of comparison (e.g., Bright and Crowley 2014).

4   European travel to southern Africa began in the 1500s, with the first recorded ships docking at the Cape of Good Hope from France in 1530, England in 1579, and the Netherlands in 1595 (Mlambo and Parsons 2019, 62). Now part of contemporary South Africa, the Cape of Good Hope was colonized by the Netherlands' West India Company and Dutch settlers in 1652 as a stopping point for those traveling around the southernmost point in Africa and to enslave the region's indigenous people.

5   Gordon (1992) provides a string of citations from the 1700s to the 1900s that all made the assertion that Khoi people were the connecting link between humans and "the brute creation," in part reliant on this categorization of their genitals as hermaphroditic. The term *eunuch* is as complicated as *hermaphrodite*; it was sometimes used synonymously and at other times indicated castration.

6   The work of A. Marius Wilson (1911) provides another example of this hierarchical thinking.

7   Anatomy was not privileged as a way to distinguish between male and female bodies until the nineteenth century, and in Europe the primary genital distinction during this time was "heat"—"the heat which causes the female vagina to 'pop out' into the morphologically identical penis" (Jones and Stallybrass 1991, 81).

8   African traditions of self-exposure as political strategies are well documented in various areas and times. See, for instance, Naminata Diabate's (2020) *Naked Agency: Genital Cursing and Biopolitics in Africa*, and Laura Grillo's (2018) *An Intimate Rebuke: Female Genital Power in Ritual and Politics in West Africa*.

9   As a point of comparison, Gordon cites Susanna Barrow's analyses of the French Third Republic and the suffrage movement in Britain. In both of these contexts, exaggerations of innate genital difference were similarly mobilized to rationalize political resistance (1992, 194).

10 Rebecca Hodes explains the convoluted routes of these ideas: "Sexual anomalies attributed to native South Africans were articulated in the writings of European scientists and travelers, and . . . wound their way into the accounts of colonial authorities stationed at the Cape, then back to the Global North, where they were revitalized in the writings of sexual scientists working across continents, chronologies, and academic disciplines. At times the steps in the process were reversed, with the accounts of travel writers, doctors, missionaries, and historians at the Cape providing the 'original' source for claims later echoed by European, British, and American scientists" (2017, 133–34).

11 Reprints of this (1894) text continue to be available on Amazon (https://www .amazon.com/Textbook-Diseases-Women-Henry-Garrigues/dp/1163502073).

12 African women's supposedly inferior pelvic structure and buttocks (so-called steatopygia) also merit dozens of pages of discussion and accompanying photographs in this chapter.

13 The authors of the Ploss compendium address debates about the origins of this "anomaly" at great length, but even when conceding that elongation may not be innate, they position the "apron" as a "symptom of primitive development" ([1885] 1935, 335). They even cite zoomorphic colonial work declaring a "remarkable resemblance between the vulva of the female chimpanzee and the local structure of the Bushwoman" (Blanchard, quoted in Ploss, Bartels, and Bartels [1885] 1935, 335).

14 Baartman is sometimes referred to as Saartjie—or by the derogatory Hottentot Venus. I choose to use the name and spelling Sara (instead of Sarah) here, as it is the name preferred by most South African activists who worked for decades to honor her history and repatriate her body. Scores of scholars have written about Baartman's exploitation; critiques of troubling representations and efforts to honor her memory include Yvette Abrahams (2000), who wrote the first book-length analysis of her life; Clifton Crais and Pamela Scully's explorations of Baartman's historical experiences and genealogical legacies (2009); and Zine Magubane's (2001) critiques and insights into discussions of Baartman and the historical emergence of blackness.

15 Colonial fascination with Africans' buttocks and thighs—and their classification as "steatopygic" (having excess tissue and fat)—has similarly been manipulated by scientists to justify theories of physical difference and inferiority.

16 Baartman has continued to be fetishized in contemporary scholarly accounts and prolific discourse that Zine Magubane describes as "a veritable theoretical industry" (2001, 817).

17 Cuvier also recommended genital surgeries to "normalize" labia that were to become common in the next century, suggesting that treatment of the "Hottentot apron" might follow a sixteenth-century Portuguese practice of surgically removing elongated labia because husbands could not abide what he called a "disgusting deformity" (Cuvier [1817] 1969, 267; Fausto-Sterling 1995, 37–38).

18 By 1822, Cuvier had 11,486 scientific preparations, including many human skeletons and skulls, used to support his theories of racial hierarchies. He built these collections by asking colonial travelers to remove (steal) bodies from any battles involving "savages" and to preserve them for his examination. Cuvier and his collaborator, Henri de Blainville, developed classification systems of living beings and theories to match at the Musée d'Histoire Naturelle. This locale became the world center for the study of the life sciences (including comparative anatomy, paleontology, morphology, and zoological taxonomy), featuring collections of plants, animals, and human bodies, which were then compared (Fausto-Sterling 1995, 24–25).

19 Innumerable Africans were transported to Europe and the United States for live displays during this period.

20 Historical details of some of these European displays of humans are spelled out in works including Thomson (1996), Lindfors (1983a, 1983b), and Altick (1978).

21 Museums also hosted scientific house journals that concretized hierarchical ideologies. Comparative anatomy theorized the world and living beings based on the random collections of bones and life-sized casts of indigenous people that they were able to obtain.

22 The systemization of ethnological and anthropological knowledge to create raced difference was given strong institutional support in South Africa after 1902, so this project was timely (Dubow 1995, 12).

23 Davison cites other primary work focusing on the genital morphology of various so-called Hottentot women, including Kirby (1954), Altick (1978), and Gould (1982).

24 Hodes (2017) points out that zoomorphism was common in descriptions of the "Hottentot apron," comparing it to an elephant ear, turkey's beak, butterfly's wings, and cockscomb, among other references.

25 Historian Paul Landau referred to this project as "medicalized tableaux," a collection in which "skulls, facial masks, and plates of photographed 'types' are grouped together in this bizarre museum according to the logic of conquest and administration" (2002, 151). As a point of comparison, see Linda Kim's (2018) analysis of the *Races of Man* exhibition that opened in Chicago in 1934, which drew well over three million visitors in its first year alone.

26 In 2013, all life casts were removed from ethnographic exhibitions in South Africa (Rassool 2015; Davison 2018).

27 It is likely that Drury also made casts of the body and genitals of /Khanako (Rassool and Hayes 2002, 128n21), and Drennan engaged in scientific scrutiny of /Khanako and her community.

28 Rassool and Hayes describe their first encounter with this image during research on a native commissioner who served in Namibia from 1915 to 1947. "In 'Cocky' Hahn's reasonably coherent photograph collection, among his studio shots of Prime Minister

Jan Smuts at the United Nations in New York to be precise, an incongruous and disturbing image fluttered out" (Rassool and Hayes 2002, 121–22; see also Hayes 1996). They document their effort to answer the questions this image raised for them, uncovering details of /Khanako's life and juxtaposing this distressing image with photos of her strong and confident leadership.

29 Anne McClintock further explains the linear temporality of this medium: "In the colonial postcard, time is reorganized as spectacle; through the choreographing of fetish icons, history is organized into a single, linear narrative of progress" (1995, 125).

30 Malatino (2019) similarly discusses the connection between such medical images and pornography.

31 In the first myth, a child represents the attributes of both parents to the extent that they are unable to decide on its sex, while the other myth represents a child as the product of parents' bodies intertwined to become joined as one (Fausto-Sterling 2000, 32). Indeed, debates about "hermaphrodites" were essentially gender theories in ancient Greek philosophy and beyond. While the older Hippocratic view suggested that "hermaphrodites" were "beings truly intermediary in sex, neither male nor female, but exactly in between" (Datson and Park 1995, 421), the Aristotelian model claimed that all people were either strictly male or female, though some might have extra genitalia which could be likened to an extra toe or nipple (Cadden 1993). According to Plato, there were originally three sexes—male, female, and hermaphrodite—but the third of these had been lost over time. Early biblical interpreters "thought that Adam began his existence as a hermaphrodite and that he divided into two individuals, male and female, only after falling from grace" (Fausto-Sterling 2000, 32–33). These and other myths and stories about gendered bodies reflected a wide range of theories of binarism.

32 As Jones and Stallybrass put it, "It was, no doubt, the very precariousness of gender hierarchy which suggested to some physicians the need to maintain differentiation by force" (1991, 87).

33 Dreger's work is grounded in extensive analyses of European history, including around three hundred accounts of hermaphroditism in humans published in British and French scientific and medical literature from 1860 to 1915 (1998, 24). In researching "The Age of Gonads" in Europe, she also points out, "It cannot be a coincidence that at the same time other historians find the emergence of the homosexual, I find the virtual extinction of the hermaphrodite" (152–53). Dreger and many other scholars have explored how hermaphroditism blurred the lines between the material body and sexual behaviors—homosexuals were often referred to as "psychic hermaphrodites"—and procreative sex was paramount.

34 The increasing attention to gonads could be linked to an increasing valorization of men's roles in reproduction in this period. Huet (1993) explains that whereas in the Renaissance, women's imaginations were thought to control the appearance of their offspring, teratology and especially teratogeny (producing "monsters" in laboratories) were indicative of a societal shift that increasingly credited men as creative geniuses who could produce and control bodies deemed monstrous.

35 See critical analyses of this period in work by Karkazis (2008) and Malatino (2009, 2019).

36 For discussion of John Edward Coke's use of the phrase "that sex which prevaileth" and deployment of this same concept by legal experts, useful historical context is provided by Fausto-Sterling (2000).

37 Dreger details Tait's reception among evolutionary theorists: "Darwin thought such a concept correct, but also amusingly scandalous. He kidded his friend, the geologist Charles Lyell, '*Our* ancestor was an animal which breathed water, had a swim bladder, a great swimming tail, an imperfect skull, and undoubtedly was an hermaphrodite! Here is a pleasant genealogy for mankind!'" (1998, 66–67).

38 Colonists' long-standing fascination with African women's buttocks, labeled as "steatopygia," can also be linked to pelvimetry and eugenic attention to reproduction. Gilman reminds us that Havelock Ellis's famous text, *Studies in the Psychology of Sex* (1905), reflects the aforementioned evolutionary "great chain of being" and links to Baartman's exploitation. Gilman details, "His discussion of the buttocks ranks the races by size of the female pelvis, a view that began with Willem Vrolik's 1826 claim that a wide pelvis is a sign of racial superiority and was echoed by R. Verneau's 1875 study of the form of the pelvis among the various races. Verneau cited the narrow pelvis of Sarah Baartman in arguing that the Hottentot's anatomical structure was primitive" (1985, 90). Ellis accepts this ranking, recognizing debates within science but still degrading "the buttocks of the Hottentot as a somewhat comic sign of the black female's primitive, grotesque nature" (Gilman 1985, 90). C. Riley Snorton positions the pelvis as "a critical site for producing racial hierarchies among nineteenth-century anatomists and sexologists intent on finding bodily 'proof' of black inferiority" and gives an example of British sexologist Havelock Ellis's (1900) argument that the supposedly larger size of African women's buttocks compensated for their allegedly smaller pelvic size (2017, 19).

39 Urology similarly developed through experimentation on the bodies of those who were dehumanized, including people who were Black, disabled, women, and/or children (Gill-Peterson 2017, 2018a).

40 When referring to Bantu Gynaecology as a specific field of medical inquiry and practice, I capitalize this phrase to indicate its institutionalization and use the preferred South African spelling of *gynaecology* (as compared to the preferred US spelling, *gynecology*).

41 As Snorton explains, almost three years of experiments on chattel persons conducted by Sims, often referred to as the father of modern gynecology, "served as 'proof' of black females' genital exceptionalism (as nonreproductive, inverted, unfeminine), even as the procedures also produced an erasure of chattel slavery's effect on black female genitalia in the state of exception" (2017, 20). Snorton further explains that Sims's archive serves as a materialization of Hortense Spiller's flesh ungendered.

42 There has been a close association between the monstrosity ascribed to women's bodies through reproduction and hermaphroditism since the Middle Ages (Huet 1993). Perhaps nowhere is this more apparent than in Bantu Gynaecology, where denigration of women's bodies, so-called hermaphroditic bodies, and African bodies converged.

43 Comparisons between pelvimetry focused on white women in the Global North and African women in the Global South during colonial periods prove important

as well. Burns addresses Ornella Moscucci's analysis of 1800–1920 England and "the inscription of a particular feminine mental, imaginative and social character in the bones of women" (1995, 416). Sally Markowitz (2001) and David Rubin (2017) also make important contributions to thinking about pelvic studies and its connections to intersex.

44 The UNESCO statement against scientific racism paradoxically reified South African racial politics. One example of this came through the reactionary journal *Mankind Quarterly*, originating in 1960 and continuing to the present as a direct commitment to extending the racial projects that predated UNESCO (Tucker 2007). While based in the United States, the journal reflected a global network of contributors and editors from India, China, Russia, Japan, Saudi Arabia, and Egypt (Saini 2019, 73). South African intellectuals such as J. D. J. Hofmeyr were centrally involved with the journal and reinforced the shift from eugenics to genetics, "geared to the defence of high apartheid" (Dubow 2015, 242). Hofmeyr led the South African Genetic Society and gave "direct support to a small but well dispersed network of international white supremacists who, in the postwar world, felt themselves to be a beleaguered scientific minority standing up for unpopular truths. These causes focused on opposition to civil rights legislation in the United States and the totemic defence of white supremacy in Rhodesia and South Africa" (242).

45 Gill-Peterson argues that normative bisexuality, then describing the concurrent existence of two sexes, has been "largely forgotten or overlooked in the history of gender, sexuality and trans medicine, [and] so too has its eugenic foundations" (2018a, 55).

46 For further critical analysis of Money's influence and scholarship, see works including Califia 1997; Kessler 1998; Fausto-Sterling 2000; Colapinto 2000; Karkazis 2000; Downing, Morland, and Sullivan 2014; Goldie 2014; Eckert 2017; and Malatino 2019.

47 Magubane (2014) also juxtaposes treatments of black and white intersex infants.

48 Traces of this can be found in the United States, including in the early work of Hugh Hampton Young in the 1930s. As Gill-Peterson writes, Young was interested in "a presumed exceptional pathology he imagined residing somewhere in black bodies" (2018b, 611).

49 Despite the supposed end of scientific racism, claims about the inferiority and difference of African genitals continued to be repeated in academic and public contexts on a transnational scale. For example, the 1963 handbook *Races of Man*, written by Sonia Cole and published by the British Museum, was hugely popular and had global influence for its depictions of race and evolution. In it, Cole takes account of post-UNESCO shifts in language about genetics and blood groupings, but her characterization includes descriptions of so-called Bushmen that reiterated a familiar portrayal of genitalia through derogatory language of comparative anatomy. Cole describes, "Certain peculiarities of the genital organs are also characteristic: the penis is often in an almost horizontal position; and in women the extension of the labia minora, forming a 'tablier' or apron, is universal, though whether this character is hereditary or acquired has been disputed" (1965, 124). In Cole's description, as in so many before, Africans' genitals are represented as unusual and inferior to those of Europeans. Fausto-Sterling notes that even the famous sexolo-

gists William Masters and Virginia Johnson's *Human Sexual Response* (1966) draws on a cited source, "a decidedly unscientific (by modern standards) compendium of female physical oddities that dates from the 1930s but draws on nineteenth-century literature of the sort discussed here" (1995, 35).

50 The follow-up volume to *Bantu Gynaecology* was titled *Gynaecology in Southern Africa* (Charlewood 1972) and included a chapter on intersex by Willem van Niekerk titled "Abnormal Sex Development."

51 Cytogenetics is a branch of biology concerned with genomes and heredity that focuses on the structure and function of chromosomes in individual cells.

52 It was also common for physicians in this time to assert a connection between so-called mental retardation and intersex, especially among black patients; Klempman asserts, "It is concluded that true hermaphroditism is the commonest form in the Bantu. A combination of abnormal sexual development with other congenital anomalies, including *mental retardation*, is often associated with abnormality of the sex chromosomes" (Klempman 1954, 236, emphasis added).

53 *African* is used synonymously with *Bantu* and *Black* here, as is *Caucasian* with *White*, reflecting common slippages among terms connoting language, geography, ethnicity, tribe, and race.

54 Though making broad claims, Wilton himself acquiesces that in a human population group, "The true incidence can only be estimated if all neonates are investigated and the intersex states recorded, this would entail detailed nuclear sexing and chromosome analysis of peripheral blood and fibroblast cultures, of large numbers of newborns" (1969, 47).

55 Princess Mariana Hospital was built in 1966 in the capital of Botswana to mark the country's independence. At this time, the hospital primarily treated patients from rural areas in advanced and acute stages of illness (Johnson 1975a).

56 Johnson notes elsewhere that as no histological services were available in Botswana, all specimens were sent to the Royal Army Medical College in London. But this case was clearly significant to him. In an article about the prevalence of advanced and varied cancers in the region, Johnson writes, "As histological specimens have to be sent outside the country and take several weeks to return, not all operation specimens are sent. This leads to an underdiagnosis of malignant conditions . . . and means that not all clinically suspected cancers are proven histologically" (1975b, 260). While many patients with life-threatening cancers did not merit laboratory analysis, this patient with minor or perhaps no medical concerns did because of the potential of a "true hermaphrodite" diagnosis.

57 Johnson himself was instrumental in postindependence allopathic medicine in Botswana, establishing the *Journal of the Medical and Dental Association of Botswana* in 1970 with the intention of stimulating interest in and funding for clinical research in Botswana. Writing at the journal's inception, Johnson muses, "While we can make no claims to being a leading medical journal, we feel we are making a contribution to the improvement of medical services and practice in Botswana" (1972, 287). Perhaps his article on "true hermaphroditism" fit Johnson's objectives of garnering attention for medicine in the region.

1 Grace's 1970 work also addresses dermatoglyphics in relation to intersex at length, and physicians often genetically link dermatoglyphics to both Turner's and Kleinfelter's syndromes.

2 Scientific and medical theories of intersex based in the Global North have always relied on juxtapositions of colonizers and colonized, and global professional networks demonstrate intellectual comraderies and competition.

3 Money published a commentary on the work of Julianne Imperato-McGinley on intersex in the Dominican Republic, arguing with her theories (Money, Imperato-McGinley, and Peterson 1976). Robert J. Stoller worked with intersex patients in the United States and then collaborated with both Imperato-McGinley and Gilbert Herdt, traveling to Papua New Guinea in efforts to diagnose and research those considered intersex. Imperato-McGinley also collaborated with Herdt to theorize and analyze those in both the Dominican Republic and Papua New Guinea as part of her development of theories of intersex in the Global South. This transnational context essentially constituted the parameters of intersex in the Global South. My brief mapping is not intended as a comprehensive review of transnational connections and citational practices in medical literature, but these exemplars point to the networks of information and collaboration that underpin ideas of intersex.

4 These three studies are Klempman (1964); Forbes and Hammar (1966); and Wilton (1969).

5 In this context, Grace was particularly fascinated with how the newly emerging field of cytogenetics and karyotypes could differentiate males from females.

6 Grace's six chapters dedicated to conditions he believes fall under the rubric of intersex are "Gonadal Dysgenesis, Turner's Syndrome and Phenotypes"; "Kleinfelter's Syndrome and Male Hypogonadism"; "Unrepresented Syndromes"; "Hormonal and Drug-Induced Intersexes"; "Male Intersexes"; "Idiopathic Female Intersexes"; "Hermaphroditism"; "'Pseudo-Intersexual' Conditions" (1970, iii–iv).

7 This is how Grace explains race: "The South African population is made up of four distinct races: the Bantu, a composite group formed from many smaller tribes of the Nguni stock; immigrant whites of European origin, and Indians from the southern provinces; and the smaller Coloured community which originated through miscegenation between early white settlers at the Cape and their Malaysian slaves and indigenous Hottentots. No population census has been made in South Africa since 1960, projections from which estimated that the 1969 population consisted of 18,000,000 Bantu; 3,750,000 whites; 1,500,000 Coloureds, and some 800,000 Indians" (1970, 4).

8 Grace goes on to state his rationale for the location of his study: "Durban [is] particularly well suited to such studies because three of the races are represented by substantial numbers and the minority, the Coloureds, are to a large extent co[n]centrated in a well-defined community so that in each case 'captive' populations for epidemiological study can easily be had" (1970, 216).

9 In Grace's later work, ongoing and shifting perceptions of the "truth" of gender and race converge in categories he uses interchangeably—Bantu, Negro, and

Black—in his different publications Analyzing the use of racialized terminology in five decades of South African medical literature points to its inconsistency and links to South African politics; Braun et al. (2007), among others, demonstrate the problems of using racial categories in medicine that assume homogeneity. It is also important to point out that class and the impacts of apartheid policies of segregation were largely left out of Grace's explicit analysis, though they were briefly acknowledged when he notes that, with regard to Indian and white patients, "a certain amount of selection was inevitable because many of the wealthier classes are precluded, either from choice or by regulation, from using the facilities at the hospitals concerned. No attempt was made to correct for this discrepancy between the social and economic status of the groups because there is no evidence to suggest that these factors have any influence over the occurrence of intersexuality; irrespective of the sampling method, the numbers involved were large enough to offset any bias" (1970, 197).

10 Hypospadias is a condition in which the urethral opening is usually on the underside of the penis rather than at the tip.

11 One of his disquieting future research recommendations is a study of everyone in the entire population, in which wide use of the sex chromatin test would determine whether the rarity of XXY males "amongst the Bantu and Indians is real." Grace suggests such studies could focus on pupils at "schools for the subnormal and patients incarcerated in hospitals for dangerous retardates" (1970, 223).

12 His language here betrays his sentiment that intersex was "rampant"—a word with an etymology referring to wild animals (e.g., "running rampant") or something spreading that is unwelcome and unrestrained—connoting colonial and apartheid perceptions of black South Africans as animalistic and uncontrollable in population, behavior, and corporeality.

13 In at least two additional publications, Grace drew on his thesis data to make similar claims involving patients, previously referenced and pictured as "Case 26" (Grace, Quantock, and Vinik 1970) and "Case 25" (Grace and Schonland 1970).

14 This is yet another example of what G. Ellison and T. de Wet (1997) refer to as the meaningless descriptive labels of ethnicity, race, and nation.

15 As detailed in chapter 1, the broader development of the field of genetics is inseparable from eugenics and grounded in histories of comparative anatomy.

16 Despite failed inquiries, Ramsay and other authors continue this quest to locate the physical basis for disproportionate "true hermaphroditism" among black South Africans for over three decades. For instance, another study that Ramsay co-authored (Spurdle, Shankman, and Ramsay 1995) replicates the intentions of Ramsay's 1988 study—to "determine the cause of the disorder"—this time through molecular investigation (53). Again, the authors claim, "Most true hermaphrodites diagnosed in southern Africa are Bantu-speaking Blacks" but admit that studies examining environmental and genetic bases for this claim as well as the molecular causes they seek to prove in their own research have not been fruitful (53). For Ramsay, the blame for not finding quantitative proof for her claims may be placed on the families of intersex children, who she posits are unwilling to share genetic information that would substantiate her unproven hypotheses.

17 The title of this film recalls the important critiques Towle and Morgan (2002) forward about the objectification and the use of the metaphor of "third" sex and gender addressed in the introduction. All transcriptions are my own.

18 Sources for these statistics for rates of intersex are not cited or mentioned.

19 Gill-Peterson explains similar perspectives shared by Hugh Hampton Young and others at the Brady Institute of Johns Hopkins University in the United States: "In many instances, black families and their communities in Baltimore were evidently quite accepting of intersex children, to the point of being skeptical of the need to accept a medical decision and binary sex. In response, physicians and social workers tried to disqualify their beliefs as unscientific or irrational" (2018a, 76).

20 Freedberg details the role of images in creating significant responses in viewers; state censorship of images deemed pornographic and aniconism—religious edicts that prohibit certain kinds of visual depictions—provide just two examples of institutionalized fears of the power that images hold. He explains: "People are sexually aroused by pictures and sculptures; they break pictures and sculptures; they mutilate them, kiss them, cry before them, and go on journeys to them; they are calmed by them, stirred by them, and incited to revolt. They give thanks by means of them, expect to be elevated by them, and are moved to the highest levels of empathy and fear" (1989, 1).

21 Campt explains that in her own work analyzing photographic archives of prisoners in Cape Town, "the haptic temporalities of the archive in question are composed of moments of contact when photographs touch us and animate reflections and responses. These temporalities include, but are in no way limited to, the moment of photographic capture; the temporality of the photographic re/production of material objects; their assembly and reconfiguration as nodes of state, social, and cultural formation; and the present and future temporalities of their interactions with researchers, archivists, and the broader community" (2017, 72).

22 Suspected diagnoses fell into a wide range of Grace's detailed "intersex" classifications already discussed here, ranging from Turner's syndrome to hypospadias.

23 A few photos in this context also represent abdominal surgeries in process and reproductive organs removed and clinically displayed.

24 Genital images in Grace's thesis collection and elsewhere, such as in Malatino's analysis of photographs in the sexological archives of the Kinsey Institute for Research in Sex, Gender, and Reproduction, are easily compared to pornography in "the privileging of close-ups over other shots, the overlighting of too often easily obscured genitalia, and the selection of positions that aim to display the intricacies of bodies and organs" (2019, 142).

25 Jacob Dlamini's *The Terrorist Album* (2020b) also speaks to the creation and power of violent images. His work analyzes the grim legacy of an album of more than seven thousand photographs taken from the 1960s to the 1990s focused on those deemed "terrorists" by the South African security police. Apartheid was fraught with failures, and Dlamini argues that when security forces were confronted with the problems and inefficiencies of this album, they would "blame the native" instead of admitting the impossibilities of racial categories revealed (2020b). His analysis exposes the confused brutality of apartheid law enforcement and the visuality of apartheid itself (2020a).

26 Other relevant publications include Grace 1975a, 1975b; and Grace and Ally 1972.

27 Grace's chapter titles indicating the extent of his interest in dermatoglyphics include the following: "Dermatoglyphics," "Dermatoglyphs of Normal South Africans," and "Dermatoglyphs in Intersexuality."

28 Dermatoglyphics was medically institutionalized in 1926 by Harold Cummins and was strongly supported through the 1980s. This field considered handprints of humans as a means of creating human hierarchies and as a point of comparison to primates; it was widely accepted as diagnostic of conditions such as epilepsy (Wertelecki and Plato 1979; Mavalwaka 1978).

29 Today, finger and handprints are also used forensically, but the objective accuracy of analyzing these ridges continues to be questioned in both scientific and juridical contexts.

30 Eyes are significant in indicating life and humanity: "Eyes . . . provide the most immediate testimony of life in living beings; in images—where substance, at the first level, excludes the possibility of movement—they are even more powerfully capable of doing so. If an image is perceived as particularly lifelike, then the absence of the eyes may inspire terror. Their presence enables the mental leap to an assumption of liveliness " (Freedberg 1989, 202). Further the use of images of people punished by the state have been sanctioned and used to shame those considered frauds and traitors—and to warn others of their presence—since the late thirteenth century (255).

31 Hausman (1995) also provides an analysis of a tradition of "before vs after" visual comparisons in early intersex medical photography in Europe.

32 Dreger's decision to include her own photo also addressed the lament she had heard from intersex people: "These people were talking about the general problem of medical textbooks showing intersexed people not just as different but as tragically deformed. But they also spoke of personal experiences. They themselves, as children and adolescents, had been repeatedly subjected to physical and visual examinations by medical students, residents, and attending physicians. Although it was certainly not the medical professionals' intentions, these 'exhibitions' had left the subjects feeling freakish and violated—'like insects tacked to a board for study'" (2000, 162).

33 As Campt reflects in her interpretation of photographs of those imprisoned under colonialism and of other South Africans: "These photos were not taken at the behest of their sitters. They are images intended to classify types rather than to identify individuals. While those in the photos may have given tacit sanction or approval, they are at best coerced and at worst compelled" (2017, 49).

34 The authors detail their fascination: "A Bantu neonate was found at birth to have epicene genitalia and perineal hypospadias. Postmortem examination revealed phallic and perineal urethrae and uterus didelphys. Cytogenetic studies demonstrated normal female sex chromatin and karyotype. The clinical history, postmortem findings and histological observations are reported. The case is of interest because the formation of a phallic urethra in a genetic female is a rare event; also, idiopathic female intersexuality is not frequently encountered in the Bantu races of southern Africa" (Grace and Schonland 1970, 1115).

35 In his discussion of the gruesome postmortem image of Emmett Till published in *Jet* magazine at his mother's bequest, Fred Moten (2002, 65) muses on the ghosts in

photographs: "An image from which one turns is immediately caught in the production of its memorialized, re-membered production. We lean into it, but we can't."

36 These representations are separate from traditions of postmortem photography
undertaken historically to memorialize and grieve family members. These practices
continue to the present in customs, for example, of stillborn photography.

37 Ellison and de Wet trace the terminological and conceptual differences found in
this literature over decades, suggesting, "For example, 'Bantu' and 'European' were
the two commonest labels used in 1950 and 1960 yet neither appeared in articles
published in 1980 and 1990. The term 'Black' or 'black' did not appear in any of the
articles published in 1950, 1960 or 1970, yet it was the commonest label used in both
1980 and 1990" (1997, 1676), reflecting popular and shifting usage in broad contexts.
They supplement this historical analysis with a table that identifies descriptive
language in the hundreds of medical articles they studied, which includes "traditional racial" terms (e.g., Caucasian and Negroid), phenotypic language (e.g., Black
and white), tribal or clan descriptions (e.g., Zulu), and language (e.g., Afrikaans).
The authors also note that of the 668 articles they analyzed, only 3 contained a
disclaimer suggesting that the authors didn't accept the validity of these categories.

38 Henrietta Lacks was a Black woman exploited for unusual and reproducible cancer cells
taken from her body without consent when she was a patient at Johns Hopkins Hospital. These cells had immeasurable use for cancer research after she passed away and
made billions of dollars in profit without the knowledge of or benefit to her family. The
life and treatment of Lacks has been the subject of numerous recent books, films, and
apologies about the ethics of racist science and medical treatment (e.g., Skloot 2010).

39 The Reimer twins' parents sought Money's expertise after seeing him on a television
program (Colapinto 2000). Morland explains the influence of popular culture on
the Reimers in this way: "Ten months after the circumcision accident, the Reimers
were watching a current affairs television program on which Money was discussing
the adult sex change surgeries being pioneered at the Johns Hopkins Hospital. The
pivotal role of television in the case has rarely received attention. Even while contemporary surgical technology foreclosed some possibilities . . . the technology of
television opened others; by the time the Reimers were watching Money in the late
1960s, television had become more popular than newspapers as a source of national
and international news for Canadians" (Morland 2015, 72).

40 I discuss David Reimer's impact in South Africa and Sally Gross's assessment of
Reimer's experiences at length in chapter 3.

41 To use Judith Butler's (1993) language, this repetition of norms that imitates no original operates citationally, despite flawed theories, troubling images, and contradictions.

3. DEFYING MEDICAL VIOLENCE AND SOCIAL DEATH

1 Gross was an active consultant for 2003 South African film, *The 3rd Sex*. This film
has no connection to the 2004 film of the same name discussed previously, which
focused on research in the United Kingdom, Dominican Republic, and South Africa.

2 Gross was a prolific writer and theorist and gave many interviews; her writings,
interviews, film contributions and archival materials are compiled and detailed in

appendix 1. GALA Queer Archive houses Sally Gross's personal collection of documents, photographs, and memorabilia, donated by her brother after her death in 2014.

3 The Triangle Project (https://triangle.org.za/) is an organization in Cape Town founded in 1981 and focused on health, community, research, and advocacy for LGBTI people and their families. It remains operational to the present and currently offers services including sexual health clinics, counseling, support groups, a phone helpline, outreach programs, and a library.

4 Slovo and Kasrils were influential anti-apartheid leaders and later politicians active in the African National Congress. In addition to Gross's writings and my interviews and communications with her, I quote at length from a three-part series on Gross's views and life authored by Stephen Coan in close collaboration with Gross in 2000 and published in the *Witness* (then called the *Natal Witness*), the longest continually published newspaper in South Africa. Gross was very proud of this set of articles and her partnership with Coan in its writing. Throughout her life, she often referenced and reshared this series of articles as a way of explaining her own biography. I also share from the article "Lifting the Veil" (1999), published in the *Mail and Guardian*, another piece that she wrote in collaboration with staff reporter Aaron Nicodemus.

5 Gross notes that at this time, the Church of England was debating the ordination of women, and her superior connected her struggles to the dismissal of women and equated intersex with issues considered to be perversions, such as pedophilia and sexual abuse (Gross 2000).

6 Dr. Harry Benjamin was one of the first physicians to work with transsexuals diagnosed (at the time) with gender dysphoria. The protocol that developed from his work, widely known in both medical and popular discussions, originated in 1979 as a set of guidelines for treating transsexuals prior to surgical interventions. It was developed collaboratively with members of the Harry Benjamin Gender Dysphoria Association, an organization that became the World Professional Association for Transgender Health (WPATH).

7 Michelle Wolff's conference paper 'Sally Gross: Mother of Transnational Intersex Activism Died Alone," presented in 2019, describes Gross's life holistically. Wolff's forthcoming biography of Gross will detail her life and ideologies, including providing a nuanced analysis of her complex relation to religion and spirituality.

8 Some of the activist work with a strong influence at this time included organizing through the Intersex Society of North America (operational until 2008, http://www.isna.org/), growing numbers of publications (such as Chase 1998), and videos such as *Hermaphrodites Speak!* (1997).

9 The organization was briefly known as the Intersex Society of South Africa at its inception, a name initially modeled on the Intersex Society of North America. But it was soon changed by Gross to Intersex South Africa to reflect its independence.

10 This article was published before Intersex South Africa had a website, and reflective of her transnational activist connections, Gross requested that the article "Lifting the Veil" include contact details for ISNA: "For information about intersexuality in general, consult the website of the Intersex Society of North America at www.isna.org" ([Gross and Nicodemus] 1999).

11 Gross continued her efforts to promote the new organization, sharing her own story in the feature series about her life in the *Witness* and in *Challenge* (a South African religious bimonthly) and interviewing on the popular Cape Town station Radio Bush.

12 Gross also found solidarity in the networks of anti-apartheid activists recommending her affiliation with Triangle, as it is locally known. She elucidates, "One of my comrades, who was at the time a senior official in the ministry with which I was doing some work suggested that I get in contact with a friend of hers . . . [who is a trustee] of Triangle Projects and ask her advice about how to go about the business of launching a group, and so on. And Heather [Adonis] thought it would be a really valuable thing to do. . . . So, I did and I chatted to Annie [Leatt] and I chatted to Graeme [Reid], who's now back studying, and I chatted to Glen [de Swardt]. And we agreed on a broad association around this issue. What I reasoned in part is that Triangle's helpline and clinic might sometimes attract people who are intersexed and don't have proper information . . . you know, that would probably give me the opportunities to get information in at that level and also to network and to build up contacts. So things went from there" (Gross 2000).

13 Gross explains details she learned about this decades later: "Some months ago, my late father sent me an email in which he expressed anger at the 'stupid' ritual circumciser, who should, on my father's account, have realised that I was a girl and should not have attempted circumcision. As I have noted, scar-tissue told me as a young adult that circumcision had been problematic. My late father's email revealed something I had not known: that the *mohel* [by Gross's own definition, "the Hebrew term for a ritual circumciser"] returned a few days later to hack at the still unhealed wounds, presumably also without anesthetic, in order to try to tidy up the mess. This shocks me" (Gross 2011, 235–36).

14 Reimer's case was most famously recounted by John Colapinto (2000) for a popular audience in a book that became a *New York Times* bestseller.

15 The fate of the Reimer twins was not anomalous. For instance, Jules Gill-Peterson describes a similarly tragic outcome for a patient named Robert Stonestreet, diagnosed with "hermaphroditism" in 1915 at Johns Hopkins University (2018a, 71). After being subjected to surgeries and other unwelcome treatment, his father withdrew him from care. But two decades later he returned to Drs. Hugh Hampton Young and William Quinby for medical proof that he was a man because a priest had heard of his childhood diagnosis and refused to marry him. The doctors refused assistance, and Stonestreet committed suicide. As Gill-Peterson explains, "Ending in suicide, Stonestreet's experience testifies to the violent and often traumatic effects of medicalizing intersex children as living laboratories of plasticity" (2018a, 75).

16 *Muti* is a Xhosa spelling, and *muthi* is the analogous spelling in Zulu.

17 I refer to Nhlanhla Mkhwanazi by his first name hereafter to differentiate him from his parents. No statistics are available on the frequency of *muti* kidnappings. Many victims of such kidnappings are murdered (Kotolo 2000; Mkhwanazi 2000), adding to the rarity of medical interventions into *muti* injuries.

18 Suzanne Kessler's (1990) adage reflecting on the tendency to assign 90 percent of babies with ambiguous genitals as girls in the United States in this period famously summarizes: "Good penis equals male, absence of good penis equals female."

19 Films speaking to health and race have long histories in South Africa; for instance, beginning in the 1930s–1940s, films focused on sexually transmitted diseases attempted to exploit black communities' engagement with cinema for eugenic purposes (Jeeves 2003). But Gross flips this historical precedent in *The 3rd Sex* (van Huyssteen 2003).

20 Susanne Klausen provides historical context on "poor whites" as descendants of those who subsisted as "itinerant pastoralists, squatters, tenant labourers, and small-scale farmers" (2001, 55).

21 These theories of scientific racism mirrored an intense sense of dread about the difficulties of maintaining British imperial dominance.

22 Coinciding with growing adoption of eugenic policies, the 1916 Medical Disorders Act criminalized characteristics associated with "poor whiteism," aiming to certify, detain, and incarcerate people with traits such as "feeble-mindedness."

23 Klausen details this history and the worries it evoked. She explains that "eugenicists, who subscribed to a biological deterministic explanation for white poverty, pushed for a restriction to be placed on the growth of the poor-white population in the name of preserving white civilization. Eugenicists attributed white poverty to inherent inferiority rather than to the effect of their social and physical environment; too many poor whites, they argued, threatened the quality of the white race. A number of eugenicists were leading members of the emergent birth-control movement" (Klausen 2001, 56).

24 As Deborah Posel aptly put it many years ago, "All versions of apartheid developed from a common starting point—a shared perception of the need to protect white supremacy and preserve the 'purity of the white race'" (1987, 125).

25 I explore apartheid's racialized gendered medical experimentation on those defined as transsexual, gay, and lesbian in *Sex in Transition*, focusing at length on the horrific treatment of white conscripts (2012, 77–107).

26 In the introduction, I document similar trends of pathologizing and experimenting on black and brown people deemed intersex in the Dominican Republic and Papua New Guinea.

27 DDT remains in use throughout Asia, South America, and Africa.

28 See, for instance, Rich et al. (2016) and Langston (2008) for discussions of the connections between EDCs and intersex in animals.

29 Endocrine-disrupting chemicals have affected human bodies intentionally, through hormonal medications, and unintentionally, through pollution and incidental consumption/absorption that lead to endocrinal changes (Kier 2010).

30 Horak, Horn, and Peters's (2021) detailed literature review in "Agrochemicals in Freshwater Systems and Their Potential as Endocrine Disrupting Chemicals: A South African Context" traces the impact of EDCs and their connections to research on intersex in fish and mammals.

31 In our conversations, Gross mentioned scientists Riana Bornman and Hindrik Bouwman by name and described their work at length (see Bornman et al. 2009;

Barnhoorn et al., 2009; Bornman, Barnhoorn, and Genthe 2010; Bornman and Bouwman 2012; Bouwman et al., 2012).

32 Bornman et al. (2009) share research that supports these statistics.

33 For instance, Rajendra Maharaj of the Malaria Research Programme at the Medical Research Council claims, "The negative effects of DDT have not been substantially proved"; similarly, the South African Health Department's spokesperson Fidel Radebe speciously argued that the Department of Health has been spraying DDT since the 1940s without any harmful effects on human health (Groenewald 2009).

34 Gross also parses medical diagnoses of intersex and their historical origins (addressed in chapter 1), pointing out that from the perspectives of physicians, "the most important thing in a person's life—and something which sets up a hell of a lot of the trauma anyway—is not the basis of this kind of very arbitrary taxonomy of true hermaphrodite, female pseudohermaphrodite, male pseudohermaphrodite, but quite simply the appearance of the external genitalia at birth" (van Huyssteen 2003).

35 Annette Brömdal's short book *Intersex: A Challenge for Human Rights and Citizenship Rights* (2008) includes an interview with Steinman that replicates his views shared in this film.

36 A published anthology, *Intersex, Theology, and the Bible,* that resulted from these conference proceedings was dedicated to Gross. In the introduction, Susannah Cornwall shares, "While this volume was in late stages of its preparation, we received the sad news that Sally Gross, the founder of Intersex South Africa, had died. Sally had been unable to travel from her home in Cape Town to Manchester for the colloquium and conference held there in March 2013, as her health prevented her from flying long distances. However, she took a full part in the proceedings via Skype, and those present were deeply moved by what she felt had been inappropriate and inhumane treatment from members of her religious order when she spoke about her intersex identity" (2015, 18).

37 Though outside the scope of this book and Gross's writings, it should be noted that extensive controversy followed the publication of Goldhagen's work, particularly his debate with Christopher Browning, focused on historical details and the role of antisemitism as a motivation for the atrocities of the Holocaust.

38 Philosophers including Claudia Card (2003) have also extended notions of social death to explain forcible loss of identity and efforts to exterminate certain groups through gendered genocide and intense mental and physical harm.

39 Snorton further conceptualizes social death in context, relating it to Frantz Fanon's discussion of "still life," Achille Mbembe's notion of "raw life," Giorgio Agamben's conception of "bare life," and Christina Sharpe's "the wake." He shows how Patterson's work and its antecedents in Black studies theorize genres of contested living and how "life and death function as schemata for systems of social valuation" (Snorton 2017, 185).

40 The term *thingification* originally comes from Aimé Césaire.

41 Keguro Macharia grapples with how "thinghood" allows space "to think about those considered not-quite-human and, at times, unhuman" in relation to histories of black diaspora and how black diasporic thinkers and artists imagined their creation of usable histories and usable lives (2019, 3).

42 The threat that intersex poses to Christianity, and its reduction to a naturalized intractable anatomy, represents centuries of history. In a comparative example from the early fourteenth century, French theologian Peter of Palude "posed the hypothetical problem of a hermaphrodite priest. Should such a person be ordained? Tellingly, his answer arose from the ways in which hermaphroditism set humans apart from nonhumans" (DeVun 2014, 465).

43 The Catholic order wanted Gross outcast, but she qualifies her assessments: "It should be noted, though, that all of this reflects the decisions and actions of a tiny handful of people who monopolised information and power in relation to my situation. The members of my former Order and Catholics and other Christians at large are not to be tarred with the same brush" (2013).

44 Jared Sexton is referencing Fanon's ([1952] 2008) assertion of black confidence in the face of white superiority in *Black Skin, White Masks*, what he describes as "an embrace of pathology without pathos" (2011, 28; see also Moten 2018, 229–30).

45 In *The 3rd Sex* (van Huyssteen 2003), Gross asserts that almost every intersexed person she has met "has at some stage attempted to commit suicide." Her comments are affirmed by an interview with psychologist Gareth Hunt in the film; he states that the categorical denial of belonging and repeated surgeries facing those deemed intersex commonly leads to suicidal ideation.

46 South African trans and intersex activists describe the personal and wide-ranging effects of restrictive gendered identity documents—including the South African inclusion of gendered honorifics in legal documents—in submissions to the South African government (SAHRC 2003). Administrative violence facing transgender people is explored by scholars including Spade (2011), Beauchamp (2019), and Camminga (2019), who detail the limits and necessities of legal social change.

47 The impetus toward "correction" as a condition for belonging is well theorized in critical intersex studies. M. Morgan Holmes puts it this way: "In the world of the clinic into which they are born, intersexed infants and children face a prevailing perception that they are so seriously damaged it is impossible even to conceive of admitting them to the category of personhood without performing extensive and immediate medical and surgical intervention on them" (2008, 170).

48 Camminga's *Transgender Refugees and the Imagined South Africa: Bodies over Borders and Borders over Bodies* (2019) provides a timely and thoughtful analysis of contemporary manifestations of the kinds of challenges for trans migration and border crossing that Gross faced in the 1990s.

49 Prominent anti-apartheid activist, parliamentarian, and professor gertrude festerwicomb explains these strategies based on her firsthand experience: "When Gross returned to South Africa, she had many problems with the Department of Home Affairs. . . . She approached a gender equality commissioner, Shelia Meintjes, and myself to enquire how we could assist her and other trans and intersex people. When i met her, i was deeply impressed by the amount of research she had done on intersex people globally. However, she was not able to do much research on their position in South Africa. I questioned whether we could not do more local research, since this would be needed if we wanted to facilitate any change in laws, and she met with Meintjes and me to share her ideas about researching the South

African situation" (2021, 81). Fester-wicomb explains the resistance and ignorance they faced and how they worked to educate and shape new ideas of gender.

50 In *Sex in Transition,* I detail the historical collusions between medicine and the law in policing the parameters of gender. In the 1960s, the Births, Marriages and Deaths Registration Act allowed legal change of gender "on the recommendation of the Secretary of Health." But from the 1970s through the end of apartheid into the 1990s, adherence to British legal precedent made it impossible to change gender on legal documents, even when medical authorities confirmed that this change was warranted. The resulting legal discrimination focused on trans people, with an impact on those who are intersex, was one of the reasons Gross focused her activism on jurisprudence and the law (Swarr 2012).

51 Ryan Thoreson explores shifts in trans and intersex activism in South Africa after 2000, characterizing agendas as focused less on rights and more on medical reconceptualizations. Further, he argues, "In their practice and rhetoric, trans and intersex activists have thus eschewed a narrow focus on borders and South African nationalism," instead embracing "a pan-African, transnational approach" and situating themselves as part of a global trans and intersex social movement (2013, 659).

52 Numerous publications, including my own, have explored gendered legal changes in South Africa (e.g., Klein 2009; Swarr 2012; Husakouskaya 2013; Thoreson 2013; Rubin 2017). It is also important to note that laws have been unevenly applied. Expectations of medical and material proof for legal changes are still often required by the Department of Home Affairs, and activist efforts continue to try to expose these hypocrisies (e.g., Camminga 2019).

53 Gross, Theron, and I wrote collaboratively about the significance of Semenya's plight for intersex activism in 2009. In this context, Gross explains the strategy behind her efforts to gain publicity and to make the amendment to the Promotion of Equality Act and its implications known through the media. "Unless I am much mistaken, the appearance of the article in the *Mail and Guardian* at this time makes it impossible for jurists, litigators and legislators to ignore it and its implications now, and the implications are in fact substantial" (Swarr, Gross, and Theron 2009, 659).

54 Gross also highlights the insufficiency of documents to affect deep-seated attitudes about intersex. Even when her identity documents matched her gender identification, medical personnel still treated her disdainfully.

55 The fundraising campaign for Gross initiated by Mitchell, started in January 24, 2014, can be found at https://www.gofundme.com/f/6gc520.

56 The only other documents on the ISSA website during this time were an article dated January 1, 2018, on substance abuse and drugs, also supposedly by Lennox, titled "Don't Let Intolerance Ruin Your Life," and a link to information titled "About Us" that replicated ISSA's organizational mission statement.

57 For instance, Behind the Mask was an extensive website of queer African histories and actions (including intersex activism) that went dormant in 2012 due to lack of funding. Activists engaged on social media may also chose to remove videos and posts that have important political significance but that compromise their safety or include personal information that they change their minds about sharing.

58 This is the organization's web address: http://www.intersex.org.za/.

1   The IAAF, an acronym that originally stood for International Amateur Athletics Federation, changed its name to World Athletics in 2019 in an effort to save its reputation after doping and corruption scandals left its president and other leaders in prison. I refer to the organization as IAAF before its name change and as World Athletics after.

2   Critiques of representations inattentive to racist and gendered histories have been incisive, yet such critics' calls have not been widely heeded (e.g. Macharia 2009; Munro 2010; Hoad 2010; Magubane 2014; and Rubin 2017).

3   I choose to refer to *gender testing* instead of *sex testing* in this chapter. As explained previously, I do not find the distinction between gender and sex useful. In my view, separating the two makes sex seem like a solid and objective scientific truth of the body, in comparison to the malleability of gender. In reality, both sex and gender are subjective historical productions better discussed together under the rubric of gender.

4   Historian Carina Ray (2009) also saw rivals' racist comments as a distraction, "sour grapes" from those deeply invested in undermining a competitor who beat them again and again, and their stakes in her career certainly belied any assumptions of objectivity. Yet reporters continued to cite these athletes' comments and feed the suspicion of Semenya. Demands like Savinova's "just look at her" suggest that a truth of gender is visible on her body. David Rubin contextualizes these comments in colonial histories of visibility, "in which black and brown female bodies and gender nonconforming bodies have long been treated as extraordinary objects of biomedical scrutiny and biopolitical regulation" (2017, 129).

5   See Moya Bailey's (2016) analysis of misogynoir in representations of Semenya in medical media.

6   One typically troubling report pronounced that the "physical evidence is damning. Her muscular development, the narrowness of her figure, the facial features, jaw line, facial hair and deep voice sent off alarm bells" (Gullan quoted in Schultz 2012, 287). Both Schultz (2012) and Miller (2015) offer extensive analyses of Semenya's visual representations in the media.

7   Height and long legs are just two of aspects of the body that may lead to success in sports like basketball and track. Olympic swimmer Michael Phelps has long been assumed to have the long limbs and flexible joints of Marfan syndrome that facilitate his swimming success. But these ungendered physical advantages are of no interest to those who regulate professional sport, and they highlight the biases of efforts targeting Semenya and other athletes.

8   Bavington demonstrates that the commonly cited rationale for gender regulations— preventing men from competing in women's events—is strikingly inconsistent with a 1936 proposal from Avery Brundage, then president of the American Olympic Committee, seeking to prevent the participation of "abnormal" women (2019, 186).

9   Heggie's historical work finds that the rules "requiring that female competitors bring a medical certificate to prove that they were eligible to compete" originated in 1946 for the IAAF and in 1948 for the IOC (2010, 159).

10 Cox was referring primarily to Black women from the United States as "hermaphrodites." No African nations entered the Olympics until the 1960s.

11 Arne Ljungqvist, chair of the IAAF Medical Commission from 1980 to 2004 and member of the IOC Medical Commission since 1987, also acknowledges that suspicions of intersex, not so-called gender fraud regarding men competing in women's events, are behind such testing. He writes that gender testing was initiated because "there had been rumours for years that there were athletes competing in the women's events who were more male than female, making it an unfair competition for 'real' women. To thwart the rumours, the IOC decided to introduce some kind of control" (2011, 183).

12 Racist histories of sport are strongly linked to eugenics (Gilroy 2004). Tavia N'yongo discusses such troubling connections among eugenics and sport in initial responses to Semenya's scrutiny (2010).

13 As Lindsay Parks Pieper points out, "US citizens disparagingly depicted women of the USSR as 'graceless, shapeless and sexless.' Degrading the Soviets' physiques as masculine and unsexed served to discredit the nation's government, suggesting that the 'ills of communism were inscribed on the bodies of women.' In addition, Americans claimed that the Soviet Union inverted the natural gender order by forcing women into labor. The hard, physical work—similar to athletic training—transformed the muscularity of the Russian women, which contradicted the United States' dominant understandings of the female form" (2016, 43). By contrast, the Soviet state favored egalitarianism in the law and the strength that comes from physical labor.

14 A 1960 proposal from American doctor Raymond Bunge called for the IOC to introduce sex chromatin testing to prevent what he referred to as "genetic doping" (Bavington 2019, 186), again conflating natural hormonal differences with fraudulent activities.

15 It is also notable that secret policies requiring athletes to take steroids in the German Democratic Republic became infamous for their damaging effects, while drug use in the United States was both ignored and enabled. In the 1980s, the US public was obsessed with suspicions about Russia, but US athletes were some of the worst drug offenders. The US Olympic Committee did not impose sanctions or even announce the eighty-six positive tests among US athletes until after the 1984 Olympics. The IOC Medical Commission then weakened the doping controls in the next Olympic games, even as it simultaneously strengthened gender testing (Pieper 2016, 123). Positive doping tests have also been routinely disregarded for more privileged athletes due to rampant corruption. Duplicity related to drug use colors all elite sport, and in 2020 Lamine Diack, IAAF president from 1999 to 2015, and other top IAAF officials were convicted of years of doping-related corruption charges.

16 Yale University endocrinologist Dr. Myron Genet detailed the motives of the Heinonen Sixteen in archival correspondence to the IOC Gender Verification Workshop Group: "As I suspected, much of this is fueled by the remarkable success of the Chinese distance runners. If there is any doubt about this, the cover article of *Keeping Track* is devoted entirely to the Chinese women runners and their recent disappearance from world level running events. There is a not-so-hidden sugges-

tion that the success of the group trained by Ma Junren was because of the use of banned substances or other nefarious maneuvers. According to the attached article from the May 4 *New York Times*, however, the success of the Chinese women runners may be more attributable to their remarkable training regimen"; Gender verification correspondence, May–September, including further correspondence regarding the "refined proposal from the Heinonen Sixteen" and the possibility of holding a conference with the sixteen athletes to discuss gender verification tests further, May 19, 1994, UGC 183/8/26, b20045645, Papers of Malcolm Andrew Ferguson-Smith, Professor of Genetics, University of Glasgow, Scotland, Wellcome Library, London, England (hereinafter Ferguson-Smith Papers).

17 There was also a condescending component of the proposal from the Heinonen Sixteen, which suggested that "educational testing" could help athletes from developing nations learn about their gender "abnormalities" before they advanced in elite sport. This article is titled "Give-and-Take on Gender Verification" (1994), gender verification correspondence, UGC 188/8/26, b20045645, Ferguson-Smith Papers.

18 See also Hida Patricia Valoria and Maria Jose Martínez-Patino's (2012) examination of "fairness" based on their experiences and their participation in these same meetings hosted by the IOC in Lausanne.

19 From its inception, gender testing has been imposed only on those competing as women, long considered a vulnerable and protected category dedicated to white femininity, and never on men.

20 Other African athletes, including Maria Mutola from Mozambique, have also been publicly targeted and are discussed later in this chapter.

21 Competitive track was reluctantly permitted for women athletes beginning in 1928, but sporting authorities were resentful and routinely portrayed those who were successful as overly masculine.

22 South Africa was banned from the Olympics from 1964 to 1992 due to worldwide reaction to apartheid.

23 Munro continues, "In modern sports, the border between male and female is inspected and policed in a quite literal sense, and Semenya is accused of being an illegal immigrant across that border. It is international sports itself, though, that has smuggled a particular set of ideas about sex differences around the world, under the guise of the universal, the natural, and the scientific" (2010, 387).

24 Judith Butler (2009) queries the broader implications of the attention focused on Semenya: "So rather than try and find out what sex Semenya or anyone else really 'is,' why don't we think instead about standards for participation under gender categories that have the aim of being both egalitarian and inclusive? Only then might we finally cease the sensationalist witch hunt antics of finding anyone's 'true sex' and open sports to the complexly constituted species of human animals to which we belong."

25 In early years, Semenya has sometimes seemed willing to give up her career, stating, "For me, running is nothing. Honestly, it's nothing," while at other times, she has been steadfast in her determination. Changing regulations and redefinitions of gender by the IAAF have consistently hindered her career, and these investigations, as Semenya explained in 2010, "have dragged on too long with no reasonable certainty

as to their end. The result is that my athletic capabilities and earning potential are being severely compromised." Over a decade later, she is engaged in the same fight.

26 Dutee Chand was another important pioneer in defiantly speaking out about the injustice she faced. After being barred from elite competition because of her naturally high testosterone levels, Chand appealed to the Court of Arbitration for Sport and was successful, leading to suspension of the IAAF's "hyperandrogynism" regulations from 2015 to 2018.

27 For instance, Francine Niyonsaba from Burundi and Maximila Imali and Margaret Wambui from Kenya have all spoken openly about the impact of the 2018 IAAF hyperandrogenism rulings on them.

28 Early representations of Semenya's perspectives can be found in the 2011 film *Too Fast to Be a Woman? The Story of Caster Semenya* (Ginnane 2011).

29 The South African government reportedly spent $15 million to defend Semenya in her most recent court case.

30 Leonard Chuene was subsequently suspended from his position, and in 2011 he was convicted for mishandling Semenya's treatment as well as for a host of other abuses of power, financial scandals, and corruption. He passed away in 2021.

31 Mandela famously stated that sport is "more powerful than governments in breaking down racial barriers" and that "sport has the power to change the world. It has the power to inspire, the power to unite people that little else has" (quoted in Levy 2009, 49).

32 The website for Xcollektiv is https://xcollektiv.wordpress.com/, and the collective also posts on Facebook and Twitter. On their website, they describe themselves in the following way: "The Xcollektiv is a creative incubator for collaborative multidisciplinary projects by visual-artists, writers, filmmakers and performers who are exploring issues of dispossession, trauma, memory and resistance through their work. Our aim is to facilitate and initiate projects that pose questions and draws attention to issues and to connect with ordinary lives through public creative processes. Our intention is to weave an 'in-cooperative' expression that will be comprised of and will infiltrate different media spaces: to reach neglected audiences, and build community and agency around issues of individual and collective importance."

33 The original cartoon's title is translated from the French as "The curious in ecstasy or shoelaces," referring to the curious woman bending down to tie her shoelaces while gazing at the exposed penis under the kilt in supposed ecstasy.

34 See the IAAF's 2018 declaration and explanation here: "IAAF Introduces New Eligibility Regulations for Female Classification," press release, World Athletics, April 2018, https://www.worldathletics.org/news/press-release/eligibility-regulations-for-female-classifica.

35 De Mérode initially presented himself as a self-styled doping expert, but Pieper (2016) argues that his expertise was based on just one academic paper (authored by Belgian doctor Albert Dirix). The prince was most likely appointed because of his public profile and influence.

36 Correspondence concerning the buccal smear test, including copies of correspondence sent to Ferguson-Smith and comments by him thereon, UGC 188/8/5, b20045438, Ferguson-Smith Papers.

37 The logistics of gender testing have always represented a failed quest to find positivist truths in the body. Before 1968, gender was verified by doctors' visual examinations of athletes' genitals, informally referred to as "nude parades," and gynecological assessments were deemed humiliating and inconclusive. The discovery of the structure of DNA in 1953 and gendered chromosomes in 1955 inspired a new consensus, as chromosomes were inaccurately equated with gender truths. When chromosomal testing was implemented for the 1968 Olympics in Mexico City, all women were forced to submit to it. But the tests were based on poor science and were predictably rife with false results.

38 When asked about better ways of determining gender, Albert de la Chapelle reflected, "How would I organize things? My final stand is, I would simply have no test at all. This view is based on the assumption that anyone who feels like a woman, looks like a woman, and has a name and passport of a woman, is a woman" (Correspondence concerning the buccal smear test, November 6, 1989, UGC 188/8/5, b20045438, Ferguson-Smith Papers).

39 Correspondence concerning the buccal smear test, November 6, 1989, UGC 188/8/5, b20045438, Ferguson-Smith Papers.

40 By the 1990s, medical associations including the American Academy of Pediatrics, American College of Obstetricians and Gynecologists, American College of Physicians, American Medical Association, American Society of Human Genetics, and the Endocrine Society all publicly opposed gender testing.

41 "Treatments"—ways to surgically and hormonally reduce natural testosterone levels—have only been offered to athletes in recent years as an alternative to withdrawing from competition. Their ugly ramifications for individual athletes are discussed below.

42 According to Bermon, while intersex occurs more frequently in the Global South, it is also less diagnosed. He blames infrequent diagnoses on indigent facilities and incompetent doctors with inadequate expertise.

43 African genital cutting has long been a problematic focus of white feminists (addressed further in chapter 5). Stanlie James (2002) documents accounts of white women from the Global North opposing African genital cutting as early as 1929.

44 Bermon condescendingly and inaccurately puts it this way: "We do nothing to 'fit people into the norm.' If a person claims to be a woman and wants to compete IN THIS PROTECTED FEMALE CATEGORY, then she should be happy to lower her testosterone level. If this is not the case one must ask questions (a) about her true sexual identity, (b) about possible secondary benefits to maintain[ing] her high testosterone levels" (quoted in Mulot 2019).

45 Paula Radcliffe and Sharon Davies are British white athletes who have publicly targeted and condemned Semenya, falsely claiming she has an "unfair advantage" and is "biologically male." I analyze Radcliffe's beef with Semenya at length in the conclusion to this chapter.

46 This publication was first brought to my attention by the brilliant analyses of Karkazis and Jordan-Young (2018). In the Fénichel paper, the specific "developing

countries" are not identified in an effort to protect patient anonymity, though critics were easily able to identify these athletes by details given. The hospitals mentioned here regularly perform unnecessary procedures on elite athletes on behalf of sports governing bodies (Fénichel et al. 2013, E1055).

47 Antidoping control officers are not medical professionals. They are minimally trained to screen patients for illegal drug use and to observe/judge athletes' genital "normality" as they urinate. In addition to genital inspections, urine drawn for doping tests may be tested for testosterone levels, often without athletes' knowledge or consent. As the authors of a Human Rights Watch report explain, "Doping control can serve as a backdoor to test any woman deemed suspicious by sports governing bodies, but it is also a route to test all women via collection of blood and urine samples" (HRW 2020, 83).

48 A 5α-reductase deficiency is an inherited autosomal condition that affects the development of reproductive and genital organs (addressed at length in the introduction).

49 The acronym SDRD5A2 refers to patients with the steroid 5α-reductase type 2 gene.

50 Testosterone-lowering medications have side effects that regularly include excessive thirst and urination, electrolyte imbalances, metabolic problems, and headaches, fatigue, and nausea (Jordan-Young, Sönksen, and Karkazis 2014, 21).

51 The mentioned references for Maimoun et al. 2011 are Imperato-McGinley et al. 1974; Imperato-McGinley et al. 1979; Imperato-McGinley et al. 1986; Imperato-McGinley et al. 1991; Jenkins et al. 1992; Thigpen et al. 1992; Cai et al. 1996; and Canto et al. 1997. The references for Houk et al. are Imperato-McGinley et al. 1974; Peterson et al. 1977; Imperato-McGinley et al. 1979; Imperato-McGinley et al. 1980; Imperato-McGinley et al. 1986; Carpenter et al. 1990; Imperato-McGinley et al. 1991; Thigpen et al. 1992; Cai et al. 1994; Cantovatchel et al. 1994; Katz et al. 1995; Cai et al. 1996; Imperato-McGinley 1997; Katz et al. 1997; and Imperato-McGinley and Zhu 2002. In addition to these links, Houk et al. 2005 cite Gilbert Herdt's similarly troubling work on Papua New Guinea discussed in the introduction (Herdt and Davidson 1988) and reference John Money's problematized protocols from the United States (Money, Hampson, and Hampson 1955; Money and Ogunro 1974).

52 I am again relying on Butler's (1993) conceptions of citationality in this formulation.

53 The 2019 film first aired on German television.

54 As Katrina Karkazis and Morgan Carpenter succinctly put it: "The alternatives available to athletes are presented under the guise of choice, but each option carries its own high price. The choice is to subjugate oneself to power: alter your body, accept being labeled, or leave. It is an impossible set of choices" (2018, 586). They thoughtfully detail the options available under the 2018 sporting regulations: submitting to constant invasive assessments and interventions, competing with men or in an imagined intersex sport category, or challenging the regulations.

55 The experiences of athletes affected by gender regulations have been largely unknown. But when comparing accounts, researchers find important patterns emerging: "Each athlete received limited information about the regulations and the procedures for their implementation, and limited information about the purpose and outcomes of the medical tests they underwent. Each was presented with a set

of options that involved medically unnecessary and potentially harmful procedures they were pressured to undergo to maintain their eligibility to compete. And each of the athletes, in this situation where they lacked information and were confronted with the loss of their career, experienced coercion" (HRW 2020, 66).

56 The film *Gender Battle* features heartbreaking interviews with the family of Indian runner Santhi Soundarajan, who attempted suicide one year after a failed gender test in 2007 (Sviridinko, Willison, and Seppelt 2019). Indian Olympian Dutee Chand experienced similar trauma following her diagnosis of hyperandrogenism in 2018. Chand has spoken publicly about the consequences of losing her career and identity, including in her testimony to the Court of Arbitration for Sport.

57 Human Rights Watch researchers reveal patterns of enforced femininity and cosmetic surgery like breast enhancements to deter suspicion of athletes in the Global South. "For example, in J. G.'s case what began as officials telling her to augment her appearance with makeup and jewelry then grew into recommendations for cosmetic genital surgery. 'Coaches told me to grow my hair long, wear lipstick and earrings, and wear a padded bra to look more like a woman,' J. G. said. The coach, she said, delivered this instruction in front of the entire team, so everyone around her was aware of the profiling taking place. Soon after that incident, officials from her local sports ministry suggested to J. G. that she undergo surgery to make her body appear more feminine: '[They] told me to do a surgery. Not related to testosterone—not specific, just because my body was different, maybe to make breasts'" (HRW 2020, 89).

58 Additional hashtags on Twitter that have waxed and waned in popularity in recent years include #IAAFMustFall, #CasterSemenya, #IStandForCaster, #IStandWithCaster, #LetHerRun, #SupportSemenya, #NaturallySuperior, #IAAFRegulating, and #WeAreCasterSemenya.

59 In Pedi, Semenya's given name—Mokgadi—means one who guides others.

60 Not only does Gladwell inaccurately (and derogatorily) describe the influence of testosterone, he invokes two additional common and false tropes. The first is the idea that gender regulations are based on an objective notion of "fairness"; fairness in women's sport has historically developed as a raced and classed notion to facilitate the success of white women in the Global North. Second, the conception of women as a "protected category" assumes both women's inherent weakness and a need for protection (from other women deemed too masculine by US and western European standards).

61 Beginning in November 2018, Cornelius would have been tasked with enforcing new regulations to restrict South African athletes with testosterone deemed "too high." He resigned because he refused to do so. Cornelius explains that if a dispute arose about an athlete's testosterone levels, he would be forced to apply rules he finds unconscionable. As a result, "Just from an ethical and moral point of view, I can't be part of it so I had to speak out against it. . . . I won't be required to enforce regulations that I think are manifestly unfair and most likely unlawful in most parts of the civilised world" (quoted in Feltham 2018).

62 Scholars of social media have celebrated the space afforded by online platforms in creating counter-publics while also addressing limitations of social media.

Critiques focus on, for instance, trans oppression due to surveillance/dataveillance (Korn and Kneese 2015; Fischer 2019; Beauchamp 2019) and racist "white savior" narratives found in online feminist spaces (Kaba et al. 2014; Tambe 2018).

63 As of 2018, 16 million South Africans used Facebook and 8 million used Twitter, where discussions about politics accounted for about 10 percent of all tweets, a number considerably higher than 1–2 percent of political hashtags in the United States and UK (Maluleke and Moyer 2020, 877–80).

64 See *Rhodes Must Fall: The Struggle to Decolonise the Racist Heart of Empire* (Chantiluke, Kwoba, and Nkopo 2018) for a range of accounts about the global impact of this movement.

65 Gavaza Maluleke and Eileen Moyer trace the roots of fallism to murdered anti-apartheid leader Steve Biko's ideology of Black consciousness (2020, 881); see also Hussen 2018.

66 *Mzansi* is a colloquial word for South Africans often used affectionately.

67 Semenya's acceptance and self-representation need to be contextualized in social media proliferation and changing ideas about gender on a global scale. In theorizing revolutionary change, social commentators have long played with a slogan of the US-based Black Panther movement coined in the 1960s—"The Revolution will not be televised." This slogan, popularized by Gil Scott-Heron's 1970 poem and song of the same title, offered a critique of corporate and popular cultures as a medium for social revolution. In 2010, journalist Malcolm Gladwell (coincidentally the negative inspiration for the #HandsOffCaster hashtag), reinvigorated debate about this phrase when he penned a widely circulated article for the *New Yorker* suggesting "The Revolution Will Not Be Tweeted" (2010). Gladwell's contention was taken up in the wake of the North African Arab Spring revolution the following year when an article in *Foreign Policy* responded, "The Revolution *Will* Be Tweeted" (Hounshell 2011, emphasis added). In discussing the silent protest that took place in front of a televised 2016 speech by accused rapist and former South African president Jacob Zuma and the related hashtag #RememberKhwezi, Gavaza Maluleke and Eileen Moyer point out that in-person, televised, and online activism can be simultaneous: "In a seeming counter to Gil Scott-Heron's 1970 poem, the revolution was not only televised, it was live-tweeted" (2020, 893). The role of foreign intervention in African activism is also foregrounded in Felogene Anumo and Valérie Bah's (2017) suggestion that for African feminist organizers, "The Revolution Will Not Be NGO-ised." As discussed in this chapter and in chapter 5, multiple forms of media and self-representation are increasingly critical to African intersex, queer, and feminist activist strategies.

68 At the time of this writing, Twitter is worth $4.4 billion, and Instagram is worth $100 billion; profit motives and political affiliations strongly affect the potential for social media as a site for radical social change.

69 Within one year, Nike's YouTube post of the ad had more than 13 million views.

70 "Just Do It: Caster Semenya," posted by Caster Semenya on Twitter (@caster800m), 1:00, September 11, 2018, https://twitter.com/caster800m/status/1039417826518491137 ?ref_src=twsrc%5Etfw%7Ctwcamp%5Etweetembed%7Ctwterm%5E103941782651 8491137%7Ctwgr%5E%7Ctwcon%5Es1_c10&ref_url=https%3A%2F%2Fwww.espn

.com%2Folympics%2Fstory%2F_%2Fid%2F24650607%2Fcaster-semenya-new-nike
-ad-was-born-do-this.

71 *Interphobia* (sometimes *intersexphobia*) is a term coined by scholar and activist
Cary Gabriel Costello in 2010. The corporatization of Pride and the rainbow flag
has been accompanied by "pinkwashing," as corporate sponsors now see queerness
as a boon for their businesses.

72 In 2014, *Time* magazine decreed that the world had reached "The Transgender
Tipping Point" due to shifts in legislation, media, and medicine (Steinmetz 2014),
but this so-called tipping point was a celebration of celebrities and assimilation
rather than an indicator of substantive changes in the lives of the majority of trans
people. Indeed, gestures toward acceptance may actually prevent revolution by
promising change while masking structural inequities (Spade 2011; Aizura 2017) or
provoking backlash.

73 Online social movements opposing oppression in countries including South Africa,
Nigeria, Sudan, Malawi, and Botswana have also relied on hashtag activism (Sebeelo 2020, 96–97). But social media in Africa has its limitations and drawbacks, at
times providing space for homophobic surveillance and homonationalist political
violence incited by those in the Global North (Currier and Moreau 2016).

74 Savinova was never subjected to the scrutiny Semenya faced, and her use of steroids
was discovered not through drug or gender testing. Instead, her own overconfi-
dent statements were captured during a doping exposé and revealed in a German
television program. The secret footage of Savinova became part of a documentary
exposing decades of doping among elite Russian athletes systemically coordinated
by Russian officials (Seppelt 2014). In it, Savinova is shown discussing her use of
anabolic steroids with the support of her husband, who, she states, had contacts in
the doping lab where athletes were tested.

75 Savinova was stripped of her gold medal, which was awarded to Semenya; Savinova's wins over the prior three years were nullified; and she was prevented from
competing again professionally until 2021. But this sanction controversially did not
affect her financial gains from sport.

76 Radcliffe even testified against Indian athlete Dutee Chand in her fight against her
exclusion from sport in 2015.

77 Current policy falsely suggests that *hyperandrogenism*, defined as excess androgen
production in women, is a medical problem. The term is used by sporting officials
as a euphemism for intersex, which is an application they invented.

78 Bermon and Garnier together are notable as the current and former directors of the
IAAF/World Athletics' Health and Sciences Department, exemplifying the incestuous
ethics of those determining the parameters of gender in sport. Their correction also
admits the need for independent research; "Ultimately, an independent, prospectively
designed, randomly controlled trial is needed to establish confirmatory scientific
evidence for the causal relationships between the variables analysed" (Bermon and
Garnier 2021, e7). But as Laine Higgins points out, "It's something critics of the study
have requested for years, likening World Athletics' research process to a cigarette
company conducting an investigation into the health effects of smoking" (2021).

79 The 2018 gender rulings by the IAAF, which continue to be upheld, are a direct result of this one study.

5. TOWARD AN "AFRICAN INTERSEX REFERENCE OF INTELLIGENCE"

1 This chapter explores both South African activism and broader Africa-wide interventions like the African Intersex Movement.

2 The acronym representing this organization has not been consistent historically, as Gross's own references in chapter 3 demonstrate. Intersex South Africa has been sometimes referred to as ISSA, ISA, and ISOA. Today it is known as ISSA, so I use that acronym consistently here. Iranti was founded in 2012 by Jabulani Pereira with an explicit focus on queer visual media, and the organization has since worked to document and advocate, in part, by "witnessing" events ranging from court cases to historic legislative gains for transgender and intersex people all over Africa (https://www.iranti.org.za/). This chapter addresses the work of only a small selection of organizations, but many others have been working in partnership over the past decade, including Transgender and Intersex Africa, Gender DynamiX, the Triangle Project, Transhope, and Matimba.

3 This work builds on the discussions in chapter 4, further emphasizing the growing power of social media for unseating interphobia.

4 I reference this important document throughout this chapter. It addresses the National Intersex Meeting that took place on December 11, 2017, and included delegates from South African NGOs, governmental departments, and academia (*National Dialogue* 2018, 36).

5 Lungile Maquba and Joshua Sehoole detail: "Sally, who worked tirelessly to ensure visibility and redress of the ongoing human rights violations of intersex people in South Africa, secured the first known mention, globally, of intersex in national law through the inclusion of 'intersex' within the definition of 'sex' in the *Promotion of Equality and Prevention of Unfair Discrimination Act*, which governs the judicial interpretation of the Equality Clause. She subsequently helped to draft legislation on the *Alteration of Sex Descriptors and Sex Status Act 49 of 2003*, which allows intersex citizens to change their sex descriptors on their identification documents" (*National Dialogue* 2018, 1).

6 For instance, a 2015 campaign by Iranti featured a photograph of South African intersex activists who are also identical twins with accompanying text that states, "there are as many intersex people as there are twins."

7 Activists are alluding to the prevalence and impact of John Money's theories of children's gender plasticity detailed in chapter 1.

8 Mokoena articulates the feelings that come from being a research subject shared by many South Africans. Gross similarly says that she didn't want to be a "specimen or lab rat," and Semenya uses the same language as Mokoena: "guinea pig."

9 After learning her surgery had been elective and unnecessary, Hendricks returned to Tygerberg Hospital in Cape Town, where the surgery had taken place, to get answers, but she was told that no files or records of her medical treatment could be found. Access to full medical records is another important priority for activists.

10 Institutionalized and traumatic visual examinations in school contexts are widely cited by intersex activists. For instance, activists share these and similar accounts: "In 2010 a principal at a school in Ga-Ntatelang village near Kuruman undressed a six-year-old child, who had ambiguous genitalia" (John 2012).

11 Tamale further describes the ramifications of colonialism: "The unhealed scars are still seen in the linear shapes of the boundaries that make up Africa's 54 nation states, in its legal, political and education systems as well as religious institutions. They are evident in the invisible tentacles that drive and direct our economies. We experience them as internalized discourses of power and submission in people's social, political and religious lives" (2020, 18).

12 Mtshawu's YouTube channel is Babalwa Mtshawu, accessed August 2021, https://www.youtube.com/c/BabalwaMtshawu; as of August 2021, it contained 153 personal vlogs.

13 At the time this vlog was recorded and posted, Mtshawu was a doctoral student in geography at the University of the Free State. In this vlog, her textbooks are visible on her desk, and the walls are decorated with a large South African map and colorful letters that read: "Wish it Dream it Do it!"

14 The music video clip was from the song titled "What" (Playboi Carti and UnoThe-Activist), ASAPROCKYUPTOWN, video, 3:38, June 29, 2016, https://www.youtube.com/watch?v=wcJVXg7gg4w.

15 Mtshawu also discusses language differences affecting gender pronouns in another vlog, *You Can't Ask That: Intersex Cringe Worthy Questions*, Babalwa Mtshawu, video, 16:35, April 2, 2020, https://youtu.be/aUKnVIcip4Q.

16 Mtshawu discusses her mixed reactions to the response to the viral BBC Africa interview and reflects on the paradoxes of visibility. While the video reached half a million views in a few days, the comments on it were "quite brutal." She explains this as yet another pitfall of wide visibility for intersex activists: "There's a lot of negativity associated with the number of views you get probably because smaller crowds tend to be nicer and bigger crowds tend to be very mean. And when you're talking about your journey within a particular topic that is considered taboo in Africa, you're going to deal with a lot of backlash" (quoted in Samanga 2019).

17 This report was published under the auspices of StopIGM.org/Zwischengeschlecht .org, an organization founded in 2007 as a self-described "international human rights non-governmental organization." This organization explains itself as led by intersex persons, partners, families, and friends. It "works to represent the interests of intersex people and their relatives, raise awareness, and fight IGM Practices and other human rights violations perpetrated on intersex people according to its motto, 'Human Rights for Hermaphrodites, too!'" (Bauer and Truffer 2016, 5). The report draws on intersex activism in Switzerland and the UK, as well as on published works by Sally Gross and ISSA, testimony by Nthabiseng Mokoena, work by South African organizations Iranti and Gender DynamiX, and the authors' own research and "personal communications with intersex people from South Africa" (Bauer and Truffer 2016, 6).

18 In this 2001 article, Wiersma's citations for this unproven claim include himself (Wiersma and Constantinides 1993), Van Niekerk (1976), Grace (1977), and Aaronson (1985); see his similar claims in Wiersma (2008). In his doctoral dissertation

a decade later, Wiersma makes the same claim: "The high incidence of OT-DSD [formerly referred to as "true hermaphroditism"] in the Southern African black population group is unusual"; but he concedes, "Despite considerable research on the condition, no explanation for this occurrence has yet been offered" (2011, 67).

19 The images of patients represented as three of Grace's cases (numbers 26, 28, and 29) are printed on pages 18–19; the authors do not explain why they chose these particular cases and photographs.

20 Infanticide is a practice documented globally and is, of course, not uniquely African. Existing research on infanticide in African contexts connects it to unplanned pregnancies (e.g., Thomas 2007) and albinism (e.g., Blankenberg 2000), among others, but not to intersex.

21 One productive activist dialogue on this issue in 2017 brought together activists, governmental officials, community health-care workers, and traditional healers. This meeting represented a collaboration between Iranti, Intersex South Africa, and the Commission for the Promotion and Protection of the Rights of Cultural, Religious and Linguistic Communities to discuss "Intersex Rights in Rural Settings."

22 The acronym LEGBO initially stood for Lesbian, Gay, Bisexual Organization.

23 Julius Kaggwa is an incredible activist, known as perhaps the first intersex person in Africa to publish on his experience (1997; 2011); he is executive director of SIPD (Support Initiative for People with Congenital Disorders, https://sipdug.org/) in Uganda. He states: "In many African countries, the traditional way of dealing with perceived sexuality 'abnormalities' has largely been staying silent—and wishing them away through various kinds of traditional rituals, which often meant killing the intersex infants." The report continues, "Moreover as a perceived 'cultural practice' infanticide can go fairly hidden, in that the numbers are largely unknown because the babies are dumped with no intention of being found. Mothers can retain their place in communities and society and avoid stigma often through taking this route or pleading ignorance regarding the actions of midwives or birth assistants" (*National Dialogue* 2018, 13)

24 Work on early representations of intersex and monstrosity includes Leah Devun's (2021) analysis, *The Shape of Sex: Nonbinary Gender from Genesis to the Renaissance*.

25 In Gross's (2013) view, governmental and religious disinterest in infanticide was another manifestation of intersex social death; she writes, "Social death strikes again, quite possibly leading to the condonation of infanticide on an industrial scale." She also discussed her views of infanticide in an interview with Trish Beaver published in *the Witness* (2012).

26 Mokoena's theories recall Oyèrónké Oyěwùmí's (1997) interrogation of gender binaries as a colonial imposition in Yorùbáland, discussed in the introduction.

27 Lack of medical care means few treatment options in rural areas, and many families are unable to afford expenses required to travel for specialized care. Mokoena details, "And that is the typical experience that when I was working at Transgender and Intersex Africa that most intersex people from Mpumulanga and the North West and Limpopo had to travel to Gauteng to have access to health because there wasn't access in their provinces" (Le Roux and Mokoena 2016).

28 The acronym FGM was first introduced by feminist activists in the Global North seeking to condemn practices in Africa without parallel considerations of similar practices in the United States and Europe or their cultural contexts. There are wide schisms between feminists from the Global North who have objectified African women through their condemnation and African women critical of these practices. Oyèrónké Oyěwùmí's "Alice in Motherland" (2003) provides a brilliant critique of this divide. Many activists and scholars prefer language such as "genital cutting" or "female genital cutting," though the word *female* itself also suggests a naturalized gendered body and anatomy that intersex activists work to unsettle.

29 ISNA's efforts to forward the correlation between FGM and IGM were shared widely. Though they had wide influence in shifting opinions, ultimately this comparison did not lead to substantive legal changes.

30 David Rubin smartly critiques comparisons that judge African practices as "backward," cautioning against the possible digression of renewed comparisons of practices in the Global North and South into what he labels "intersex imperialism" (2017, 118).

31 South African intersex activists are critical of the legal condemnation of indigenous African practices because laws against such practices have had contradictory effects. They explain, "In many countries, FGM is, actually, illegal although this does not stop the practice. In fact, some research suggests that the legal injunction against it has only made the practice more dangerous by driving it underground" (*National Dialogue* 2018, 10).

32 Activists identify and call out particular pediatric centers where elective surgeries are still practiced in South Africa as the Red Cross War Memorial Hospital in Cape Town, Chris Hani Baragwanath Hospital, the Department of Paediatric Surgery at Free State University, Tygerberg Hospital, East London Hospital, and the University of KZN's Paediatric Department (*National Dialogue* 2018, 16). The support of the South African state for such surgeries while also acknowledging intersex harm makes it complicit. As Bauer and Truffer contend, "The State party is responsible for these violations constituting a harmful practice, violence against children, and torture or at least ill-treatment, perpetrated by publicly funded doctors, clinics, and universities, as well as in private clinics, all relying on money from the mandatory health insurance, and public grants" (2016, 18).

33 South African activists report that a global study of trans and intersex organizations in 107 countries concludes that intersex activist groups are severely underresourced and excluded from funding by international donor agencies and governments, with fewer than one in five intersex groups employing full-time paid staff (*National Dialogue* 2018, 26).

34 In August 2020, Iranti collaboratively launched a mutual aid fund distributed throughout southern and East Africa: Burundi, Kenya, Lesotho, Namibia, Tanzania, Uganda, and Zimbabwe. They explain, "Iranti has decided to take a 'solidarity not charity' approach to our relief efforts in the region as we also see it as the responsibility of people taking care of each other during this time" (Iranti 2020b).

35 One anonymous person recounts, "It is often difficult for me to explain myself every time I visit a health facility. When they look at my particulars (ID) and the person

before them, it raises more questions to them. The humiliation is just too much that they tend to call one health official after the other. The same thing happened when I tried to get vaccinated and was turned away after going through that dehumanising experience" (Matimaire 2021). Betha Tsitsi Masvibga Ndabambi of the Intersex Community Trust of Zimbabwe explains that many of those who were able to get the first vaccine dose had not been able to get the second dose for these same reasons.

36 Iranti explains this difficulty: "While the clear majority of media outlets had set out to report on this issue with significant sympathy for and deference to the trans, gender-diverse, and intersex communities, there was a significant lack of nuance and understanding of the issues at hand and of Iranti's specific advocacy goals. The third option was, for example, referred to over and over again as 'third gender,' which would not be an accurate descriptor for a country as socially and culturally diverse as South Africa" (Iranti 2021).

37 Activists held a webinar on the issue, and representatives of the DHA who attended acknowledged that they had already begun learning from this feedback from trans, nonbinary, and intersex activists (Igual 2021; Nortier 2021).

38 At the time of this writing (May 2021), this policy was under review by the DHA. But as this book was going to press, the DHA began offering x marker options on identity documents. Iranti partnered with the DHA undertaking multiple joint events in 2022 to help with ID, gender, and name changes, "in hopes of alleviating some of the difficulties and discrimination" faced by trans, intersex, and gender diverse people "when attempting to attain official documents that accurately reflect their identity" (Iranti [@irantiorg], Instagram, June 14, 2022, https://www.instagram .com/p/CeyxhPCDPTU/?hl=en).

Aaronson, I. A. 1985. "True Hermaphroditism: A Review of 41 Cases with Observations on Testicular Histology and Function." *British Journal of Urology* 57: 775–79.

Abrahams, Yvette. 2000. "Colonialism Dysfunction and Dysjuncture: The Historiography of Sara Bartmann." PhD diss., University of Cape Town, South Africa.

Abrahams, Yvette. 2021. "Bringing Water to Krotoa's Gardens: Decolonisation as Direct Action." In *Surfacing: On Being Black and Feminist in South Africa*, edited by Desiree Lewis and Gabeba Baderoon, 274–83. Johannesburg: Wits University Press.

Acutt, Robin, dir. 2016. *Through the Wormhole*. Season 7, episode 3, "Are There More Than Two Sexes?" Aired September 13, 2016, on the Science Channel. https://www .sciencechannel.com/video/through-the-wormhole-with-morgan-freeman-science -atve-us/are-there-more-than-two-sexes.

AIM (African Intersex Movement). 2017. "Public Statement by the African Intersex Movement." December 14. https://www.astraeafoundation.org/stories/public -statement-african-intersex-movement/.

AIM (African Intersex Movement). 2019. "African Intersex Movement—Africa's Regional Intersex Network—Established." July 3. https://www.astraeafoundation.org /stories/african-intersex-movement-statement/.

AIM (African Intersex Movement). 2020. "African Intersex Movement (AIM) Intersex Awareness Day Statement." October 26. Author's collection.

Aizura, Aren. 2017. "Introduction." *South Atlantic Quarterly* 116 (3): 606–11.

Aizura, Aren. 2018. *Mobile Subjects: Transnational Imaginaries of Gender Reassignment.* Durham, NC: Duke University Press.

Akoob, Rumana. 2018. "Laws Need to Be Put in Place to Protect Rights of Intersex People." *Daily Vox* (Johannesburg), February 2. http://www.thedailyvox.co.za/laws -need-to-be-put-in-place-to-protect-rights-of-intersex-people-rumana-akoob/.

Ally, F. E., and H. J. Grace. 1979. "Chromosome Abnormalities in South African Mental Retardates." *South African Medical Journal* 55 (18): 710–12.

Altick, R. D. 1978. *The Shows of London.* Cambridge, MA: Belknap Press of Harvard University Press.

Amadiume, Ifi. 1987. *Male Daughters, Female Husbands: Gender and Sex in African Society.* London: Zed.

Anthropology Today. 2000. "News Follow-Up." 16 (1): 26.

Anumo, Felogene, and Valérie Bah. 2017. "'The Revolution Will Not Be NGO-ised': Four Lessons from African Feminist Organising." *OpenDemocracy*, July 31. https://www.opendemocracy.net/en/5050/four-lessons-african-feminist-organising/.

Appiah, Kwame Anthony. 2020. "The Case for Capitalizing the *B* in Black." *Atlantic*, June 18. https://www.theatlantic.com/ideas/archive/2020/06/time-to-capitalize-blackand-white/613159/.

Arondekar, Anjali R. 2009. *For the Record: On Sexuality and the Colonial Archive in India*. Durham, NC: Duke University Press.

Asher, Kiran, and Priti Ramamurthy. 2020. "Rethinking Decolonial and Postcolonial Knowledges beyond Regions to Imagine Transnational Solidarity." *Hypatia* 35: 542–47.

Athletics Weekly. 2019. "Caster Semenya Case among 'Most Pivotal' Ever Heard, Says Court." February 22. https://www.athleticsweekly.com/athletics-news/caster-semenya-case-among-most-pivotal-ever-heard-says-court-1039920946/.

Austin, Naomi, and Martin Johnson, dirs. 2015. *Countdown to Life: The Extraordinary Making of You*. Aired September 14, 21, and 28, 2015, on BBC. https://www.bbc.co.uk/programmes/b06dsmn1.

Azoulay, Ariella. 2008. *The Civil Contract of Photography*. New York: Zone.

Bailey, Moya. 2016. "Misogynoir in Medical Media: On Caster Semenya and R. Kelly." *Catalyst: Feminism, Theory, and Technoscience* 2 (2): 1–31.

Barnhoorn, I. E. J., M. S. Bornman, C. Jansen van Rensburg, H. Bouwman. 2009. "DDT Residues in Water, Sediment, Domestic and Indigenous Biota from a Currently DDT-Sprayed Area." *Chemosphere* 77 (9): 1236–41.

Bauer, Markus, and Daniela Truffer. 2016. *Intersex Genital Mutilations: Human Rights Violations of Children with Variations of Sex Anatomy*. StopIGM.org/Zwischengeschlecht.org, August 15. http://intersex.shadowreport.org/public/2016-CRC-ZA-NGO-Zwischengeschlecht-Intersex-IGM.pdf.

Bavington, L. Dawn. 2019. "Sex Control in Women's Sport: A History of the Present Regulations on Hyperandrogenism in Female Athletes." In *Sex, Gender, and Sexuality in Sport: Queer Inquiries*, edited by Vikki Krane, 181–201. New York: Routledge.

BBC Trending. 2016. "Rio 2016: 'Hands Off Caster' Trends in South Africa." BBC News, August 16. https://www.bbc.com/news/blogs-trending-37095600.

Bearak, Barry. 2009. "Inquiry about Sprinter's Sex Angers South Africans." *New York Times*, August 25. https://www.nytimes.com/2009/08/26/world/africa/26safrica.html.

Beauchamp, Toby. 2019. *Going Stealth: Transgender Politics and US Surveillance Practices*. Durham, NC: Duke University Press.

Beaver, Trish. 2012. "The In-Betweeners." *Witness* (Pietermaritzburg), February 11. https://www.news24.com/witness/archive/the-in-betweeners-20150430.

Bermon, Stéphane, and Pierre-Yves Garnier. 2021. "Correction: *Serum Androgen Levels and the Relation to Performance in Track and Field: Mass Spectrometry Results from 2127 Observations in Male and Female Elite Athletes*." *British Journal of Sports Medicine* 55 (17): e7.

Blankenberg, Ngaire. 2000. "That Rare and Random Tribe: Albino Identity in South Africa." *Critical Arts: South-North Cultural and Media Studies* 14 (2): 6–48.

Boellstorff, Tom, Mauro Cabral, Micha Cárdenas, Trystan Cotten, Eric A. Stanley, Ka-laniopua Young, and Aren Z. Aizura. 2014. "Decolonizing Transgender: A Round-table Discussion." *Transgender Studies Quarterly* 1 (3): 419–39.

Bornman, M. S., I. E. J. Barnhoorn, and B. Genthe. 2010. *DDT for Malaria Control: Effects in Indicators and Health Risk*. Report to the Water Research Commission, WRC Report no. 1674/1/09, February.

Bornman, M. S. (Riana), and Hindrik Bouwman. 2012. "Environmental Pollutants and Diseases of Sexual Development in Humans and Wildlife in South Africa: Harbingers of Impact on Overall Health." *Reproduction in Domestic Animals* 47: 327–32.

Bornman, Riana, Christiaan de Jager, Zeleke Worku, Paulina Farias, and Simon Rief. 2009. "DDT and Urogenital Malformations in Newborn Boys in a Malarial Area." *BJU International* 108: 405–11.

Botha, Kellyn. 2016. "ISSA Reborn: Hopeful Future for Intersex South Africa." Iranti, September 6. http://www.iranti.org.za/. No longer available.

Botha, Kellyn. 2021. "Adding a 'Third Gender Option' on IDs: A Small Step in the Right Direction." *Mamba Online*, March 14. https://www.mambaonline.com/2021/03/14/opinion-adding-a-third-gender-option-on-ids-a-small-step-in-the-right-direction/.

Bouwman, Hindrik, Henrik Kylin, Barbara Sereda, and Riana Bornman. 2012. "High Levels of DDT in Breast Milk: Intake, Risk, Lactation Duration, and Involvement of Gender." *Environmental Pollution* 170: 63–70.

Boykoff, Jules. 2019. "#HandsOffCaster: Why the Policing of Female Athletes' Testosterone Levels Needs to Stop." *Bitch Media*, February 20. https://www.bitchmedia.org/article/science-testosterone-female-athletes-olympics-problems-caster-semenya-dutee-chand-feminist.

Brain, P., and H. J. Grace. 1968. "On the Haemagglutinin of the Snail *Achatina Granulata*." *Vox Sanguinis* 15: 297–99.

Braun, Lundy, Anne Fausto-Sterling, Duana Fullwiley, Evelynn M. Hammonds, Alondra Nelson, William Quivers, Susan M. Reverby, and Alexandra E. Shields. 2007. "Racial Categories in Medical Practice: How Useful Are They?" *PLoS Medicine* 4 (9): 1423–28.

Braun, Lundy, and Evelynn Hammonds. 2014. "The Dilemma of Classification: The Past in the Present." In *Genetics in the Unsettled Past: The Collision of DNA, Race, and History*, edited by Keith Wailoo, Alondra Nelson, and Catherine Lee, 67–80. New Brunswick, NJ: Rutgers University Press.

Brenner, Steve. 2021. "Caster Semenya: 'They're Killing Sport. People want Extraordinary Performances.'" *Guardian* (London), April 23. https://www.theguardian.com/sport/2021/apr/23/caster-semenya-theyre-killing-sport-people-want-extraordinary-performances.

Bright, Jennifer Burns, and Ronan Crowley. 2014. "'A Quantity of Offensive Matter': Private Cases in Public Places." In *Porn Archives*, edited by Tim Dean, Steven Roszczycky, and David Squires, 103–26. Durham, NC: Duke University Press.

Brömdal, Annette. 2008. *Intersex: A Challenge for Human Rights and Citizenship Rights*. Saarbrücken, Germany: VDM Verlag Dr. Müller.

Bryson, Donna. 2009. "SA Rallies behind Runner in Gender Storm." *Mail and Guardian* (Johannesburg), August 22. https://mg.co.za/article/2009-08-22-sa-rallies-behind-runner-in-gender-storm.

Burns, Catherine Eileen. 1995. "Reproductive Labors: The Politics of Women's Health in South Africa, 1900–1960." PhD diss., Northwestern University.

Butler, Judith. 1993. *Bodies That Matter: On the Discursive Limits of Sex*. New York: Routledge, 1993.

Butler, Judith. 2009. "Wise Distinctions." *London Review of Books* (blog), November 20. http://www.lrb.co.uk/blog/2009/11/20/judith-butler/wise-distinctions/.

Cacho, Lisa Marie. 2012. *Social Death: Racialized Rightlessness and the Criminalization of the Unprotected*. New York: New York University Press.

Cadden, Joan. 1993. *Meanings of Sex Difference in the Middle Ages: Medicine, Science, and Culture*. Cambridge: Cambridge University Press.

Cahn, Susan K. 2015. *Coming on Strong: Gender and Sexuality in Women's Sport*. Reprint, Urbana: University of Illinois Press.

Cai, Li-Qun, Carmel M. Fratianni, Teofilo Gautier, and Julianne Imperato McGinley. 1994. "Dihydrotestosterone Regulation of Semen in Male Pseudohermaphrodites with 5α-Reductase-2 Deficiency." *Journal of Clinical Endocrinology and Metabolism* 79 (2): 409–14.

Cai, Li-Qun, Yuan-Shan Zhu, Melissa D. Katz, Cecilia Herrera, José Baéz, Mariano DeFilo-Ricart, Cedric H. L. Shackleton, and Julianne Imperato-McGinley. 1996. "5α-Reductase-2 Gene Mutations in the Dominican Republic." *Journal of Clinical Endocrinology and Metabolism* 81 (5): 1730–35.

Califia, Pat. 1997. *Sex Changes: The Politics of Transgenderism*. San Francisco: Cleis Press.

Camminga, B. 2019. *Transgender Refugees and the Imagined South Africa: Bodies over Borders and Borders over Bodies*. New York: Palgrave Macmillan.

Campt, Tina M. 2017. *Listening to Images*. Durham, NC: Duke University Press.

Canovatchel, William J., David Volquez, Sophie Huang, Elizabeth Wood, Martin L. Lesser, Teofilo Gautier, and Julianne Imperato-McGinley. 1994. "Luteinizing Hormone Pulsatility in Subjects with 5α-Reductase Deficiency and Decreased Dihydrotestosterone Production." *Journal of Clinical Endocrinology and Metabolism* 78 (4): 916–21.

Canto, Patricia, Felipe Vilchis, Bertha Chávez, Osvaldo Mutchinick, Julianne Imperato-McGinley, Gregorio Pérez-Palacios, Alfredo Ulloa-Aguirre, and Juan Pablo Méndez. 1997. "Mutations of the 5α-Reductase Type 2 Gene in Eight Mexican Patients from Six Different Pedigrees with 5α-Reductase-2 Deficiency." *Clinical Endocrinology* 46: 155–60.

Card, Claudia. 2003. "Genocide and Social Death." *Hypatia* 18 (1): 64–79.

Carpenter, Thomas O., Julianne Imperato-McGinley, Susan D. Boulware, Robert M. Weiss, Cedric Shackleton, James E. Griffin, and Jean D. Wilson. 1990. "Variable Expression of a 5α-Reductase Deficiency: Presentation with Male Phenotype in a Child of Greek Origin." *Journal of Clinical Endocrinology and Metabolism* 71 (2): 318–22.

Carson, Rachel. 1962. *Silent Spring*. Boston: Houghton Mifflin.

Chantiluke, Roseanne, Brian Kwoba, and Athinangamso Nkopo, eds. 2018. *Rhodes Must Fall: The Struggle to Decolonise the Racist Heart of Empire*. London: Zed.

Charlewood, G. P. 1956. *Bantu Gynaecology*. Johannesburg: Photo Publishing and Witwatersrand University Press.

Charlewood, G. P., ed. 1972. *Gynaecology in Southern Africa*. Johannesburg: Witwatersrand University Press.

Chase, Cheryl, dir. 1997. *Hermaphrodites Speak!* Rohnert Park, CA: Intersex Society of North America.

Chase, Cheryl. 1998. "Hermaphrodites with Attitude: Mapping the Emergence of Intersex Political Activism." GLQ: *A Journal of Gay and Lesbian Studies* 4 (2): 189–211.

Chase, Cheryl. 2002. "'Cultural Practice' or 'Reconstructive Surgery'?: U.S. Genital Cutting, the Intersex Movement, and Medical Double Standards." In *Genital Cutting and Transnational Sisterhood: Disrupting U.S. Polemics*, edited by Stanlie M. James, 126–51. Chicago: University of Chicago Press.

Cherry, Gene. 2019. "Semenya Vows No World Championships if She Can't Run 800 Meters." *Reuters*, June 30. https://www.reuters.com/article/us-athletics-diamond-prefontaine-idUSKCN1TV0X0.

Citizen. 2018. "Caster Responds to IAAF Policy against Her with Awesome Tweets." *Citizen* (Johannesburg), April 28. https://citizen.co.za/sport/south-africa-sport/sa-athletics-south-africa-sport/1909116/caster-responds-to-iaaf-policy-against-her-with-awesome-tweets/.

Clare, Eli. 2017. *Brilliant Imperfection: Grappling with Cure.* Durham, NC: Duke University Press.

Clarey, Christopher, and Gina Kolata. 2009. "Gold Awarded amid Dispute over Runner's Sex." *New York Times*, August 20. https://www.nytimes.com/2009/08/21/sports/21runner.html.

Coan, Stephen. 2000. "The Journey from Selwyn to Sally." *Natal Witness*, February 21.

Colapinto, John. 2000. *As Nature Made Him: The Boy Who Was Raised as a Girl.* New York: HarperCollins.

Cole, Sonia. 1965. *Races of Man.* Reprint, London: Trustees of the British Museum, Natural History.

Collison, Carl. 2018. "Intersex Babies Killed at Birth Because 'They're Bad Omens.'" *Mail and Guardian* (Johannesburg), January 24. https://mg.co.za/article/2018-01-24-00-intersex-babies-killed-at-birth-because-theyre-bad-omens.

Collison, Carl. 2021. "Proposed Identity Law Changes 'Send a Strong Message.'" *New Frame*, January 21. https://www.newframe.com/proposed-identity-law-changes-send-a-strong-message/.

Collison, Carl. 2022. "A Sangoma Campaigns to Protect Intersex Newborns.'" *New Frame*, April 29. https://www.newframe.com/a-sangoma-campaigns-to-protect-intersex-newborns/.

Cook, James. 1797. *The Three Voyages of Captain James Cook around the World to the Pacific Ocean.* Boston: Manning and Loring for Thomas and Andrews and D. West.

Coovadia, Hoosen, Rachel Jewkes, Peter Barron, David Sanders, and Diane McIntyre. 2009. "The Health and Health System of South Africa: Historical Roots of Current Public Health Challenges." *Lancet* 374: 817–34.

Cornwall, Susannah, ed. 2015. *Intersex, Theology, and the Bible: Troubling Bodies in Church, Text, and Society.* New York: Palgrave Macmillian.

Costello, Cary Gabriel. 2010. "Interphobia—Not Cured by Hiding Us Away." *Intersex Roadshow* (blog), September 12. https://intersexroadshow.blogspot.com/2010/09/interphobia-not-cured-by-hiding-us-away.html.

Costello, Cary Gabriel. 2016. "Intersex and Trans Communities: Commonalities in Tensions." In *Transgender and Intersex: Theoretical, Practical, and Artistic Perspectives*, edited by Stefan Horlacher, 83–113. New York: Palgrave Macmillan.

Crais, Clifton, and Pamela Scully. 2009. *Sara Baartman and the Hottentot Venus: A Ghost Story and a Biography*. Princeton, NJ: Princeton University Press.

Craven, Emily, and the Joint Working Group. 2009. "Joint Working Group Statement on Caster Semenya." August 23.

Creighton, S., J. Alderson, S. Brown, and C. L. Minto. 2002. "Medical Photography: Ethics, Consent and the Intersex Patient." *BJU International* 89: 67–72.

Curran, Andrew S. 2011. *The Anatomy of Blackness: Science and Slavery in an Age of Enlightenment*. Baltimore, MD: Johns Hopkins University Press.

Currier, Ashley, and Julie Moreau. 2016. "Digital Strategies and African LGBTI Organizing." In *Digital Activism in the Social Media Era: Critical Reflections on Emerging Trends in Sub-Saharan Africa*, edited by Bruce Mutsvairo, 231–47. Cham, Switzerland: Palgrave Macmillan.

Curtis. 2007. "Why We Do Not Use 'Disorder of Sex Development.'" 2007. Organisation Internationale des Intersexués—Organization Intersex International, October 12. https://oiiinternational.com/697/why-we-do-not-use-disorder-of-sex-development/.

Cuvier, Georges. (1817) 1969. *Discours sur les révolutions de la surface du globe; et sur les changements qu'elles ont produits dans le règne animal*. Brussels: Culture et Civilisation.

Daniels, Glenda. 2016. "Scrutinizing Hashtag Activism in the #MustFall Protests in South Africa in 2015." In *Digital Activism in the Social Media Era: Critical Reflections on Emerging Trends in Sub-Saharan Africa*, edited by Bruce Mutsvairo, 175–93. Cham, Switzerland: Palgrave Macmillan.

Dariawo, Ben, Titus Pameko, Daniel Meian, Mark Nawokre, Joseph Simbaisipta, Joel Amburi, Wevin Meyande, Kevin Kambarumo, and Nason Aguleko. 1999. "Breach of Contract?" *Anthropology News* 40 (7): 4.

Dart, Raymond A. 1937. "The Physical Characters of the /?Auni-≠Khomni Bushmen." *Bantu Studies* 11 (1): 175–246.

Datson, Lorraine, and Katherine Park. 1995. "The Hermaphrodite and the Orders of Nature: Sexual Ambiguity in Modern France." *GLQ: A Journal of Gay and Lesbian Studies* 1: 419–38.

Davison, Patricia. 1993. "Human Subjects as Museum Objects: A Project to Make Life-Casts of 'Bushmen' and 'Hottentots,' 1907–1924." *Annals of the South African Museum* 102 (5): 165–83.

Davison, Patricia. 2018. "The Politics and Poetics of the Bushman Diorama at the South African Museum." *International Council of Museums* 46: 81–97.

de la Chapelle, Albert. 1986. "Invited Editorial: The Use and Misuse of Sex Chromatin Screening for 'Gender Identification' in Athletes." *Journal of the American Medical Association* 256 (14): 1920–23.

Derrida, Jacques. 1994. *Specters of Marx: The State of Debt, the Work of Mourning, and the New International*. Translated by Peggy Kamuf. New York: Routledge.

de Souza, J. J. L., P. Barnett, C. D. Kisner, and J. P. Murray. 1984. "True Hermaphrodit- ism: A Case Report with Observations on Its Bizarre Presentation." *South African Medical Journal* 66 (22): 855–58.

DeVun, Leah. 2014. "Animal Appetites." GLQ: *A Journal of Gay and Lesbian Studies* 20 (4): 461–90.

DeVun, Leah. 2021. *The Shape of Sex: Nonbinary Gender from Genesis to the Renaissance.* New York: Columbia University Press.

Diabate, Naminata. 2020. *Naked Agency: Genital Cursing and Biopolitics in Africa.* Dur- ham, NC: Duke University Press.

DiPietro, Pedro J., Jennifer McWeeny, and Shireen Roshanrava. 2019. "Like an Earth- quake to the Soul: Experiencing the Visionary Philosophy of María Lugones." In *Speaking Face to Face: The Visionary Philosophy of María Lugones,* edited by Pedro J. DiPietro, Jennifer McWeeny, and Shireen Roshanrava, 1–30. Albany, NY: SUNY Press.

Dixon, Robyn. 2009. "Gender Issue Has Always Chased Her." *Los Angeles Times,* August 21. https://www.latimes.com/archives/la-xpm-2009-aug-21-fg-south-africa -runner21-story.html.

Dlamini, Jacob. 2020a. *African Studies in Conversation: Jacob Dlamini, "The Terror- ist Album."* With Amanda Swarr, Ron Krabill, and Danny Hoffman, University of Washington, UWJSIS, video, 59:36, November 19. https://www.youtube.com/watch?v =sI6kj8oXru4.

Dlamini, Jacob. 2020b. *The Terrorist Album: Apartheid's Insurgents, Collaborators, and the Security Police.* Cambridge, MA: Harvard University Press.

Downing, Lisa, Iain Morland, and Nikki Sullivan, eds. 2015. *Fuckology: Critical Essays on John Money's Diagnostic Concepts.* Chicago: University of Chicago Press.

Dreger, Alice Domurat. 1998. *Hermaphrodites and the Medical Invention of Sex.* Cam- bridge, MA: Harvard University Press.

Dreger, Alice Domurat, ed. 1999. *Intersex in the Age of Ethics.* Hagerstown, MD: Univer- sity Publishing Group.

Dreger, Alice Domurat. 2000. "Jarring Bodies: Thoughts on the Display of Unusual Anatomies." *Perspectives in Biology and Medicine* 43 (2): 161–72.

Driskill, Qwo-Li. 2016. *Asegi Stories: Cherokee Queer and Two-Spirit Memory.* Tucson: University of Arizona Press.

Drury, James, and Matthew Drennan. 1926. "The Pudendal Parts of the South African Bush Race." *Medical Journal of South Africa* 22: 113–17.

Dubow, Saul. 1995. *Scientific Racism in Modern South Africa.* New York: Cambridge University Press.

Dubow, Saul. 1996. "Human Origins, Race Typology, and the Other Raymond Dart." *African Studies* 55 (1): 1–30.

Dubow, Saul. 2006. *A Commonwealth of Knowledge: Science, Sensibility, and White South Africa.* Oxford: Oxford University Press.

Dubow, Saul. 2015. "Racial Irrendentism, Ethnogenesis, and White Supremacy in High- Apartheid South Africa." *Kronos* 41: 236–64.

Du Plessis, Rory. 2014. "Photographs from the Grahamstown Lunatic Asylum, South Africa, 1890–1907." *Social Dynamics* 40 (1): 12–42.

Dworkin, Shari L., Amanda Lock Swarr, and Cheryl Cooky. 2013. "(In)Justice in Sport: The Treatment of South African Track Star Caster Semenya." *Feminist Studies* 39 (1): 40–69.

Eckert, Lena. 2017. *Intersexualization: The Clinic and the Colony*. New York: Routledge.

Ellison, G. T. H., and T. de Wet. 1997. "The Use of 'Racial' Categories in Contemporary South African Health Research: A Survey of Articles Published in the *South African Medical Journal* between 1992 and 1996." *South African Medical Journal* 87 (12): 1671–79.

Epstein, David. 2012. "Caster Semenya Will Face Judgement Whether She Runs Fast or Slow." *Sports Illustrated*, August 9. https://www.si.com/more-sports/2012/08/09 /caster-semenya-800-meter-final.

Epstein, Randi Hutter. 2010. "Pioneer Reflects on Future of Reproductive Medicine." *New York Times*, March 23.

Fanon, Frantz. (1952) 2008. *Black Skin, White Masks*. Translated by Charles Lam Markmann. Reprint, New York: Grove.

Fausto-Sterling, Anne. 1995. "Gender, Race, and Nation: The Comparative Anatomy of 'Hottentot' Women in Europe, 1815–1817." In *Deviant Bodies: Critical Perspectives on Difference in Science and Popular Culture*, edited by Jennifer Terry and Jacqueline Urla, 19–47. Bloomington: Indiana University Press.

Fausto-Sterling, Anne. 2000. *Sexing the Body: Gender Politics and the Construction of Sexuality*. New York: Basic.

Feltham, Luke. 2018. "Bad Science Won't Undo Semenya." *Mail and Guardian* (Johannesburg), May 4. https://mg.co.za/article/2018-05-04-00-bad-science-wont-undo -semenya.

Fénichel, Patrick, Françoise Paris, Pascal Philibert, Sylvie Hiéronimus, Laura Gaspari, Jean-Yves Kurzenne, Patrick Chevallier, Stéphane Bermon, Nicolas Chevalier, and Charles Sultan. 2013. "Molecular Diagnosis of 5α-Reductase Deficiency in 4 Elite Young Female Athletes through Hormonal Screening for Hyperandrogenism." *Journal of Clinical Endocrinology and Metabolism* 98 (6): E1055–E1059.

fester-wicomb, gertrude. 2021. "Querying the Queer." In *Surfacing: On Being Black and Feminist in South Africa*, edited by Desiree Lewis and Gabeba Baderoon, 73–89. Johannesburg: Wits University Press.

Fischer, Mia. 2019. *Terrorizing Gender: Transgender Visibility and the Surveillance Practices of the U.S. Security State*. Lincoln: University of Nebraska Press.

Flanagan, Jane. 2016. "'Haters, Be Patient . . . I Have so Much More for You': Gender Row Runner Caster Semenya's Fans Launch #HandsOffCaster Twitter Campaign at Haters Who Say She Shouldn't Run in Rio as a Woman." *Daily Mail* (London), August 16. Updated August 14, 2017. http://www.dailymail.co.uk/news/article -3741488/Haters-patient-Gender-row-runner-Caster-Semenya-s-fans-launch -HandsOffCaster-Twitter-campaign-haters-say-shouldn-t-run-Rio-woman.html.

Forbes, J. I., and B. Hammar. 1966. "Intersex among Africans in Rhodesia." *Archive of Diseases of Childhood* 41: 102–7.

Foucault, Michel. (1963) 1994. *The Birth of the Clinic: An Archaeology of Medical Perception*. Translated by Alan Sheridan. Reprint, New York: Vintage.

Freedberg, David. 1989. *The Power of Images: Studies in the History and Theory of Response*. Chicago: University of Chicago Press.

Ganie, Yasmeen, Colleen Aldous, Yusentha Balakrishna, and Rinus Wiersma. 2017. "The Spectrum of Ovotesticular Disorders of Sex Development in South Africa: A Single Centre Experience." *Hormone Research in Paediatrics* 87: 307–14.

Garrigues, Henry Jacques. 1894. *A Textbook of the Diseases of Women*. Philadelphia: W. B. Saunders.

Geddes, Patrick, and J. Arthur Thomas. 1890. *The Evolution of Sex*. New York: Scribner and Welford.

Gill-Peterson, Jules. 2017. "Implanting Plasticity into Sex and Trans/Gender: Animal and Child Metaphors in the History of Endocrinology." *Angelaki* 22 (2): 47–60.

Gill-Peterson, Jules. 2018a. *Histories of the Transgender Child*. Minneapolis: University of Minnesota Press.

Gill-Peterson, Jules. 2018b. "Trans of Color Critique before Transsexuality." *Transgender Studies Quarterly* 5 (4): 606–20.

Gilman, Sander L. 1985. *Difference and Pathology: Stereotypes of Sexuality, Race, and Madness*. Ithaca, NY: Cornell University Press.

Gilroy, Paul. 2004. *Between Camps: Nations, Culture, and the Allure of Race*. New York: Taylor and Francis.

Ginnane, Maxx, dir. 2011. *Too Fast to Be a Woman? The Story of Caster Semenya*. Kuchu Times, video, 49:14, August 27, 2015. https://www.youtube.com/watch?v=f-UXoLE_tCg.

Gladwell, Malcolm. 2010. "Small Change: Why the Revolution Won't Be Tweeted." *New Yorker*, September 27. https://www.newyorker.com/magazine/2010/10/04/small-change-malcolm-gladwell.

Gladwell, Malcolm, and Nicholas Thompson. 2016. "Caster Semenya and the Logic of Olympic Competition." *New Yorker*, April 12. https://www.newyorker.com/news/sporting-scene/caster-semenya-and-the-logic-of-olympic-competition.

Godden, Maryse. 2017. "Inside the Baffling Caribbean Village where Little Girls Turn into Boys at the Age of 12 . . . and Even Suddenly Grow Penises." *The Sun*, August 7. https://www.thesun.co.uk/news/4187004/guevedoces-girls-turn-into-boys-salinas/.

Goldhagen, Daniel Jonah. 1996. *Hitler's Willing Executioners: Ordinary Germans and the Holocaust*. New York: Knopf.

Goldie, Terry. 2014. *The Man Who Invented Gender: Engaging the Ideas of John Money*. Vancouver: University of British Columbia Press.

Goldschmidt, Richard. 1917. "Intersexuality and the Endocrine Aspect of Sex." *Endocrinology* 1 (4): 433–56.

Gordon, Avery. 2008. *Ghostly Matters: Haunting and the Sociological Imagination*. Minneapolis: University of Minnesota Press.

Gordon, Robert J. 1992. "The Venal Hottentot and the Great Chain of Being." *African Studies* 51 (2): 185–201.

Gould, S. J. 1982. "The Hottentot Venus." *Natural History* 10: 22–27.

Gqola, Pumla Dineo. 2009. "Semenya as the 21st Century Bartmann?" *Loudrastress: Afrikan Feminist Musings and Reflections* (blog), August 24. http://pumlagqola.wordpress.com/2009/08/24/semenya-as-the-21st-century-bartmann/.

Gqola, Pumla Dineo. 2015. *Rape: A South African Nightmare*. Auckland Park, SA: MF Books.

Grace, H. J. 1970. "Intersex in Four South African Racial Groups in Durban." Master's thesis, University of Natal, South Africa.

Grace, H. J. 1974. "Palmar Dermatoglyphics of South African Negroes and Coloureds." *Human Heredity* 24: 167–77.

Grace, H. J. 1975a. "Digital and Palmar Dermatoglyphics of South African Whites." *Human Heredity* 25: 234–47.

Grace, H. J. 1975b. "Distribution of Hypothenar Radial Arches." *Humangenetik* 28: 325–28.

Grace, H. J. 1976. "Concentration of Similar Finger Print Patterns in Four Race Groups." *Human Heredity* 26: 306–9.

Grace, H. J. 1977. "Studies of Intersexuality in South Africa." PhD diss., University of Natal, South Africa.

Grace, H. J., and F. E. Ally. 1972. "Dermatoglyphic Features of South African Coloureds." *Human Heredity* 22: 351–55.

Grace, H. J., and F. E. Ally. 1973. "Dermatoglyphs of the South African Negro." *Human Heredity* 23: 53–58.

Grace, H. J., F. E. Ally, A. P. Nelemans, and Bernadette Kint. 1979. "Cytogenetic Study of a Mentally Retarded Population in South Africa." *South African Medical Journal* 55 (18): 707–9.

Grace, H. J., and W. E. B. Edge. 1973. "A White Hermaphrodite in South Africa." *South African Medical Journal* 47 (34): 1553–54.

Grace, H. J., O. P. Quantock, and A. Vinik. 1970. "An Unusual Cause of 'Haematuria' in an xx/xy Hermpahrodite." *South African Medical Journal* 44 (2): 40–43.

Grace, H. J., and Mary Schonland. 1970. "Penile Urethra in a Bantu Female Intersex." *South African Medical Journal* 44 (39): 1112–15.

Grace, H. J., and G. Uhlenbruck. 1969. "The Agglutination of Abantu and Other Human Erythrocytes by Reagents from Snails." *Journal of Forensic Medicine* 16 (4): 139–42.

Graham, Stuart. 2016. "Mosquito Pesticide Linked to Births of Intersex Children." *London Times*, August 19.

Green, Amy. 2018. "Government Urged to Ban Intersex Genital Mutilation." *Health-E News*, January 15. https://www.health-e.org.za/2018/01/15/government-urged-ban-intersex-genital-mutilation/.

Grillo, Laura. 2018. *An Intimate Rebuke: Female Genital Power in Ritual and Politics in West Africa.* Durham, NC: Duke University Press.

Groenewald, Yolandi. 2009. "Lesser of Two Evils." *Mail and Guardian* (Johannesburg), November 20. https://mg.co.za/article/2009-11-20-lesser-of-two-evils/.

Gross, Sally. 2000. Interview by Amanda Swarr and Sam Bullington. March 16. Transcript.

Gross, Sally. 2009a. "Intersex and the Law." *Mail and Guardian* (Johannesburg), September 19. https://mg.co.za/article/2009-09-19-intersex-and-the-law.

Gross, Sally. 2009b. "Life in the Shadow of Gender." *Witness* (Pietermaritzburg), August 29.

Gross, Sally. 2009c. "Response on the Mistreatment of Caster Semenya." *Intersex Initiative.* Accessed June 26, 2018. http://www.intersexinitiative.org/media/castersemenya.html.

Gross, Sally. 2009d. "Updated Feature Article" [Re: Stephen Coan's "The Journey from Selwyn to Sally," published in 2000]. *Witness* (Pietermaritzburg). Sally Gross Collection, GALA at the University of the Witwatersrand, Johannesburg.

Gross, Sally. 2011. "The Chronicle of an Intersexed Activist's Journey." In *African Sexualities: A Reader*, edited by Sylvia Tamale, 235–37. Cape Town: Pambazuka Press.

Gross, Sally. 2013. "Not in God's Image: Intersex, Social Death, and Infanticide." Paper presented via Skype at the Intersex, Theology and the Bible conference, University of Manchester, March 12.

[Gross, Sally, and Aaron Nicodemus]. 1999. "Lifting the Veil on Intersexuality." *Mail and Guardian* (Johannesburg), August 13. https://mg.co.za/article/1999-08-13-lifting-the -veil-on-intersexuality.

Haraway, Donna J. 1989. *Primitive Visions: Gender, Race, and Nature in the World of Modern Science*. New York: Routledge.

Haraway, Donna J. 1991. *Simians, Cyborgs, and Women: The Reinvention of Nature*. New York: Routledge.

Haraway, Donna J. 1997. *Modest_Witness@Second_Millenium. FemaleMan©_Meets_ OncoMouse™: Feminism and Technoscience*. New York: Routledge.

Hausman, Bernice L. 1995. *Changing Sex: Transsexualism, Technology, and the Idea of Gender*. Durham, NC: Duke University Press.

Hayes, Patricia. 1996. "'Cocky' Hahn and the 'Black Venus': The Making of a Native Commissioner in South West Africa, 1915–46." *Gender and History* 8 (3): 364–92.

Heggie, Vanessa. 2010. "Testing Sex and Gender in Sports: Reinventing, Reimagining and Reconstructing Histories." *Endeavour* 34 (4): 157–63.

Herdt, Gilbert. 1981. *Guardians of the Flutes: Idioms of Masculinity*. New York: McGraw-Hill.

Herdt, Gilbert. 1987. *The Sambia: Ritual and Gender in New Guinea*. New York: Holt, Rinehart and Winston.

Herdt, Gilbert. 1999. "Response to Dariawo." *Anthropology News* 40 (7): 4.

Herdt, Gilbert H., and Julian Davidson. 1988. "The Sambia 'Turnim-Man': Sociocultural and Clinical Aspects of Gender Formation in Male Pseudohermaphrodites with 5-Alpha-Reductase Deficiency in Papua New Guinea." *Archives of Sexual Behavior* 17 (1): 33–56.

Herdt, Gilbert H., and Robert J. Stoller. 1985. "Sakulambei—A Hermaphrodite's Secret: An Example of Clinical Ethnography." *Psychoanalytic Study of Society* 11: 115–56.

Hewat, Matthew L. 1905. *Bantu Folk Lore*. Cape Town: T. Maskew Miller.

Heyns, O. S. 1956. "Some Ethnic Relations of the Bantu in South Africa." In *Bantu Gynaecology*, by G. P. Charlewood, 1–11. Johannesburg: Photo Publishing and Witwatersrand University Press.

Higgins, Laine. 2021. "The Study That Blocked Caster Semenya from the Tokyo Olympics Has Been Corrected by Its Publishers." *Wall Street Journal*, August 19. https:// www.wsj.com/articles/caster-semenya-tokyo-olympics-testosterone-11629382859.

Hoad, Neville. 2010. "'Run, Caster Semenya, Run!' Nativism and the Translations of Gender Variance." *Safundi: The Journal of South African and American Studies* 11 (4): 397–405.

Hodes, Rebecca. 2017. "The 'Hottentot Apron': Genital Aberration in the History of Sexual Science." In *A Global History of Sexual Science, 1880–1960*, edited by Veronika Fuechter, Douglas E. Haynes, and Ryan M. Jones, 118–38. Oakland: University of California Press.

Holmes, M. Morgan. 2008. "Mind the Gaps: Intersex and (Re-productive) Spaces in Disability Studies and Bioethics." *Bioethical Inquiry* 5 (2–3): 169–81.

Horak, Ilzé, Suranie Horn, and Rialet Peters. 2021. "Agrochemicals in Freshwater Systems and Their Potential Endocrine Disrupting Chemicals: A South African Context." *Environmental Pollution* 268: 1–13.

Houk, Christopher P., D. Damiani, and Peter A. Lee. 2005. "Choice of Gender in 5α-Reductase Deficiency: A Moving Target." *Journal of Pediatric Endocrinology and Metabolism* 18: 339–45.

Hounshell, Blake. 2011. "The Revolution Will Be Tweeted: Life in the Vanguard of the New Twitter Proletariat." *Foreign Policy*, June 20.

HRW (Human Rights Watch). 2020. "'They're Chasing Us Away from Sport': Human Rights Violations in Sex Testing of Elite Women Athletes." Human Rights Watch, December 4. https://www.hrw.org/report/2020/12/04/theyre-chasing-us-away-sport /human-rights-violations-sex-testing-elite-women.

Huet, Marie-Hélène. 1993. *Monstrous Imagination*. Cambridge, MA: Harvard University Press.

Husakouskaya, Nadzeya. 2013. "Rethinking Gender and Human Rights through Trans-gender and Intersex Experiences in South Africa." *Agenda* 27 (4): 10–24.

Hussen, Tigist Shewarega. 2018. "Social Media and Feminist Activism: #RapeMustFall, #NakedProtest, and #RUReferenceList Movements in South Africa." In *Engaging Youth in Activism, Research, and Pedagogical Praxis: Transnational and Intersectional Perspectives on Gender, Sex, and Race*, edited by Tamara Shefer, Jeff Hearn, Kopano Ratele, and Floretta Boonzaier, 199–214. New York: Routledge.

Igual, Roberto. 2021. "Give Your Feedback on Proposed Gender ID Changes." *Mamba Online*, February 2. https://www.mambaonline.com/2021/02/02/give-your-feedback -on-proposed-gender-id-changes/.

Imperato-McGinley, Julianne. 1997. "5 Alpha-Reductase-2 Deficiency." *Current Therapy in Endocrinology and Metabolism* 6: 384–87.

Imperato-McGinley, Julianne, Teofilo Gautier, Marino Pichardo, and Cedric Shackle-ton. 1986. "The Diagnosis of 5α-Reductase Deficiency in Infancy." *Journal of Clinical Endocrinology and Metabolism* 63 (6): 1313–18.

Imperato-McGinley, Julianne, Luis Guerrero, Teofilo Gautier, and Ralph E. Peterson. 1974. "Steroid 5α-Reductase Deficiency in Man: An Inherited Form of Male Pseudo-hermaphroditism." *Science* 186 (4170): 1213–15.

Imperato-McGinley, J., M. Miller, J. D. Wilson, H. E. Peterson, C. Shackleton, and D. C. Gajdusek. 1991. "A Cluster of Male Pseudohermaphrodites with 5α-Reductase Defi-ciency in Papua New Guinea." *Clinical Endocrinology* 34: 293–98.

Imperato-McGinley, Julianne, Ralph E. Peterson, Teofilo Gautier, and Erasmo Sturla. 1979. "Androgens and the Evolution of Male-Gender Identity among Male Pseu-dohermaphrodites with a 5α-Reductase Deficiency." *Obstetrical and Gynecological Survey* 34 (10): 769–71.

Imperato-McGinley, Julianne, Ralph E. Peterson, Mark Leshin, James E. Griffin, George Cooper, Suzanne Draghi, Magdalena Berenyi, and Jean D. Wilson. 1980. "Steroid 5α-Reductase Deficiency in a 65-Year-old Male Pseudohermaphrodite: The Natural

History, Ultrastructure of the Testes, and Evidence for Inherited Enzyme Heterogeneity." *Journal of Clinical Endocrinology and Metabolism* 50 (1): 15–22.

Imperato-McGinley, Julianne, and Yuan-Shan Zhu. 2002. "Androgens and Male Physiology the Syndrome of 5α-Reductase-2 Deficiency." *Molecular and Cellular Endocrinology* 198: 51–59.

Iranti. 2017. *Intersex Day of Solidarity with ISSA*. Iranti Media, video, 5:46, November 8. https://www.youtube.com/watch?v=4to7TY83EcA.

Iranti. 2018. *National Intersex Meeting 2017*. Iranti Media, video, 5:56, March 8. https://www.youtube.com/watch?v=4ESKhysCaFA.

Iranti. 2020a. "African Intersex Movement (AIM) Intersex Awareness Day Statement." Iranti, press release, October 26. https://www.iranti.org.za/.

Iranti. 2020b. *The Iranti COVID-19 Newsletter*. Editions 1 and 2, August. https://www.iranti.org.za/. No longer available.

Iranti. 2021a. "Human Rights Day Should Also Be for Intersex Children." Iranti, press release, March 21. https://www.iranti.org.za/?p=4249.

Iranti. 2021b. "Iranti Hosts Media Briefing on Home Affairs's ID Gender Policy." Iranti, press release, March 12. https://www.iranti.org.za/?p=4237.

Iranti and Intersex South Africa. 2020. "Swiss Court Upholds Discriminatory Practices against Caster Semenya." Joint statement and press release, September 9. https://www.iranti.org.za/?p=4134.

James, Stanlie M. 2002. "Listening to Other(ed) Voices: Reflections around Female Genital Cutting." In *Genital Cutting and Transnational Sisterhood: Disrupting U.S. Polemics*, edited by Stanlie M. James, 87–113. Chicago: University of Chicago Press.

Jansen, Jonathan D. 2009. *Knowledge in the Blood: Confronting Race and the Apartheid Past*. Stanford, CA: Stanford University Press.

Jeeves, Alan. 2003. "The State, the Cinema, and Health Propaganda for Africans in Pre-Apartheid South Africa, 1932–48." *South African Historical Journal* 48 (1): 109–29.

Jenkins, Elizabeth, Stefan Andersson, Julianne Imperato-McGinley, Jean D. Wilson, and David W. Russell. 1992. "Genetic and Pharmacological Evidence for More Than One Human Steroid 5α-Reductase." *Journal of Clinical Investigation* 89 (1): 293–300.

John, Victoria. 2012. "Gentle Man's Brutal Murder Turns Spotlight on Intolerance." *Mail and Guardian* (Johannesburg), June 28. https://mg.co.za/article/2012-06-28-gentle-mans-brutal-murder-turns-spotlight-on-intolerance/.

Johnson, R. H. 1972. "The Journal of the Medical and Dental Association of Botswana." *Botswana Notes and Records* 4: 286-87.

Johnson, R. H. 1974. "A Case of True Hermaphroditism Presenting as an Undescended Testicle." *South African Medical Journal* 48 (36): 1540.

Johnson, R. H. 1975a. "Bowel Obstruction in a Botswana Hospital." *East African Medical Journal* 52 (6): 319–25.

Johnson, R. H. 1975b. "The Cases of Cancer Seen at a Botswana Hospital, 1968–1972." *Central African Journal of Medicine* 21 (12): 260–64.

Jones, Ann Rosalind, and Peter Stallybrass. 1991. "Fetishizing Gender: Creating the Hermaphrodite in Renaissance Europe." In *Body Guards: The Cultural Politics of Gender Ambiguity*, edited by Julia Epstein and Kristina Straub, 80–111. New York: Routledge.

Jones, Howard W., Jr. 1976. "Discussion of 'True Hermaphroditism': An Analytic Review with a Report of 3 New Cases' by Van Niekerk, W. A." *American Journal of Obstetrics and Gynecology* 26 (7): 905.

Jordan-Young, Rebecca M., and Katrina Karkazis. 2019. "4 Myths about Testosterone." *Scientific American*, June 18. https://blogs.scientificamerican.com/observations/4-myths-about-testosterone/.

Jordan-Young, Rebecca M., Peter Sönksen, and Katrina Karkazis. 2014. "Sex, Health, and Athletes." *BMJ* 348: 20–21.

Judd, Bettina. 2014. *Patient*. New York: Black Lawrence Press.

Kaba, Mariame, Andrea Smith, Lori Adelman, and Roxane Gay. 2014. "Where Twitter and Feminism Meet." *Nation*, April 17. https://www.thenation.com/article/archive/where-twitter-and-feminism-meet/.

Kaggwa, Julius. 1997. *From Juliet to Julius: In Search of My True Gender Identity*. Kampala: Fountain.

Kaggwa, Julius. 2011. "Intersex: The Forgotten Constituency." In *African Sexualities: A Reader*, edited by Sylvia Tamale, 231–34. Cape Town: Pambazuka Press.

Karkazis, Katrina. 2000. *Fixing Sex: Intersex, Medical Authority, and Lived Experience*. Durham, NC: Duke University Press.

Karkazis, Katrina. 2008. "The Art of Medicine—Naming the Problem: Disorders and Their Meanings." *Lancet* 372: 2016–17.

Karkazis, Katrina, and Morgan Carpenter. 2018. "Impossible 'Choices': The Inherent Harms of Regulating Women's Testosterone in Sport." *Journal of Bioethical Inquiry* 15 (4): 579–87.

Karkazis, Katrina, and Rebecca Jordan-Young. 2018. "The Powers of Testosterone: Observing Race and Regional Bias in the Regulation of Women Athletes." *Feminist Foundations* 30 (2): 1–39.

Katz, Melissa D., Li-Qun Cai, Yuan-Shan Zhu, Cecilia Herrera, Mariano DeFillo-Ricart, Cedric H.L. Shackleton, and Julianne Imperato-McGinley. 1995. "The Biochemical and Phenotypical Characterization of Females Homozygous for 5α-Reductase-2 Deficiency." *Journal of Clinical Endocrinology and Metabolism* 80 (1): 3160–67.

Katz, Melissa D., Isaac Kligman, Li-Qun Cai, Yuan-Shan Zhu, Carmel M. Fratianni, Ioannis Zervoudakis, Zev Rosenwaks, and Julianne Imperato-McGinley. 1997. "Paternity by Intrauterine Insemination with the Sperm from a Man with 5α-Reductase-2 Deficiency." *New England Journal of Medicine* 336 (14): 994–97.

Keeping Track. 1994. "Give-and-Take on Gender Verification." 1994. *Keeping Track: International Track and Field Newsletter*, no. 6 (May): 2–3.

Kessler, Suzanne. 1990. "The Medical Construction of Gender." *Signs: Journal of Women and Culture* 16 (1): 3–26.

Kessler, Suzanne. 1998. *Lessons from the Intersexed*. New Brunswick, NJ: Rutgers University Press.

Kier, Bailey. 2010. "Interdependent Ecological Transsex: Notes on Re/production, 'Transgender' Fish, and the Management of Populations, Species, and Resources." *Women and Performance: A Journal of Feminist Theory* 20 (3): 299–319.

Kim, Linda. 2018. *Race Experts: Sculpture, Anthropology, and the American Public in Malvina Hoffman's "Races of Mankind."* Lincoln: University of Nebraska Press.

Kirby, Percival R. 1940. "Robert Knox and His South African Research." *South African Medical Journal* 14 (13): 254–61.

Kirby, Percival R. 1954. "The Hottentot Venus of the Musee de L'Homme, Paris." *South African Journal of Science* 50 (12): 319–22.

Klausen, Susanne M. 2001. "'Poor Whiteism,' White Maternal Mortality, and the Promotion of Public Health in South Africa: The Department of Public Health's Endorsement of Contraceptive Services, 1930–1938." *South African Historical Journal* 45: 53–78.

Klausen, Susanne M. 2017. "Eugenics and the Maintenance of White Supremacy in Modern South Africa." In *Eugenics at the Edges of Empire: New Zealand, Australia, Canada and South Africa*, edited by Diane B. Paul, John Stenhouse, and Hamish G. Spencer, 289–309. New York: Palgrave Macmillan.

Klein, Thamar. 2009. "Intersex and Transgender Activism in South Africa." *Liminalis* 3: 15–24.

Klempman, Sarah. 1964. "The Investigation of Developmental Sexual Abnormalities." *South African Medical Journal* 38 (12): 234–36.

Knox, Robert. 1850. *The Races of Men: A Fragment*. Philadelphia: Lea and Blanchard.

Knox, Robert. 1855. "Some Remarks on the Aztecque and Bosjieman Children, Now Being Exhibited in London, and on the Races to Which They Are Presumed to Belong." *Lancet* 65 (65): 357–60.

Korn, Jenny Ungbha, and Tamara Kneese. 2015. "Feminist Approaches to Social Media Research: History, Activism, Values." *Feminist Media Studies* 15 (4): 707–10.

Kotolo, McKeed. 2000. "Three Held in 'Muti' Murder." *Sowetan* (Johannesburg), August 14.

Lahood, Grant, dir. 2012. *Intersexion*. San Francisco, CA: Frameline.

Landau, Paul. 2002. "Empires of the Visual: Photography and Colonial Administration in Africa." In *Images and Empires: Visuality in Colonial and Postcolonial Africa*, edited by Paul Landau and Susan Griffin, 141–71. Berkeley: University of California Press.

Langston, Nancy. 2008. "The Retreat from Precaution: Regulating Diethylstilbestrol (DES), Endocrine Disruptors, and Environmental Health." *Environmental History* 13 (1): 41–65.

Layden, Tim. 2016. "Is It Fair for Caster Semenya to Compete against Women at the Rio Olympics?" *Sports Illustrated*, August 11. https://www.si.com/olympics/2016/08/11/caster-semenya-2016-rio-olympics-track-and-field.

Lepule, Tshego. 2021. "Department of Home Affairs Seeks to Amend Identity Laws to Include a Third Gender." *Weekend Argus* (Cape Town), January 10. https://www.iol.co.za/weekend-argus/news/department-of-home-affairs-seeks-to-amend-identity-laws-to-include-a-third-gender-3fe3df48-cca6-4313-9a46-5bdd0cce52fd.

Le Roux, Gabrielle, and Nthabiseng Mokoena. 2016. *Reclaiming Intersex while Black Genderqueer + Feminist in South Africa*. Video, 27:50, April 19, 2017. https://vimeo.com/213891894.

Levy, Ariel. 2009. "Either/Or: Sports, Sex, and the Case of Caster Semenya." *New Yorker* 85 (39): 46–59.

Lewis, Desiree, and Gabeba Baderoon. 2021. "Being Black and Feminist." In *Surfacing: On Being Black and Feminist in South Africa*, edited by Desiree Lewis and Gabeba Baderoon, 1–14. Johannesburg: Wits University Press.

Lindfors, Bernth. 1983a. "Circus Africans." *Journal of American Culture* 6 (2): 9–14.

Lindfors, Bernth. 1983b. "'The Hottentot Venus' and other African Attractions in Nineteenth-Century England." *Australasian Drama Studies* 1 (2): 82–104.

Ljungqvist, Arne. 2011. *Doping's Nemesis*. Reprint, Cheltenham, UK: Sports Books.

Longman, Jeré. 2018. "Caster Semenya Will Challenge Testosterone Rule in Court." *New York Times*, June 18. https://www.nytimes.com/2018/06/18/sports/caster-semenya -iaaf-lawsuit.html.

Lugones, María. 2007. "Heterosexualism and the Colonial/Modern Gender System." *Hypatia* 22 (1): 186–209.

Lugones, María. 2010. "Toward a Decolonial Feminism." *Hypatia* 25 (4): 742–59.

Macharia, Keguro. 2009. "On Caster Semenya." *Gukira* (blog), September 20. https:// gukira.wordpress.com/2009/09/20/on-caster-semenya/.

Macharia, Keguro. 2015. "Archive and Method in Africa Studies." *Agenda* 29 (1): 140–46.

Macharia, Keguro. 2016. "On Being Area-Studied: A Litany of Complaint." *GLQ: A Journal of Gay and Lesbian Studies* 22 (2): 183–89.

Macharia, Keguro. 2019. *Frottage: Frictions of Intimacy across the Black Diaspora*. New York: New York University Press.

Magadla, Siphokazi, Babalwa Magoqwana, and Nthabiseng Motsemme. 2021. "Thirty Years of *Male Daughters, Female Husbands*: Revisiting Ifi Amadiume's Questions on Gender, Sex and Political Economy." *Journal of Contemporary African Studies* 39 (4): 517–33.

Magubane, Zine. 2001. "Which Bodies Matter?: Feminism, Poststructuralism, Race, and the Curious Theoretical Odyssey of the 'Hottentot Venus.'" *Gender and Society* 15 (6): 816–34.

Magubane, Zine. 2014. "Spectacles and Scholarship: Caster Semenya, Intersex Studies, and the Problem of Race in Feminist Theory." *Signs: Journal of Women in Culture and Society* 39 (3): 761–85.

Maguire, Bernadette. 2019. "Caught in Intersex No-Person's Land." *Daily Maverick* (Johannesburg), May 22. https://www.dailymaverick.co.za/article/2019-05-22-caught -in-the-intersex-no-persons-land/.

Mail and Guardian (Johannesburg). 2009. "Politicians Weigh in on Semenya Debate." August 26. https://mg.co.za/article/2009-08-26-politicians-weigh-in-on-semenya-debate.

Maimoun, Laurent, Pascal Philibert, Benoit Cammas, Françoise Audran, Philippe Bouchard, Patrick Fenichel, Maryse Cartigny, et al. 2011. "Phenotypical, Biological and Molecular Heterogeneity of 5α-Reductase Deficiency: An Extensive International Experience of 55 Patients." *Journal of Clinical Endocrinology and Metabolism* 96 (2): 296–307.

Malatino, Hil. 2009. "Situating Bio-logic, Refiguring Sex: Intersexuality and Coloniality." In *Critical Intersex*, edited by Morgan Holmes, 73–94. New York: Routledge.

Malatino, Hil. 2019. *Queer Embodiment: Monstrosity, Medical Violence, and Intersex Experience*. Lincoln: University of Nebraska Press.

Maluleke, Gavaza, and Eileen Moyer. 2020. "'We Have to Ask for Permission to Become': Young Women's Voices, and Mediated Space in South Africa." *Signs: Journal of Women in Culture in Society* 45 (4): 871–900.

Mama, Amina. 2001. "Challenging Subjects: Gender and Power in African Contexts." In *Identity and Beyond: Rethinking Africanity*, edited by Souleymane Bachir Diagne,

Amina Mama, Henning Melber, and Francis B. Nyamnjoh, 9–18. Uppsala: Nordiska Afrikainstitutet.

Markowitz, Sally. 2001. "Pelvic Politics: Sexual Dimorphism and Racial Difference." *Signs* 26 (2): 389–414.

Matebeni, Zethu. 2014a. "How Not to Write about South Africa." In *Reclaiming Afrikan: Queer Perspectives on Sexual and Gender*, edited by Zethu Matebeni, 61–63. Athlone, South Africa: Modjaji Press.

Matebeni, Zethu, ed. 2014b. *Reclaiming Afrikan: Queer Perspectives on Sexual and Gender Identities.* Athlone, South Africa: Modjaji Press.

Matebeni, Zethu. 2021. "*Nongayindoda*: Moving beyond Gender in a South African Context." *Journal of Contemporary African Studies* 39 (4): 565–75.

Matimaire, Kenneth. 2021. "Intersex Community Struggles to Access Covid Vaccines." *New Zimbabwe*, July 29. https://www.newzimbabwe.com/intersex-community -struggles-to-access-covid-vaccines/.

Mavalwaka, Jamshed, ed. 1978. *Dermatoglyphics: An International Perspective.* Chicago: Mouton.

McClintock, Anne. 1995. *Imperial Leather: Race, Gender, and Sexuality in the Colonial Contest.* New York: Routledge.

McRae, Donald. 2009. "Caster Semenya: 'People Want to Stare at Me, to Touch Me. I Don't Think I Like Being Famous So Much.'" *Guardian* (London), November 14. https://www.theguardian.com/sport/2009/nov/14/caster-semenya-donald-mcrae -training-camp.

McWhorter, Ladelle. 2009. *Racism and Sexual Oppression in Anglo-America.* Bloomington: Indiana University Press.

"Media." 1998. *Anthropology Today* 14 (4): 30.

Miller, Shane Aaron. 2015. "'Just Look at Her!': Sporting Bodies as Athletic Resistance and the Limits of Sport Norms in the Case of Caster Semenya." *Men and Masculinities* 18 (3): 293–317.

Mkhwanazi, Muzi. 2000. "Soweto Sangomas Face Trial for Muti Murder." *Sowetan* (Johannesburg), August 14.

Mlambo, Alois S., and Neil Parsons. 2019. *A History of Southern Africa.* London: Red Globe.

Mohamed, Ashfak. 2021. "Caster Semenya Is Racing for Justice after Study Correction." *IOL* (Cape Town), August 25. https://www.iol.co.za/sport/athletics/caster-semenya-is -racing-for-justice-after-study-correction-docff7aa-64c5-4088-a70a-dee56b3290d7.

Mokoena, Nthabiseng. 2015. "Remembering Sally, and the Intersex Movement in South Africa." Iranti, October 22. http://www.iranti-org.co.za/content/Profiles/Sally-Gross -Remembering-Nthabiseng-Mokoena.html. No longer available.

Money, John. 1952. "Hermaphroditism: An Inquiry into the Nature of a Human Paradox." PhD diss., Harvard University.

Money, John, J. Hampson, and J. L. Hampson. 1955. "Hermaphroditism: Recommendations concerning Alignment of Sex, Change of Sex and Psychological Management." *Bulletin Johns Hopkins Hospital* 97: 284–300.

Money, John, Julianne Imperato-McGinley, and Ralph E. Peterson. 1976. "Gender Identity and Hermaphroditism." *Science* 191 (4229): 872.

Money, John, and C. Ogunro. 1974. "Behavioral Sexology: Ten Cases of Genetic Male Intersexuality with Impaired Prenatal and Pubertal Androgenization." *Archives of Sexual Behavior* 3 (3): 181–205.

Montañola, Sandy, and Aurélie Olivesi. 2016. "Introduction." In *Gender Testing in Sport: Cases and Controversies*, edited by Sandy Montañola and Aurélie Olivesi, 1–12. New York: Routledge.

Morgan, Tom. 2019. "Paula Radcliffe Reveals 'Aggressive' Abuse Suffered Online since Supporting IAAF Landmark Legal Battle with Caster Semenya." *Telegraph* (London), April 18. https://www.telegraph.co.uk/athletics/2019/04/18/paula-radcliffe-reveals -aggressive-abuse-suffered-online-since/.

Morland, Iain. 2011. "Intersex Treatment and the Promise of Trauma." In *Gender and the Science of Difference: Cultural Politics of Contemporary Science and Medicine*, edited by Jill Fisher, 147–63. New Brunswick, NJ: Rutgers University Press.

Morland, Iain. 2014. "Keywords: Intersex." *Transgender Studies Quarterly* 1 (1–2): 111–15.

Morland, Iain. 2015. "Gender, Genitals, and the Meaning of Being Human." In *Fuckology: Critical Essays on John Money's Diagnostic Concepts*, edited by Lisa Downing, Iain Morland, and Nikki Sullivan, 69–98. Chicago: University of Chicago Press.

Moten, Fred. 2002. "Black Mo'nin'." In *Loss: The Politics of Mourning*, edited by David L. Eng and David Kazanjian, 59–76. Berkeley, CA: University of California Press.

Moten, Fred. 2018. *Stolen Life*. Durham, NC: Duke University Press.

Mtshawu, Babalwa. 2017a. *Intersex Struggles: I Do Not Love Doctors*. Babalwa Mtshawu, video, 12:52, March 13. https://www.youtube.com/watch?v=h15gddqDI5k.

Mtshawu, Babalwa, and Thando Hlope. 2019. "I'm Intersex, I Don't Get Periods and I'm Going through Menopause." *BBC News Africa*, video, 3:35, April 18. https://www .youtube.com/watch?v=ovBEq-MorJA.

Mulot, Rachel. 2019. "Athleticism: 'If You Want to Compete in the Feminine Category, Then You Must Not Oppose a Treatment.'" *Sciences et Avenir*, June 25. https://www .sciencesetavenir.fr/sante/athetism-if-you-want-to-compete-in-the-feminine -category-then-you-must-not-oppose-a-treatment_134846.

Munro, Brenna. 2010. "Caster Semenya: Gods and Monsters." *Safundi: The Journal of South African and American Studies* 11 (4): 383–96.

National Dialogue on the Protection and Promotion of the Human Rights of Intersex People. 2018. National Intersex Meeting Report. https://www.justice.gov.za/vg/lgbti /2018-NationalIntersexMeetingReport.pdf.

Ngoasheng, Asanda. 2021. "Debunking the Apartheid Spatial Grid: Developing a Socially Just Architecture Curriculum at a University of Technology." *Journal of Asian and African Studies* 56 (1): 135–49.

Ngqakamba, Sesona. 2018. "Semenya Ruling—South African Fans Are Furious." *Huffington Post*, April 26. https://www.huffingtonpost.co.uk/2018/04/26/semenya-ruling -south-african-fans-are-furious_a_23420824/.

Nortier, Christi. 2021. "Call for Home Affairs to Make a Third 'Unspecified' Option for Recording Gender Available to Anyone." *Daily Maverick* (Johannesburg), March 9. https://www.dailymaverick.co.za/article/2021-03-09-call-for-home-affairs-to-make-a -third-unspecified-option-for-recording-gender-available-to-anyone/.

Nyong'o, Tavia. 2010. "The Unforgivable Transgression of Being Caster Semenya." *Women and Performance: A Journal of Feminist Theory* 20 (1): 95–100.

OII (Organization Intersex International). 2014. "Remembering Sally Gross." OII Intersex Network, February 21. https://oiiinternational.com/2930/remembering-sally-gross/.

Ovington, John. 1697. *A Voyage to Surat in the Year 1689 Giving a Large Account of That City and Its Inhabitants and of the English Factory There: Likewise a Description of Madeira, St. Jago, Annobon, Cabenda and Malemba (upon the Coast of Africa), St. Helena, Johanna, Bombay, the City of Muscatt, and Its Inhabitants in Arabia Felix, Mocha, and Other Maritine Towns upon the Red-Sea, the Cape of Good Hope, and the Island Ascension.* London: Printed for Jacob Tonson, at the Judges Head in Fleet-street, near the Inner-Temple-Gate.

Owens, Deirdre Cooper. 2017. *Medical Bondage: Race, Gender, and the Origins of American Gynecology.* Athens: University of Georgia Press.

Oyěwùmí, Oyèrónkẹ́. 1997. *The Invention of Women: Making an African Sense of Western Gender Discourses.* Minneapolis: University of Minnesota Press.

Oyěwùmí, Oyèrónkẹ́. 2003. "Alice in Motherland: Reading Alice Walker on Africa and Screening the Color 'Black.'" In *African Women and Feminism: Reflecting on the Politics of Sisterhood,* edited by Oyèrónkẹ́ Oyěwùmí, 159–85. Trenton, NJ: Africa World Press.

Paré, Ambroise. 1634. *Of Monsters and Prodigies.* Translated by Thomas Johnson. London: T. Cotes and R. Young.

Patterson, Orlando. 1982. *Slavery and Social Death: A Comparative Study.* Cambridge, MA: Harvard University Press.

Peterson, Ralph E., Julianne Imperato-McGinley, Teofilo Gautier, and Erasmo Sturla. 1977. "Male Pseudohermaphroditism Due to Steroid 5α-reductase Deficiency." *American Journal of Medicine* 62: 170–91.

Petit, Michael. 2013. "Becoming Glandular: Endocrinology, Mass Culture, and Experimental Lives in the Interwar Age." *American Historical Review* 118 (4): 1052–76.

Petkar, Sofia. 2017. "The Mysterious Caribbean Village Where Young Girls Morph into Boys." *UK Express* (London). August 8. https://www.express.co.uk/news/world /838588/dominican-republic-girls-become-boys-sex-hormones-caribbean-puberty.

Pielke, Roger, Jr., Ross Tucker, and Erik Boye. 2019. "Scientific Integrity and the IAAF Testosterone Regulations." *International Sports Law Journal* 19 (1–2): 18–26.

Pieper, Lindsay Parks. 2016. *Sex Testing: Gender Policing in Women's Sports.* Urbana: University of Illinois Press.

Pink News. 2017. "There's a Village in the Caribbean Where 'Girls' Grow Penises at Age 12." *Pink News* (London). August 10 https://www.pinknews.co.uk/2017/08/10/theres -a-village-in-the-caribbean-where-girls-grow-penises-at-age-12/.

Pinney, Christopher. 2011. *Photography and Anthropology.* London: Reaktion.

Ploss, Hermann Heinrich, Max Bartels, and Paul Bartels. (1885) 1935. "The Female Genitalia: Racial and Ethnographical Characteristics." In *Woman: An Historical, Gynecological and Anthropological Compendium,* vol. 1, edited by Hermann Heinrich Ploss, Max Bartels, and Paul Bartels, 276–379. Reprint, London: William Heinemann (Medical Books).

Posel, Deborah. 1987. "The Meaning of Apartheid before 1948: Conflicting Interests and Forces within the Afrikaner Nationalist Alliance." *Journal of Southern African Studies* 14 (1): 123–39.

Radcliffe, Paula. 2016. "Radcliffe: Caster Semenya Rio Gold 'Won't Be Sport.'" BBC *Live at 5 Sport*, July 21. https://www.bbc.co.uk/programmes/p0425m52.

Ramsay, Michèle, Renee Bernstein, Esther Zwane, David C. Page, and Trefor Jenkins. 1988. "XX True Hermaphroditism in Southern African Blacks: An Enigma of Primary Sexual Difference." *American Journal of Human Genetics* 43: 4–13.

Ramsay, M., W. Pfaffenzeller, E. Kotze, L. Bhengu, F. Essop, and T. de Ravel. 2009. "Chimerism in Black Southern African Patients with True Hermaphroditism 46,XX/44XY,+21 and 46,XX/46,XY." *Annals of the New York Academy of Sciences* 1151: 68–70.

Rao, Rahul. 2020. *Out of Time: The Queer Politics of Postcoloniality*. New York: Oxford University Press.

Rassool, Ciraj. 2015. "Re-storing the Skeletons of Empire: Return, Reburial and Rehumanisation in Southern Africa." *Journal of Southern African Studies* 41 (3): 653–70.

Rassool, Ciraj, and Patricia Hayes. 2002. "Science and the Spectacle: /Khanako's South Africa, 1936–1937." In *Deep hiStories: Gender and Colonialism in Southern Africa*, edited by Wendy Woodward, Patricia Hayes, and Gary Minkley, 117–61. Amsterdam: Rodopi.

Ray, Carina. 2009. "Caster Semenya: 21st Century 'Hottentot Venus'?" *New African*, no. 489, 18–19.

Republic of South Africa. 2004. "Alteration of Sex Description and Sex Status Bill." No. 331. *Government Gazette*, Republic of South Africa, vol. 465, no. 26148, March 15.

Rich, Alisa L., Laura M. Phipps, Seweta Tiwari, Hemanth Rudaraju, and Philip O. Dospesi. 2016. "The Increasing Prevalence in Intersex Variation from Toxicological Dysregulation in Fetal Reproductive Tissue Differentiation and Development by Endocrine-Disrupting Chemicals." *Environmental Health Insights* 10: 163–71.

Roberts, Jack, dir. 2004. *The Third Sex*. Princeton, NJ: Films for the Humanities and Sciences.

Rubin, David A. 2017. *Intersex Matters: Biomedical Embodiment, Gender Regulation, and Transnational Activism*. Albany, NY: SUNY Press.

SAHRC (South African Human Rights Commission). 2003. "Submission—Alteration of Sex Description and Sex Status Bill [37–2003]." Portfolio Committee on Home Affairs, September 9.

Said, Nick. 2019. "Semenya Accuses IAAF of Using Her as a 'Human Guinea Pig.'" *Reuters*, June 18. https://www.reuters.com/article/us-athleticssemenya/semenya-accuses-World%20Athletics-of-using-her-as-a-human-guinea-pig-idUSKCN1TJ22P.

Saini, Angela. 2019. *Superior: The Return of Race Science*. Boston: Beacon.

SALC (South African Law Commission). 1995. *Examination of the Legal Consequences of Sexual Realignment and Related Matters*. Project 52. Pretoria: SALC.

Salo, Elaine. 2016. "'Caster Semenya—The Ancients Would Have Called Her God': The International Re-imagining and Remaking of Sex and the Art of Silence." In *Gender Testing in Sport: Cases and Controversies*, edited by Sandy Montañola and Aurélie Olivesi, 150–67. New York: Routledge.

Samanga, Rufaro. 2019. "Influenced: Meet Babalwa Mtshawu—The YouTuber Unapologetically Sharing Her Intersex Journey with the World." *OkayAfrica*, August 1. https://www.okayafrica.com/meet-our-influencer-babalwa-mtshawu-unapologetic-intersex-youtuber/.

Sawer, Patrick, and Sebastian Berger. 2009. "Gender Row over Caster Semenya Makes Athlete into a South African Cause Célèbre." *Telegraph* (London), August 23. https://www.telegraph.co.uk/news/worldnews/africaandindianocean/southafrica/6073980/Gender-row-over-Caster-Semenya-makes-athlete-into-a-South-African-cause-celebre.html.

Schiebinger, Londa. 2013. *Nature's Body. Gender in the Making of Modern Science*. Reprint, New Brunswick, NJ: Rutgers University Press.

Schultz, Jaime. 2012. "The Accidental Celebritisation of Caster Semenya." *Celebrity Studies* 3 (3): 283–96.

Scott, David. 2000. "The Re-enchantment of Humanism: An Interview with Sylvia Wynter." *Small Axe*, no. 8: 119–207.

Scully, Pamela. 2010. "The Trials of Caster Semenya." *Defenders Online*, July 16. www.thedefendersonline.com. No longer available.

Sebeelo, Tebogo B. 2020. "Hashtag Activism, Politics and Resistance in Africa: Examining #ThisFlag and #RhodesMustFall Online Movements." *African Studies* 13 (1): 95–109.

Semenya, Caster. 2010. "Caster Semenya's Comeback Statement in Full." *Guardian* (London), March 30. https://www.theguardian.com/sport/2010/mar/30/caster-semenya-comeback-statement.

Seppelt, Hajo. 2014. *The Secrets of Doping: How Russia Makes Its Winners*. Lucky Loser Tennis, video, 58:05, April 27, 2015. https://www.youtube.com/watch?v=iu9B-ty9JCY.

Sexton, Jared. 2011. "The Social Life of Social Death: On Afro-Pessimism and Black Optimism." *InTensions*, no. 5 (Fall–Winter): 1–47.

Sharpley-Whiting, T. Denean. 1999. *Black Venus: Sexualized Savages, Primal Fears, and Primitive Narratives in French*. Durham, NC: Duke University Press.

Silva, Joseli Maria, and Marcio Jose Orrat. 2016. "Transfeminism and Decolonial Thought: The Contribution of Brazilian *Travestis*." *Transgender Studies Quarterly* 3 (1–2): 220–27.

Sindane, Lucky. 2009. "Semenya's Saga: Chuene's Trail of Lies." *Mail and Guardian* (Johannesburg), September 18. https://mg.co.za/article/2009-09-18-semenya-saga-chuenes-trail-of-lies.

Skloot, Rebecca. 2010. *The Immortal Life of Henrietta Lacks*. New York: Broadway.

Skotnes, Pippa, ed. 1996. *Miscast: Negotiating the Presence of the Bushmen*. Cape Town: University of Cape Town Press.

Skotnes, Pippa. 2002. "The Politics of Bushman Representations." In *Images and Empires: Visuality in Colonial and Postcolonial Africa*, edited by Paul Landau and Susan Griffin, 253–74. Berkeley: University of California Press.

Smith, David. 2009. "Caster Semenya Row: 'Who Are White People to Question the Makeup of an African Girl? It Is Racism.'" *Guardian* (London), August 22. https://www.theguardian.com/sport/2009/aug/23/caster-semenya-athletics-gender.

Snorton, C. Riley. 2017. *Black on Both Sides: A Racial History of Trans Identity*. Minneapolis: University of Minnesota Press.

Sontag, Susan. 1977. *On Photography*. New York: Farrar, Straus and Giroux.

Spade, Dean. 2011. *Normal Life: Administrative Violence, Critical Trans Politics, and the Limits of Law*. Cambridge, MA: South End Press.

Spillers, Hortense. 1987. "Mama's Baby, Papa's Maybe: An American Grammar Book."
    Diacritics 17 (2): 64–81.
Spurdle, Amanda D., Sara Shankman, and Michèle Ramsay. 1995. "xx True Hermaph-
    roditism in Southern African Blacks: Exclusion of sry Sequences and Uniparental
    Disomy of the X Chromosome." *American Journal of Medical Genetics* 55: 53–56.
Steinmetz, Katy. 2014. "The Transgender Tipping Point." *Time,* May 28.
Stern, Curt. 1967. "Richard Benedict Goldschmidt, April 12, 1878–April 24, 1958." In
    Biographical Memoirs, vol. 39, 141–92. New York: Columbia University Press.
Sviridinko, Olga, Edmund Willison, and Hajo Seppelt, dirs. 2019. *Gender Battle: The
    Abandoned Women of Sport.* The Dark Side of Sport, video, 59:22, September 29.
    https://www.youtube.com/watch?v=Af4CIrCL3Do.
Swarr, Amanda Lock. 2012. *Sex in Transition: Remaking Gender and Race in South
    Africa.* Albany, NY: suny Press.
Swarr, Amanda Lock, with Sally Gross and Liesl Theron. 2009. "South African Intersex
    Activism: Caster Semenya's Impact and Import." *Feminist Studies* 35 (3): 657–62.
Sze, Julie. 2006. "Boundaries and Border Wars: des, Technology, and Environmental
    Justice." *American Quarterly* 58 (3): 791–814.
Tait, Lawson. 1876. "Hermaphroditism." *Transactions of the American Gynecological
    Association* 1: 318–25.
Tamale, Sylvia. 2020. *Decolonization and Afro-Feminism.* Ottawa: Daraja Press.
Tambe, Ashwini. 2018. "Reckoning with the Silences of #MeToo." *Feminist Studies* 44 (1):
    197–202.
Tempelhoff, Elise. 2009. "'Thousands' like Caster." *News24* (Cape Town), September 15.
    https://www.news24.com/southafrica/news/thousands-like-caster-20090915.
Thiele, Susanne, Ute Hoppe, Paul-Martin Holterhus, and Olaf Hiort. 2005. "Isoenzyme of
    Type 1 of 5alpha-Reductase Is Abundantly Transcribed in Normal Human Genital Skin
    Fibroblasts and May Play an Important Role in Masculinization of 5alpha-Reductase
    Type 2 Deficient Males." *European Journal of Endrocrinology* 152 (6): 875–80.
Thigpen, Anice, Daphne L. Davis, Athena Milatovich, Berenice B. Mendonca, Julianne
    Imperato-McGinley, James E. Griffin, Uta Francke, Jean D. Wilson, and David W.
    Russell. 1992. "Molecular Genetics of Steroid 5α-Reductase 2 Deficiency." *Journal of
    Clinical Investigation* 90 (3): 799–809.
Thomas, Lynn. 2007. "Gendered Reproduction: Placing Schoolgirl Pregnancies in Afri-
    can History." In *Africa after Gender,* edited by Catherine Cole, 48–62. Bloomington:
    Indiana University Press.
Thomson, Rosemarie Garland, ed. 1996. *Freakery: Cultural Spectacles of the Extraordi-
    nary Body.* New York: New York University Press.
Thoreson, Ryan. 2013. "Beyond Equality: The Post-apartheid Counternarrative of Trans
    and Intersex Movements in South Africa." *African Affairs* 112 (449): 646–65.
Towle, Evan B., and Lynn M. Morgan. 2002. "Romancing the Transgender Native: Re-
    thinking the Use of the 'Third Gender' Concept." *glq: A Journal of Gay and Lesbian
    Studies* 8 (4): 469–97.
Tshwaku, Khanyiso. 2017. "Caster Semenya Refuses to Speak Ill of Disgraced Russian
    Rival Savinova." *Times Live* (Johannesburg), March 16. https://www.timeslive.co.za

/sport/2017-03-16-caster-semenya-refuses-to-speak-ill-of-disgraced-russian-rival
-savinova/.

Tuck, Eve, and K. Wayne Yang. 2012. "Decolonization Is Not a Metaphor." *Decolonization, Indigeneity, Education, and Society* 1 (1): 1–40.

Tucker, William H. 2007. *The Funding of Scientific Racism: Wickliffe Draper and the Pioneer Fund*. Champaign: University of Illinois Press.

Urological Sciences Research Foundation. 2022. "The 'Guevedoces' of the Dominican Republic." Accessed April 22, 2022. https://www.usrf.org/news/010308-guevedoces.html.

Valoria, Hida Patricia, and Maria José Martínez-Patiño. 2012. "Reexamining Rationales of 'Fairness': An Athlete and Insider's Perspective on the New Policies on Hyperandrogenism in Elite Female Athletes." *American Journal of Bioethics* 12 (7): 17–33.

Van der Westhuizen, Fantie. 1992. "Verandering van Geslag is Seuntjie se Enigste Hoop (Sex Change a Boy's Only Hope)." Translated by Taghmeda Achmat. *Johannesburg Beeld*, July 21.

Van Dongen, L. G. R. 2003. "Godfrey Phillips Charlewood: In Memoriam." *South African Medical Journal* 93 (7): 511.

Van Huyssteen, Wessel, dir. 2003. *3rd Sex*. Johannesburg: Tin Rage Productions for SABC3.

Van Niekerk, Willem A. 1974. *True Hermaphroditism: Clinical, Morphologic and Cytogenetic Aspects*. Hagerstown, MD: Harper and Row.

Van Niekerk, Willem A. 1976. "True Hermaphroditism: An Analytic Review with a Report of 3 New Cases." *American Journal of Obstetrics and Genetics* 26 (7): 890–907.

Waits, Mira Rai. 2016. "The Indexical Trace: A Visual Interpretation of the History of Fingerprinting in Colonial India." *Visual Culture in Britain* 17 (1): 18–46.

Ward, N. A., T. Ward, and R. H. Johnson. 1973. "A Case of Appendicitis Simulating Ruptured Ectopic Pregnancy." *South African Medical Journal* 47 (5): 191.

Washington, Harriet A. 2006. *Medical Apartheid: The Dark History of Medical Experimentation on Black Americans from Colonial Times to the Present*. New York: Harlem Moon.

Wertelecki, Wladimir, and Chris C. Plato, eds. 1979. *Dermatoglyphics—Fifty Years Later*. New York: Alan R. Liss.

Wharton, David. 2019. "In the Case of Star South African Runner Caster Semenya, a Sports Arbitration Court Must Determine the Definition of a Woman." *Los Angeles Times*, March 16. https://www.latimes.com/sports/la-sp-caster-semenya-gender
-20190313-story.html.

Wicomb, Zoë. 2021. "Representing Sara Baartman in the New Millennium." Interview by Desiree Lewis. In *Surfacing: On Being Black and Feminist in South Africa*, edited by Desiree Lewis and Gabeba Baderoon, 28–46. Johannesburg: Wits University Press.

Wiersma, Rinus. 2001. "Management of the African Child with True Hermaphroditism." *Journal of Pediatric Surgery* 36 (2): 397–99.

Wiersma, Rinus. 2004. "True Hermaphroditism in Southern Africa: The Clinical Picture." *Pediatric Surgery International* 20 (5): 363–68.

Wiersma, Rinus. 2008. "Overview of Bladder Exstrophy: A Third World Perspective." *Journal of Pediatric Surgery* 43 (8): 1520–23.

Wiersma, Rinus. 2011. "OvoTesticular Disorder of Sex Development in Southern Africa." PhD diss., University of KwaZulu-Natal.

Wiersma, R., and C. G. Constantinides. 1993. "Intersex: An Investigative Problem." *South African Journal of Paediatric Surgeons* 31 (1): 35.

Wiersma, Rinus, and P. K. Ramdial. 2009. "The Gonads of 111 South African Patients with Ovotesticular Disorder of Sex Differentiation." *Journal of Pediatric Surgery International* 44: 556–60.

Wilson, Gina. 2011. "Eighth Day of Intersex: Sally Gross." *Intersex Human Rights Australia* (formerly OII Australia), November 2. https://ihra.org.au/15234/eighth-day-intersex-sally-gross/.

Wilson, A. Marius. 1911. "The Nymphae (Anthropological)." In *Transactions of the South African Medical Congress, 12th Meeting,* 228–33. Cape Town: Transactions Committee.

Wilton, E. 1969. "A Cytogenetic Study of Patients with Anomalous Sexual Development." *South African Journal of Surgery* 7 (2): 45–48.

Wolff, Michelle. 2019. "Sally Gross: Mother of Transnational Intersex Activism Died Alone." Paper presented at the annual meeting for the National Women's Studies Association, San Francisco, November 14–17.

Wolff, Michelle, David Rubin, and Amanda Lock Swarr. 2022. "The Intersex Issue: An Introduction." *Transgender Studies Quarterly* 9 (2): 143–59.

Wynter, Sylvia. 2000. "Africa, the West and the Analogy of Culture." In *Symbolic Narratives/African Cinema: Audiences, Theory, and the Moving Image,* edited by June Givanni, 25–76. London: British Film Institute.

Yacob-Haliso, Olajumoke. 2021. "Decolonisation and Disputations in African Women's Studies." Paper presented via Zoom, sponsored by the Centre for Social Change, University of Johannesburg.

Yacob-Haliso, Olajumoke, and Toyin Falola, eds. 2021. *The Palgrave Handbook of African Women's Studies.* Cham: Palgrave Macmillan. https://doi.org/10.1007/978-3-030-28099-4.

Page numbers followed by f refer to figures.

Abrahams, Yvette, 5, 176n14

activism: African decolonial, 7, 122; anti-apartheid, 74, 76, 89; Gross's, 74, 87–89, 95, 96–97, 192n50; hashtag, 120–27, 150, 199n58, 200n67, 201n73; Hendricks's, 139; online, 126, 200n67; in South Africa, 14, 122, 152, 202n11. *See also* intersex activism

African Intersex Movement (AIM), 7, 19, 140–41, 165–66

African National Congress (ANC), 75, 91–93, 109, 187n4

Age of Gonads, 37, 39, 178n33

Alteration of Sex Description and Sex Status Act (2003), 94, 99

Amadiume, Ifi, 4, 171n5

apartheid, 15, 17–18, 42–44, 53, 55, 62, 68, 75, 90–93, 100, 105, 107, 156, 183n9, 184n25, 188n44; abortion under, 82; architects of, 9, 74; childbirth under, 41–42, 82, 84; end of, 77, 150, 192n50; eugenics and, 42, 180n44; law enforcement, 184n25; Olympics and, 107, 195n22; raced categories of, 51, 53, 67, 182–83; sport boycotts and, 109; transition to democracy from, 93; white gay and lesbian conscripts under, 83, 189n25; white supremacy and, 189n24

athletes, 18, 103, 108–9, 114, 116–19, 122–24; African, 107, 115, 119–20, 195n20; Chinese, 106, 113; finasteride use by, 173n19; gender testing/verification of, 105, 119–20, 195nn16–17, 197n37, 198n47, 198–99nn54–55; from the Global South, 103, 113, 115, 199n57; intersex, 115, 129; professional, 125; Russian, 201n74,

South African, 199n61; Soviet, 106; steroid use by, 173n19, 194n15; white, 107, 110, 128–30, 197n45; women, 121, 129, 131, 195n21

Baartman, Sara, 30–31, 35–36, 48, 108, 176n14, 176n16, 179n38; Semenya and, 109–13, 127, 159. *See also* Xcollektiv

Baderoon, Gabeba, 123, 172n7, 172n9

Bantu Gynaecology, 17, 41–42, 44–45, 67, 82, 175n1, 179n40, 179n42

Bantu Gynaecology (Charlewood), 23–24, 28, 31, 34, 44–46, 156–57, 175n1, 181n50

Bauer, Markus, 144–45, 158, 205n32

Bavington, L. Dawn, 105, 120, 193n8

Bermon, Stéphane, 114–17, 119, 128, 130–31, 197n42, 197n44, 201n78

Bill of Rights (South Africa), 92–93

black intersex frequency, 2, 52, 57–58, 60, 68, 70, 84, 171n3

blackness, 91, 120; gender indefiniteness and, 6; historical emergence of, 176n14; intersex and, 2–3, 18, 50–51, 54, 81

Burns, Catherine, 25, 34, 41, 180n43

Butler, Judith, 68, 107, 171n2, 186n41, 195n24, 198n52

Campt, Tina, 61, 63, 184n21, 185n33

"Casting Project, The" 32–33, 67

Charlewood, Godfrey Phillips, 23–24, 44, 156, 175n1. See also *Bantu Gynaecology*

Charon, Louis François, 111, 112f, 159

Chase, Cheryl, 65, 76, 149–50. *See also* Intersex Society of North America (ISNA)

Chuene, Leonard, 108–9, 196n30
circumcision, 69, 150, 188n13; accidents, 79, 186n39; medical, 78; religious, 77. *See also* Reimer, David; Reimer twins (Reimers)
citational chains, 3, 17–18, 27, 29–30, 39, 49–51, 66, 68–69, 103, 116, 129, 144–45, 156–58, 182n3; Grace and, 56–57, 68; Imperato-McGinley and, 118; Van Niekerk and, 56–57, 68–69
citationality, 68, 171n2, 198n52
class, 18, 74, 81–82, 84, 106, 183n9
clitoridectomy, 18, 103, 115–17, 145, 150
concealment, 135–37, 145; culture of, 82
Cornelius, Steve, 122, 199n61
Cox, Norman, 105–6, 114, 194n10
critical intersex studies, 7, 37, 191n47
Cuvier, Georges, 30–31, 36, 110, 177nn17–18
cytogenetics, 181n51; Cytogenetics Unit of the South African Institute for Medical Research, 45–46

Davidson, Julian, 12, 173n24
Davies, Sharron, 116, 197n45
Davison, Patricia, 32, 177n23
DDT (dichlorodiphenyltrichloroethane), 18, 85–87, 189n27, 190n33
De Blainville, Henri, 30, 177n18
decolonial intersex critique/analysis, 5, 9
decoloniality: feminist, 7; intersex, 5–6, 159
decolonization, 5, 172n9, 173n15; Africa's, 17, 140; of gender testing, 103; intersex, 4, 6, 18, 158
De la Chapelle, Albert, 114, 197n38
De Mérode, Alexandre, 113–14, 128, 196n35
Department of Home Affairs (DHA), 92, 153, 191n49, 192n52, 206nn37–38
dermatoglyphics, 52, 54, 64, 182n1, 185nn27–28
Derrida, Jacques, 159, 171n2
disorders of sex development (DSD), 16, 174nn33–34; ovotesticular (OT), 50, 56, 59, 204n18
Dominican Republic, 118; Guevedoces and, 11; intersex and, 9, 25, 44, 52, 61, 117, 182n3, 189n26; *The Third Sex* (Roberts) and, 58, 61, 186n1; visual scrutiny and, 13. *See also* Imperato-McGinley, Julianne
Dreger, Alice, 37, 39, 63, 65, 178n33, 179n37, 185n32
Drury, James, 32–34, 177n27
Dubow, Saul, 31, 81
Du Plessis, Rory, 62–63

Eckert, Lena, 13, 174n32
endocrine-disrupting chemicals (EDCs), 85–86, 189n28, 189n30. *See also* DDT
environmental racism, 87; intersex and, 18; intersex critique of, 86. *See also* DDT
eugenics, 40–42, 64, 180n44, 183n15; ideologies of, 107; racist histories of sport and, 194n12; in South Africa, 81

Fanon, Frantz, 91, 190n39, 191n44
female genital mutilation (FGM), 149–50, 197n43, 205nn28–29, 205n31. *See also* Intersex Genital Mutilation (IGM)
feminisms, 123; African, 4–5, 172n7, 172n9; decolonial, 5, 7, 172n8
femininity, 5, 103–4, 172n12; enforced, 199n57; fragile, 106; Western standards of, 125; white, 110–11, 195n19
feminists, 173n15; African, 4–5; South African, 123; from the Global North, 5, 149, 205n28; white, 197n43
Fénichel paper, 116–19, 197n46
fester-wicomb, gertrude, 98–99, 191–92n49
5α-reductase deficiency, 10–11, 116–17, 198nn48–49
Forbes, J. L., 45, 182n4

GALA Queer Archive (University of the Witwatersrand), 15, 74, 174n31, 187n2
Garnier, Pierre-Yves, 130, 201n78
gaze, 8, 14, 111; camera's, 10, 63, 157; clinical, 174n28; colonial, 6; consumptive, 24, 36; medical, 50–51, 63, 82, 89, 137; photographic, 61–62; scientific, 74; spectacularizing, 113; white, 5
gender binaries, 4–6, 15, 39, 58, 77, 87, 96, 103, 147, 154, 204n26; colonial racism and, 120; hermaphroditism and, 35, 37–38; *muti* and, 80; policing, 9, 113; raced, 4, 66; racialized, 34; violence of, 160
gender binarism, 3, 5–6, 8, 25, 52, 68, 130
gender dimorphism, 4, 24, 37–39, 47, 172n12
Gender DynamiX, 133, 202n2, 203n17
gender regulations, 18, 120, 122, 130, 193n8, 198n55, 199n60
gender testing, 14, 18, 103, 105–9, 113–15, 119–20, 193n3, 194n11, 194n15, 195n19, 199n56; international, 117; logistics of, 197n37; opposition to, 197n40; racialized history of, 134
gender verification, 96, 102, 105, 114–15, 131, 195nn16–17

genital ambiguity, 35, 46, 76
Gill-Peterson, Jules, 41, 43–44, 84, 173n16, 180n45, 180n48, 184n19, 188n15
Gilman, Sander, 28, 179n38
Gladwell, Malcolm, 121–22, 199n60, 200n67
Global North, 18, 25, 51–52, 57, 152, 159, 173n13, 201n73; athletes from, 104, 106–7, 129; banning of DDT in, 85; clitoridectomy and, 113; feminists in, 5, 149, 205n21; FGM and, 150, 197n43, 205n28; finasteride and, 173n19; gender and sexuality and, 15; hermaphroditism in, 38–39, 47; intersex and, 182n2; intersex imperialism and, 205n30; male bodies in, 41; pelvimetry and, 179n43; race and, 17; racism of, 109, 125; sexual anomalies and, 176n12; universalizations of, 126; white women in, 179n43, 197n43, 199n60
Global South, 10, 117; athletes from, 103, 113, 115, 119–20, 199n57; black intersex frequency in, 57, 118, 171n3; DDT in, 85; EDCs in, 86; gender binaries in, 15, 153; genital surgeries and, 150; intersex in, 8–9, 11–12, 14, 18, 50, 61, 73, 103, 114–15, 118, 128–29, 182n3, 197n42; intersex and blackness in, 2; intersex research in, 47, 55; pelvimetry and, 179n43; raced gender binarism and, 52; true hermaphroditism in, 38–39. See also Dominican Republic; Papua New Guinea; South Africa
Goldhagen, Daniel, 89–90, 190n37. See also social death
gonadectomy, 18, 103, 116–17, 119, 141, 143
Gqola, Pumla Dineo, 24, 110–11
Grace, H. J. (Hatherley James), 57, 63, 70, 74, 81, 83–84, 182n5, 182–83nn8–9, 183n11, 183n13, 184n22, 184n24, 204n19; master's thesis, 17–18, 49, 51–55, 62, 64–69, 145, 157–58, 182n1, 182n6, 185n27; on race, 52–55, 182n7
Gross, Sally, 9, 14, 16, 18, 73–78, 80–101, 110, 132, 135, 138, 147, 152, 157–58, 186n40, 187n2, 187nn4–5, 187n7, 187–88nn9–13, 189n31, 190n34, 190nn36–37, 191n43, 191–92nn49–50, 192nn54–55, 202n8; The 3rd Sex and, 186n1, 189n19, 191n45; activism of, 74, 87–89, 93, 96–97, 192n50; on infanticide, 204n25; publications by, 203n17; on Semenya, 192n53; trans migration and border crossing and, 191n48; Triangle Project, 74, 77, 187n3, 188n12, 202n12. See also Intersex South Africa

Hammar, B., 45, 182n4
Haraway, Donna, 63, 86, 174n29
haunting, 61, 157, 159
Hayes, Patricia, 33, 177n28
health care, 99, 136, 148; gender-affirming, 152; providers, 140; in South Africa, 83–84; workers, 204n20
health insurance, 84, 205n32
Heggie, Vanessa, 105, 193n9
Heinonen Sixteen, 106–7, 194–95nn16–17
Hendricks, Crystal, 134, 136–39, 145, 152, 202n9
Herdt, Gilbert, 12–13, 173–74nn23–26, 182n3, 198n51
hermaphrodite, 16, 24, 27, 35, 37, 60, 67, 138, 156, 178n31, 178n33, 191n42; eunuch and, 175n5; pseudo, 37; spurious, 36, 39. See also true hermaphrodite
hermaphroditism, 3, 5, 9, 17, 24, 36, 38, 55, 58–60, 87, 110, 178n33, 188n15, 191n42; African, 26; in Bantu Gynaecology, 45; black South Africans and, 52, 54, 105; European, 39; monstrosity and, 179n42. See also true hermaphroditism
Higgins, Laine, 130, 201n78
Hodes, Rebecca, 29, 176n10, 177n24
Hofmeyr, J. D. J., 44, 180n44
hormones, 1–2, 52, 79, 128, 171n4. See also testosterone
"Hottentot apron" fallacy, 17, 26–32, 34–35, 39–40, 47, 110, 177n17
Huet, Marie-Hélène, 36, 178n34
Hunt, Gareth, 81, 191n45
hyperandrogenism, 121, 128, 196n27, 199n56, 201n77
hypervisibility, 133, 151; of Baartman, 31

Imperato-McGinley, Julianne, 9–12, 58, 67, 117–18, 173n24, 182n3, 198n51
infanticide, 145–48, 204n20, 204n23, 204n25
International Association of Athletics Federations (IAAF)/World Athletics, 102, 106–10, 113–19, 122–25, 130–31, 193n1, 193n9, 196n34; gender rulings (2018), 202n79; Health and Sciences Department, 201n78; #IAAFMustFall, 19, 122–23, 199n58; Medical Commission, 194n11; officials, 194n15; regulations, 195–96nn25–27
International Olympic Committee (IOC), 1, 105, 107, 193n9, 194n14, 195n18; Gender Verification Workshop Group, 194n16; Medical Commission, 113, 194n11, 194n15

intersex: decoloniality, 5–6, 159; decolonization of, 4, 6, 18, 158; definitions of, 2–3, 59, 94; frequency, 2, 18, 50, 53, 55, 68, 115, 129; in the Global South, 8–9, 11–12, 14, 18, 50, 61, 73, 103, 114–15, 118, 128–29, 182n3, 197n42; killings, 140, 145; medical theories of, 59, 64, 74, 78, 87, 182n2; and race, 14, 54, 57, 58, 69, 105; raced, 49–50, 55, 58, 67–68; representation and, 2, 4, 146, 157, 159, 204n24; science, 18, 50, 67, 73, 103, 132

intersex activism, 76, 97, 203n17; African, 18, 132, 192n57; legislative gains, 202n2; rights, 140–41, 146, 151, 202n5; Semenya and, 95–96; 133–34; 192n53; South African, 70, 99, 135, 151, 192n51

intersex activists, 87, 98, 132, 134, 137–40, 158–59, 203n10; African, 2, 4–5, 7, 9, 15, 19, 131, 140, 145, 149, 160, 203n16; FGM and, 205n28; self-representations of, 9, 19, 133, 141, 154, 160; South African, 133, 136, 147, 150–52, 155, 191n46, 192n51, 202n6, 205n31, 206n37; in the United States, 65, 88

intersex genital mutilation (IGM), 136, 149–51, 203n17, 205n29

intersex medicine, 2–3, 16–17, 19, 82–84, 131–32, 150, 158; care and, 84, 136, 204n27; colonial ideologies and, 49; concealment and pathologization in, 137; racist, 103; scrutiny and, 138, 144; taxonomies imposed by, 74, 87; visibility in, 135; whiteness and, 81

Intersex Society of North America (ISNA), 76–77, 149, 187n10, 205n29

Intersex Society of South Africa, 187n9

Intersex South Africa (ISSA), 18, 66, 83, 99, 134–35, 139, 159, 187n9, 192n56, 202n2; anti-apartheid activism and, 74; Gross and, 77, 81–82, 88, 92, 94, 96–99, 147, 152; publications by, 203n17; website, 99–100

intersexuality, 7, 77, 93; diagnostic category of, 17, 46, 183n9, 187n10; invisibility of, 80; race and, 52, 54, 56, 134, 185n34, 187n10; true hermaphroditism and, 56

invisibility, 63, 76, 80, 133, 135–36, 147, 151, 155

Iranti, 134–35, 139, 151, 159, 202n2, 202n6, 203n17, 204n21, 205n34, 206n36, 206n38

Johnson, R. H., 47, 56, 181nn56–57
Jones, Howard W., 56, 68–69
Jordan-Young, Rebecca, 118, 197n46

Kaggwa, Julius, 132, 173n18, 204n23
Karzakis, Katrina, 118, 178n35, 197n46, 198n54
Kasril, Ronnie, 75, 187n4
Klebs, Theodor Albrecht Edwin, 37, 39
Klempman, Sarah, 45, 181n52, 182n4

Lacan, Jacques, 68, 171n2
LEGBO Northern Cape, 145–46, 204n22
Lewis, Desiree, 123, 172n7, 172n9
longue durée: of intersex and race, 58, 105; of racialized intersex, 3
Lugones, María, 5–6, 172n12

McClintock, Anne, 14, 34, 178n29
Macharia, Keguro, 3–4, 15, 23, 44–45, 156, 190n41
Magubane, Zine, 47, 176n14, 176n16, 180n47
malaria, 85–86. See also DDT
Malatino, Hil, 7, 38, 63–65, 178n30, 178n35, 184n24
Mandela, Nelson, 92, 109, 196n31
masculinity, 5, 104–5; intersex and, 171n4; Kratochilova's, 123; Semenya's, 124, 128
Matebeni, Zethu, 15, 171n5
medicine, 7, 9, 35, 86, 151, 201n72; allopathic, 39, 83, 147, 181n57; contemporary, 51; gendered, 54; harms of, 158; law and, 92, 192n50; modern, 61; racial categories in, 183n9; racist, 143; racist histories of, 2; South African, 88; surveillance and, 89; traditional, 50; trans, 43, 180n45. See also intersex medicine; muti; teratology
Mitchell, Mani Bruce, 97–99, 192n55
Mokoena, Nthabiseng, 99, 134–35, 137–40, 147–48, 150, 152, 154–55, 202n8, 203n17, 204nn26–27
Money, John, 52, 68–69, 74, 180n46, 182n3, 186n39; gender theories of, 43–44, 77–81, 202n7; protocols of, 18, 78, 80–81, 83, 198n51. See also Grace, H. J.; Jones, Howard W.; Reimer, David; Reimer twins (Reimers)
monstrosity, 18, 36, 38, 110, 179n42, 204n24; critique of, 87–88; infanticide and, 147; of intersex, 90. See also teratology
Morgan, Lynn M., 8–9, 184n17
Morland, Iain, 2–3, 7, 43, 171n4, 186n39
Moten, Fred, 61, 185n35
Mtshawu, Babalwa, 134, 141–44, 203nn12–13, 203nn15–16
Munro, Brenna, 107, 195n23
muti, 79–81, 188nn16–17

mutilation, 80, 88, 137, 158; genital, 136; penile, 79. *See also* female genital mutilation (FGM); intersex genital mutilation (IGM)

Ngoasheng, Asanda, 17, 174nn35–36
Nike, 125–27, 200n69
normality, 36, 58, 105; gender, 52; genital, 198n47; of intersex, 88

Olympics, 102, 113, 121, 127, 194n15; African nations in, 194n10; chromosomal testing and, 197n37; South Africa and, 107, 195n22; Tokyo (2021) 130
Ovington, John, 26–27
Oyěwùmí, Oyèrónké, 4, 172n6, 204n26, 205n28

Papua New Guinea, 173n24, 174n26, 198n51 hermaphroditism in, 12; intersex and, 9, 13, 25, 44, 52, 117, 182n3, 189n26. *See also* Herdt, Gilbert
pathologization, 2, 7, 89, 159; African, 70; of Chinese women in athletics, 106; colonial, 110; of intersex, 55, 88, 100, 137
Patterson, Orlando, 89–91, 190n39
pelvimetry, 40, 179n38, 179n43
Pereira, Jabulani, 153, 202n2
photography, 4, 13–15, 144, 151; clinical, 65, 135–36; colonial, 61; Gross's experience of, 89; Hendricks's experience of, 139; intersex, 89, 145, 158; medical, 3, 9–10, 18, 51, 62–63 137, 159, 185n31; postmortem, 66, 186n36; Semenya's experience of, 104, 109, 124
Pieper, Lindsay Parks, 106, 194n13, 196n35
Pinney, Christopher, 66, 173n20
plasticity, 17, 41–42, 188n15, 202n7; gender, 43, 78–79; intersex infants', 69; medicalized, 44, 84; racial, 42–43
poor whites, 81–82, 84, 189n20, 189n23; poor whiteism, 81–82, 189n22
pornography, 12–13, 34, 175n3, 178n30, 184n20, 184n24
poverty, 96; intersex and, 74; medicalized, 97; white, 81, 189n23
Promotion of Equality and Prevention of Unfair Discrimination Act, 94, 192n53

queer politics, 4, 126

race, 16, 33, 42–43, 53, 67, 180n49, 181n53; colonialism and, 103; gender binarism and,

3, 5; gender testing and, 18; Grace on, 52–55, 182n7, 182n9; health and, 189n19; improvement, 40; intersex and, 2–3, 14, 54, 57–58, 69, 84, 86, 89, 103, 105; intersexuality and, 134; as meaningless, 183n14; science of, 31; sexuality and, 110; theories of, 17, 24
racial purity, 17, 32, 55
racism, 31, 42, 62, 74, 123, 131; colonial, 120; environmental, 18, 86–87; FGM and, 150; global, 25; of the IAAF, 102; intersex health and, 85. *See also* scientific racism
Radcliffe, Paula, 116, 128–30, 197n45, 201n76
Ramsay, Michèle, 57–60, 183n16
Rasool, Ciraj, 33, 177n28
Ray, Carina, 109, 111, 193n4
Reimer, David, 69–70, 78–80, 186n40, 188n14
Reimer twins (Reimers), 69, 186n39, 188n15
representation, 19, 24, 30, 33, 45, 193n2; of African women's bodies, 25, 27, 29, 32, 34; of Baartman, 110, 176n14; of hermaphroditism, 5–6, 17, 23, 34, 39; of the Global South, 14; of Guevedoces, 10–11; of intersex, 2, 4, 146, 157, 159, 204n24; of Semenya, 110, 120, 124–26, 193nn5–6, 196n28; visual, 3, 18, 40, 50–51, 61, 67–68, 104. *See also* intersex activists: self-representations

Saint-Hilaire, Isidore Geoffroy, 36, 85. *See also* teratology
Savinova, Mariya, 104, 127–28, 193n4, 201nn74–75
scientific racism, 29, 42, 44–46, 53, 70, 118, 180n44, 180n49; British imperial dominance and, 189n21; intersex genetics and, 64; intersex medicine and, 2, 51; Lamprey grid and, 173n20; poor whiteism and, 81
scrutiny, 3–4, 18, 33, 35, 50–51, 67–68, 119, 139, 157; Baartman and, 31, 159; black intersex and, 58; of intersex medicine, 144; medical, 51, 83, 95, 133, 136, 138, 193n4; scientific, 177n27; Semenya and, 1, 85, 103, 108–9, 194n12, 201n74; visual, 13
Scully, Pamela, 110, 176n14
Sebidi, Dimakatso, 154–55
Semenya, Caster, 1–2, 18–19, 86, 94–96, 102–4, 107–13, 120–31, 133–34, 193n4, 193n7, 195nn23–25, 196nn28–30, 197n45, 199n59, 201n75, 202n8; Baartman and, 109–13, 127, 159 (*see also* Xcollektiv); #HandsOffCaster, 18, 103,

Semenya (continued)
120–22, 124–25, 129, 200n67; intersex activism and, 192n53; representation of, 110, 120, 124–26, 193nn5–6, 196n28; scrutiny of, 1, 85, 103, 108–9, 194n12, 201n74; self-representation, 200n67; visibility of, 96, 108, 121
shadow existence, 91, 95, 105
Sharpeville massacre, 44, 150
Simpson, James Young, 36–37
Sims, J. Marion, 41, 179n41
Slovo, Joe, 75, 187n4
Snorton, C. Riley, 6, 41, 90, 179n38, 179n41, 190n39
social death, 89–90, 190nn38–39; intersex, 74, 90–91, 93–94, 96, 204n25
social media, 4, 9, 14, 18–19, 30, 103, 107, 192n57, 200n68, 201n73, 202n3; Baartman and Semenya in, 111–13; critique of, 125–27, 199n62, 200nn67–68; hashtag campaigns, 121–24; intersex activism and, 132, 135, 141–44, 151; Semenya's self-representation on, 120–21, 124–27, 128
Soldaat, Nombulelo, 74, 89, 158
South African Museum, 31, 33, 67
Spillers, Hortense, 6
sport, 109, 194n15, 196n31; gender testing in, 14, 103, 105, 107, 113–15, 134, 195n17; intersex, 198n54; leaders of global, 18; parameters of gender in, 113, 131, 201n78; professional, 95, 193n7; racist histories of, 194n12; regulatory changes in, 121; science, 19, 103; white womanhood and, 116; women's, 1, 95, 106–7, 113, 128–29, 199n60
Steinman, Christie, 88–89, 190n35
Stoller, Robert, 12–13, 173nn24–25, 182n3
strategies of raced intersex science, 50–51, 67–70; definition as, 18, 37, 50–51, 67; of sex, 94, 98, 202n5; justification as, 18, 26, 31, 42, 50–51, 67, 69; repetition as, 18, 27, 50–51, 56–57, 67–69, 186n41; scrutiny as, 3–4, 18, 33, 35, 50, 67–68, 119, 139, 157. See also scrutiny

Tamale, Sylvia, 5, 17, 140, 203n11
teratology, 36, 74, 85, 110, 147, 178n34; critiques of, 18, 87–89. See also monstrosity
testosterone, 1, 76, 108, 116–17, 121, 123, 130–31, 196n26, 197n41, 197n44, 198n47, 199n60; blockers, 10; IAAF policing of, 113; regulation of, 114, 199n61; synthetic, 128; testosterone-lowering medications, 117, 198n50

Theron, Liesl, 133, 192n53
thingification, 90, 190n40
third gender, 8–9, 153, 206n36
Third Sex, The (Roberts), 11, 58–59, 61
3rd Sex, The (van Huyssteen), 73–74, 77, 81, 88–89, 157–58, 186n1, 189n19, 191n45
Towle, Evan B., 8–9, 184n17
true hermaphrodite, 24, 35–39, 46, 50, 61, 67, 175n2, 183n16, 190n34
true hermaphroditism, 17, 24, 37–39, 43–49, 52, 59, 61, 66, 181n57; South Africans and, 45–46, 54, 56–58, 68–70, 144, 181n52, 183n16, 204n18
Truffer, Daniela, 144–45, 158, 205n32

United Nations Educational, Scientific and Cultural Organization (UNESCO), 42–43, 180n44, 180n49
United States (US): athletes from, 106, 194n15; civil rights legislation in, 180n44; early intersex and trans medicine in, 43; gender diagnoses and treatments in, 47, 52; hermaphroditic diagnoses in, 37, 194n10; intersex activism in, 76; intersex activists in, 65, 88; intersex medicine in, 84, 180n48, 182n3, 189n18; objectification in, 35; slavery in, 6, 89–90, 177n19; treatment of impotence in, 40; true hermaphroditism in, 38, 46; white intersex in, 44

vaginoplasty, 79, 116–17
Van Niekerk, Willem A., 46, 56, 67–69, 181n50, 203n18; True Hermaphroditism, 24, 46, 67
visibility, 19, 95, 139, 144, 203n16; colonial histories of, 193n4; intersex, 134–36, 202n5; intersex organizations and, 152; public, 133; Semenya's, 96, 108, 121. See also hypervisibility; invisibility
voyeurism, 11, 111

whiteness, 44, 81, 84; in South Africa, 18, 74
white supremacy, 2, 42, 44, 82, 180n44, 189n24
Wiersma, Rinus, 144–45, 203–4n18
Wilton, E., 46, 181n54, 182n4

Xcollektiv, 111–13, 159, 196n32

Yacob-Haliso, Olajumoke, 5, 172n10, 173n15

Zimbabwe, 152–53

www.ingramcontent.com/pod-product-compliance
Lightning Source LLC
Chambersburg PA
CBHW020857270326
41928CB00006B/741